Rainer Maria Rilke

PROSE
AND POETRY

The German Library: Volume 70

Volkmar Sander, General Editor

Rainer Maria Rilke

PROSE
AND
POETRY

Edited by Egon Schwarz
Foreword by Howard Nemerov

CONTINUUM · NEW YORK

1984

The Continuum Publishing Company
370 Lexington Avenue, New York, NY 10017

Copyright © 1984 by The Continuum Publishing Company

Foreword © 1984 by Egon Schwarz
Introduction © 1984 by Howard Nemerov

Library of Congress Cataloging in Publication Data

Rilke, Rainer Maria, 1875–1926.
Prose and poetry.

(The German library ; v. 70)
Includes index.
I. Schwarz, Egon, 1922– . II. Title. III. Series.
PT2635.I65A2 1984   831'.912 [B]   83-27311
ISBN 0-8264-0286-0

Acknowledgments will be found on page 262,
which constitutes an extension of the copyright page.

Contents

Contents · vii

Foreword

Rilke happened to me early on, when I was still an undergraduate and just beginning at my own verses. Memory shows me on a Cape Cod beach that summer, a copy of the *Duino Elegies* in my hands, the just-published translation by J. B. Leishman and Stephen Spender, reading to a girl. Memory insists, indeed, on the book's being in my hands, for it had a blue dust jacket, turquoise or aquamarine, of low brilliance but great pathos, and the blue came off on my fingers, where it stayed indelibly for many days. So much for memory, also indelible for many days. I have forgotten the girl's name. And the summer ended and the war began.

The impression made by the *Elegies* on a young man innocent of German except for an ambition to sing Wagner is easier described—angels, great glamor, a certain emptiness as to content and sense—than accounted for: the young man was innocent of vastly more than the German language, and when told this was the book of a Great Poet he accepted that for fact and read with reverence, if not with judgment.

Rilke was not entirely absent from his thoughts in the forty-five years following, during which he read, among other things, Leishman's translations of *New Poems*, M. D. Herter Norton's translations of *The Sonnets to Orpheus* and *Translations from the Poetry of Rainer Maria Rilke*, as well as her English version of *The Notebooks of Malte Laurids Brigge*, and took account, especially in the past few years, of a fair number of new renderings of the *Elegies* and other things. He even got a little, a very little, homemade and bookish German in an attempt to see what was really going on, what a Great Poet was, and why Rilke was one, if he was. The attempt has not been altogether successful, for the ideas of a Great Poet, and of Modernism, and what its canon came to be, and how and by whom established, remain largely hidden, sometimes in mystery and sometimes in mere confusion, obscurantism, and special pleading. But what he is able to say is as follows.

A Great Poet does not become one, it appears, solely in virtue of his verses, for above a fairly low level of competence one lot of poems is about as good as another. There must also be The Life, followed by The Letters, followed by a vast accumulation of scholarship, criticism, biography, analysis, and legend.

Like the other masters who made the modern canon between 1910 and 1930 or so, Rilke was born to the old world of the nineteenth century and lived—just half his life—into the new world of the twentieth. Like those others, too, his productive life had to cross the Great Divide of 1914, of which Valéry wrote five years later the somber, brooding sentence that begins one of his essays: "We know now, we other civilizations, that we too are mortal."

Rilke's life was exemplary almost to the point of parody for the myth of the modern poet, or the romantic and symbolist poet born late into a strange new age in which Byronic loneliness and destiny came costumed à la Charlie Chaplin. If Hollywood were given to epics of The Life of the Poet, Rilke's life would be the ideal subject, as offering the maximum concentration of characteristics together with what, seen unsympathetically from outside, would look like low comedy tending to farce in its perfecting, taking to the end of the line, traits that other lives show only in solution and complexity.

Even from his birth, in Prague but of German-speaking parents, he was the prototypical displaced or stateless person. His mother raised him as a girl, and if that were not a good enough start, his father then gave over his further upbringing to a couple of military schools in which he was, expectably, miserable. He lived his life in a series of self-imposed exiles, had no homeland nor, it seems, cared to have one, and restlessly peregrinated Europe from Russia to Spain, from Paris to Switzerland and Italy, learning as well as Dante did, though voluntarily, about other people's stairs and other people's bread. His inner life was dominated by an introspection so intense and so unsatisfied that it sometimes seems objectless and empty of content, introspection for its own sake; while at the same time, and without contradiction, his eye for the outside world was shrewd and his observation of it precise. Indeed, it was the putting together of inward and outward that gave him, poetically, his greatest troubles and his greatest triumphs in equal measure. His artistic life was marked by prolonged periods of aridity and depression, punctuated in legendary romantic manner by such breakthroughs and furious spurts of inspiration as gave him and us the first of the *Elegies* in 1912 and their completion, with the unexpected gift of *The Sonnets to Orpheus,* in 1922. To complete the account, he was generally miserable in love and about love, and when he died of leukemia at only age fifty, the legend put about of his being poisoned by the thorn of a rose got some credibility from the legend he made to be inscribed on his tomb:

> O Rose, reiner Widerspruch, Lust,
> Niemandes Schlaf zu sein unter so viel Lidern.

> Rose
> o you
> paradox
> pure and simple
> pleasing yourself
> to be
> under all those eyelids
> the sleep of
> no one

—tr. Elizabeth Sewell[1]

The translators of the present selection, Leishman (with Spender for the *Elegies*) and Herter Norton, remain my favorites, not only because I came upon them first. They seem to me superior also in giving the literal sense without adding things of their own invention to eke out the measure; even so, Leishman's courageous will-

[1] In her book *Acquist* (Durham, N.C., 1983).

ingness to undertake the rimes of the original leads him quite often into serious awkwardnesses of diction and lapses from English idiom:

> Praising, that's it! As a praiser and blesser
> he came like the ore from the transient mine.
> Came with his heart, oh, transient presser,
> for men, of a never-exhaustible wine.

> —*The Sonnets to Orpheus*, I, 7, first stanza

The opening sounds like a cheerleader exhorting, or an ad for a product named Praising, and while the meaning of "presser" is quite clear the overtone from dry cleaning rather gets in the way. The passage illustrates also two out of three trivial but nevertheless real difficulties for the reader of English: Rilke says "O" a great deal, which the translator's rendering as "oh" makes just slightly more embarrassing; Rilke is also ever so fond of the exclamation point, which must have an entirely different tonality in German than it does in English, where it usually means that something has gone frightfully wrong with the writing. The third such difficulty is italicizing as a means to providing intensity where it would not otherwise exist:

> And he himself as he lay there in such relief,
> dissolving, under his drowsy eyelids, the sweetness
> of your light shaping into the sleep he had tasted,
> *seemed* to be under protection . . . *Within,* though:
>   who could avert,
> divert, the floods of origin flowing within him?
> Alas, there *was* no caution within that sleeper; . . .

> —The Third Elegy

That passage will illustrate also a major difficulty. Checking it against the original as far as I am able, I can see that the translators have followed the syntax of the German faithfully, and I sympathize with what I imagine must often have been their thought:

"That's what it says, isn't it?" as they grit their teeth and plough on through, italics and all, but still must record my impression that English just doesn't sound that way. It is perhaps reassuring, but not a present help, to be told that

> The *Duino Elegies,* Rilke's greatest work, are exceedingly difficult. . . . Even the German reader must struggle with their uncommon use of common words, with their sentences that tear open to let displaced parts of speech press into the gap, with their obscure allusions and mystifying or wildly farfetched metaphors (when fully understood, they will appear wonderfully apt and illuminating).[2]

To my complaints about idiom the translators might reasonably reply that they are trying to represent not merely a foreign tongue but also a style and manner in that tongue that is in the highest degree idiosyncratic and personal to its author: no wonder it sounds odd. And it is one of our cherished tenets about modern work that the really new (and hence the truly valuable?) will not sound like the poetry of the past at all. Against this, though, we should put the opinion of M. D. Herter Norton: "One is easily trapped, in one's absorption with the German, into certain inversions that accord neither with English idiom nor with the natural prose sequence of modern poetry, whereas Rilke's style being straightforward and simple, the translator is liable to misrepresent it if he departs from the simple and straightforward idiom of his own language."[3]

If the poets are full of contradiction, and they are—between the life and the work, between this work and that—it is the essence of their vocation to represent to us that we are full of contradiction too, contradiction which our ordinary lives with their ordinary language will neither account for nor take account of. The disagreement of translators as to whether Rilke is exceedingly difficult or simple and straightforward in such things as diction and syntax may be duplicated among his critics: his admirers have their doubts of him, his detractors doubt themselves.

[2] Gregor Sebba in *The Poem Itself,* ed. Stanley Burnshaw (New York: Horizon, 1983).
[3] Foreword to *Translations from the Poetry of Rainer Maria Rilke* (New York: Norton, 1938).

For instance. An American scholar, Walter Kaufmann, begins an essay called "Rilke: Nirvana or Creation" with the plain statement that "Rilke was one of the greatest poets of all time," which one would have thought enough. But he follows on at once with some half-dozen generous concessions to the other side, for example: he wrote bad poems (who doesn't?); he does not come across as an exemplary human being; the person depicted (in the Letters) is weak, precious, lacking in humor; many poems are marred by affectations, and even some of the best narrowly miss self-parody ("But they do miss it"); and, maybe most telling of all, the *Elegies* are uneven "and might be accounted a noble failure" but that the poet replaced the Fifth with a new one at the last moment; even so, fully half the ten are inferior. And then the essayist bases his claim for "one of the greatest poets of all time" on *theme:* "the choice between . . . intensity and peace," adding that Moses himself had offered the same choice some time before: Choose life or death this day.

That Moses had recommended the choice first is no obstacle, save that Moses was unequivocal about it, which Kaufmann does not claim for his poet: "It cannot be proved which choice is better, and a poet's business is not with proofs or arguments. He can try to explore experiences and show us what they are like. This is what Rilke does superbly."[4]

"Superbly" appears to substitute the arbitrary for the argument; or, as Freud said, "we must not be misled by the evidence." I bring up the instance not to criticize Kaufmann, but to suggest briefly the problems raised by the assertion, as by the denial, of "greatness" in poetry.

For my own part, and to conclude, I should locate the essential tension for Rilke not in theme but in method, in the tension between inside and outside. There are at the one extreme the *Ding-Gedichte,* or Object-poems, in which, as E. M. Butler and J. B. Leishman handsomely say, Rilke spoke not merely of things but for them; and, at the other, the quasi-religious assertions of the *Elegies* and the sometimes empty praise of the Orpheus poems, from which things and their thingness have largely departed.

Bringing together the inwardness of mind and the outwardness

---

[4] In *Rilke: The Alechemy of Alienation,* ed. Frank Baron, Ernst S. Dick, and Warren R. Maurer (Lawrence, Kans.: Regents Press of Kansas, 1980).

of world has always been implicit in the poetic attempt, though it seems to have become more of a critical question for the poets of this century than it was for their precursors. I like Rilke best—indeed love him best—when he appears to accomplish this with the least possible forcing of thoughts on things. For example, in "The Courtesan" of *New Poems,* included in this volume, where the courtesan and Venice, bridge, canal, and sea are brought together by subtle yet probable bonds of high civilization, culture, preciosity, the city founded in the sea, leading to the conclusion, so striking and at the same time just,

> And many a hopeful youth of high extraction
> will not survive my mouth's envenoming.

But at the same time, right in the course of this triumphal progression, there comes in that silly dog, whom people envy for her resting her hand on him, where the tone goes to pieces, Groucho Marx replaces Charlie Chaplin for an instant, and one can see the point of Hans Egon Holthusen's remark on Rilke's humorlessness and want of irony as "a highly gifted tastelessness."

What Rilke is best at, superb at, to revert to Kaufmann's word, is farewell, and especially to childhood. From the poet's life one might conclude that the escape from childhood was matter for congratulation; but in the fictive projection of Malte, and in the poetry, losing childhood is worse, losing "that land that long remains in sight/ before it ultimately disappears," and towards which we are always looking back:

> Just as he,
> on the last hill, that shows him all his valley
> for the last time, will turn and stop and linger,
> we live our lives, for ever taking leave.

> —The Eighth Elegy

And it is, because poetry is full of contradictions, the poet's and our own, when he puts together the elements that dominate his thought, or obsess it—childhood, aristocracy, the figure of the poet, and death—that Rilke seems most to triumph over, or be recon-

ciled with, his narcissism, snobbery, and vanity. For poetry re-
moves the poison and the curse from these traits, and allows the
poet to undertake in verse, as he was so little able to do in life, the
burden of the reality of others and the outside, his inwardness not
lost but re-enforced by all those famous "things." So it is in my
last instance, "The Singer Sings before a Child of Princes," an el-
egy for Paula Becker-Modersohn, which ends so appealingly in
image, inheritance, aesthetic, and lament scarce to be distin-
guished from praise:

> You pale child, you make the singer rich
> with your destiny that can so well be sung:
> So a great garden festival is mirrored
> with many lights in the astonished pool.
>
> In the dark poet silently each thing
> repeats itself: a star, a house, a wood.
> And many things that he would celebrate
> are standing round about your moving form.
>
> —tr. M. D. Herter Norton

This, and some others like it, continue to move me, after so many
years, as they did at first when I was nearer childhood. In it, Rilke
is neither "the Santa Claus of loneliness" (W. H. Auden) nor "the
Saint Francis of the Will to Power" (Erich Heller), but the legend
of himself, free of all doctrine, even his own.

HOWARD NEMEROV

Introduction

Rilke was an alienated poet. It seems he was alienated before he became a poet. Alienation is of course endemic in modern times. Its presence is general and atmospheric. In Rilke's case, however, it is possible to indicate some very specific causes: the neurotic personality of his mother who raised René as a girl; her frustrated social ambitions and foible for the aristocracy; her exaggerated Catholicism, suffused with spiritualism and superstition (all of which reemerge in her son, albeit in greatly modified form); the parents' bad marriage which was dissolved when he was still a boy; the tensions between the ruling minority of Germans to whom Rilke's family belonged and the repressed but rebellious Czech masses in his native Prague with whom he sympathized.

But the most traumatic experience seems to have been the military academy where he was sent at the age of ten. Toward the end of the nineteenth century—Rilke was born in 1875—the Austro-Hungarian army was a highly prestigious institution whose corps of officers offered the boys of impecunious but ambitious families attractive careers. Meticulous historical studies have shown that the military schools of St. Pölten and Mährisch-Weißkirchen which the cadet René Rilke attended from 1886 to 1891 were not at all the harsh and mindless prisons Rilke still remembered in outbursts of unmitigated pain decades later. But there is no doubt that the sensitive unathletic boy remained a despised outsider among his more robust and sports-minded comrades and that, subjectively, he lived in agonies of solitude and humiliation until a kind of nervous breakdown forced his family to remove him from this environment.

Back in Prague private tutors prepared him for the Gymnasium examination which he passed with flying colors. But the damage had been done, and René was spoiled for any of the bourgeois occupations his relatives still had in mind for him. As a matter of fact, he was spoiled for a conventional life altogether. From then on a profound disdain for the middle classes, their pleasures and attitudes, their state and institutions, their entire history and civilization constituted the core of his world view. But since he was not a revolutionary he sought orientation in the arts and the aristocratic values of the past against the industrial materialism of his society. This ideological mixture was not without its dangers and probably accounts for Rilke's admiration of Mussolini in the last years of his life. For a while he still attended the university, but what he now wanted was to be a writer and a poet. Indefatigably he corresponded with other writers, joined literary societies, organized poetic readings, published journals, and became a literary busybody in Prague. But above all he began to write. His linguistic facility was prodigious. He turned out large amounts of short stories, plays, and verse in the style of the period. A glance at the products of those years makes one realize that only an extraordinary exertion of the will and the mobilization of an exceptional but hidden talent could change the producer of these feeble beginnings into a great poet.

What saved him from the perils of mediocrity was his flight to Munich in 1896 and the love of a cultured, well-connected woman, Lou Andreas-Salomé. It is to her civilizing influence that the gauche lad from the provinces owed all-important impulses. She gave him self-confidence; she introduced him to the upper-class public on whose patronage he would always depend; under her expert guidance he took two trips to Russia whose devoutly religious, aristocratic-agrarian world he henceforth regarded as his spiritual home; and it was she who made him change his name to Rainer Maria, inseparable from his fame. Even after they ceased being lovers she remained a trusted friend to whom the inveterate correspondent Rilke wrote the most honest and therefore most revealing letters about his intimate life.

One should not underestimate the importance of Rilke's participation in the artists' colony of Worspwede near Bremen of which Heinrich Vogeler and Paula Modersohn-Becker were residents, his marriage to another member, the sculptress Clara Westhoff, the birth of their daughter Ruth. But Rilke was not made for marital life, and when the opportunity arose he left his family to join Auguste Rodin for the purpose of writing a monograph on the already famous sculptor.

This step proved to be of momentous significance for Rilke's development. He arrived in Paris in 1902. Until then he had written many works of prose and poetry, some of them quite popular, such as the *Stories of the Good Lord, The Lay of the Love and Death of the Cornet Christopher Rilke,* and *The Book of Hours.* The last work was often misunderstood as religious poetry because the individual poems present themselves as prayers spoken by a fictitious Russian monk at every hour of the day (hence the title). But at that time Rilke had long lost the literal faith of his childhood. The constant attempts at capturing God in ever-new formulations are masterly *études* in which Rilke perfected the mobility and articulateness of his poetic expression, rather than manifestations of pious belief. Only in the third and last part of the cycle, "The Book of Poverty and Death," with its invective against the big cities, symbols of the modern age, does the poet express his newest and most earnest concerns. But this section of *The Book of Hours* already incorporates his Parisian experiences.

The *New Poems* and *The Notebooks of Malte Laurids Brigge,* written from 1902 to 1910, constitute the main works of his middle period and are characterized by the impact of French culture. Referring to *The Book of Hours,* Rilke later said that he could have continued writing verses in its vein forever. That he did not is the reason why he is still being read today. In Paris, deeply impressed by Baudelaire's poetry, in close proximity to his successors, to Cézanne and the tireless Rodin whose motto was "travailler, toujours travailler," Rilke changed his aesthetic views. He now understood that poetry was "work," that it rested on respect for the outside world and on painstaking observation of "things." He now wandered through the city, with pencil and notebook in hand, through the parks and the boulevards, the museums and the zoo, putting down what he *saw.* No wonder the *New Poems* and *Malte* are replete with references to eyes, eyelids, gaze, etc., and with the effort of "learning to see." Of course, his new approach to writing did not obliterate the need to express his feelings, even his most subjective metaphysical whims. On the contrary, this fusion of outer reality with Rilke's innermost self, this language no longer based on "inspiration" alone, for the first time produced works of that kind of rich texture that is destined to last.

The *New Poems* all have a similar structure. They are "emblematic" poems. Their title conjures up a concrete thing, a town, a building, an *objet d'art,* a mythical or historical figure whose "reality" is skillfully recreated in language. What emerges is at first the conventional view. But all of a sudden, a "reversal" occurs, a switch in perspective that alters the nature of the person or thing, showing it in its "true" reality in Rilke's nonconformist illumination. Such is the case with the "Archaic Torso of Apollo" where the onlooker, let us say the visitor to a museum, in full possession of his senses and limbs, faces a disfigured piece of rock to which he is tempted to feel superior. But not for long. The inexorable law of art, imprinted on the stone, forces him to reverse his judgment. Such is the perfection of the sculpture, the density of its structure, that every square inch can take over the function of the whole. It sparkles, it vibrates, it "sees" so dynamically that it forces on the viewer the realization of his inferior existence and the need to change his life.

Or take "The Swan." It describes quite accurately three stages in the bird's movements: its clumsy gait on land, its fluttering descent into the water, its graceful progress once it finds itself in its true element. But all of this is allegory. With the swan as an example, the poem intimates that the tribulations of life may be preparatory for a freer, more dignified existence. Similarly, the "Roman Sarcophagi" are not what they seem, repositories of decay, symbols of transitoriness. The "switch" occurred sometime in history when they were put to a life-serving use as the water fountains one can see in many South European villages. Rilke's need to reinterpret accepted reality is obsessive. It does not spare the incarnations of Christianity. At the risk of blasphemy they are stripped of their divinity and revealed in their human, all too human agonies. Entire civilizations must undergo this Rilkean transformation. His Venice poems illustrate the principle. Cleverly the courtesan is likened to Venice, the point of comparison being the decadence of the city from its proud and beautiful past to its present venal status as tourist attraction. But the "alchemy" of poetry takes effect, the reversal sets in: not the city, it turns out, is moribund—it is already immortal—but those who frequent her in pursuit of easy pleasures, totally incognizant of any danger, perish in the unequal encounter. "Late Autumn in Venice" repeats the exercise. After the tourists are gone, the true character of the city reveals itself in all its historical glory to the lonely self of the poet who has stayed behind, defying the inhospitable fall weather. His vision of an energetic medieval city is tantamount to the rejection of its cult as the embodiment of death and beauty by many fin-de-siècle artists.

It is no accident that *The Notebooks of Malte Laurids Brigge* contain a similar reinterpretation of Venice. The thematic correspondences between the prose work and the cycle of poems are numerous. Almost every New Poem has its parallel in *Malte*. Nor is this the only indication that it is "a poet's novel." The individual "entries" in the fictitious diary are prose poems, circular in structure, metaphorical, associative, self-referential, and decipherable by the same methods of analysis as other hermetic poems. But *Malte* is more: one of the first modernistic novels ever written. No longer is there a plot, an omniscient narrator, a known historical, philosophical, or metaphysical reality against which the events, feelings, and thoughts of the protagonist can be measured. Instead, the reader is confronted with a thoroughly modern despair and disorientation, the self-projection of an inner life in process, agonizingly searching for meaning in an increasingly absurd world. Sociologically speaking, the personality thus presented is also frighteningly up-to-date. Malte's is the consciousness of a *déclassé*, a young Danish aristocrat who has lost his home, his fortune, his social status, his every certainty, one of thousands of refugees in the *cité lumière* of which he sees, with the incorruptible eye of the poet, the seedy side, the human refuse, the debris of a perverse civilization which he describes with the biting sarcasm of a deeply wounded satirist. Surrounded by the city's millions of sick, poor, twisted, insane or otherwise defective outcasts, empty husks of erstwhile human existences, threatened with becoming one of their number, the desperate poet seeks strength and solace in the memories of his "pre-revolutionary" childhood, in venerable cultural heroes (such as Baudelaire, Jammes, Beethoven, Ibsen, the Duse), and fraternal figures of history. Finally he takes recourse to metaphysical constructs, the most notorious of which is the dogma of "intransitive" or "nonpossessive" love. Since it recurs, basically unmodified in his later works including the *Duino Elegies* which he regarded as his *magnum opus,* it is not unfair to label it the "Rilke doctrine." It has aroused much controversy among Rilke scholars and has caused a great deal of doubt. But historically speaking, it is not too different from the fin-de-siècle conviction that life and art are mutually exclusive; and it also bears resemblance to the neo-Platonic belief that the seeker after truth must progress from sexual love to spiritual love, from the love of a fellow human being to that of creation and finally of God. Rilke's version would have it that traditionally women alone have carried the heavy burden and demonstrated the glory of love, whereas men have remained dilettantes in this difficult art. But the true lovers, the models for all great poets, were the women abandoned by their partners who, in their dereliction, had turned the pain of their lament into poetry. Beginning with the fictitious Abelone and ending with an array of female figures from history, Malte Laurids Rilke celebrates the origin of poetry and of the utopian "other vision" that will correct the evils of modern society in such unrequited love. Personal or possessive love stifles the partner and keeps the rays of love from reaching beyond him (or her) into the universe. The book ends therefore in a rewriting or "contraposto" of the parable of the Prodigal Son whose story is "the legend of him who did not want to be loved." He leaves his family because their love prevents him from developing his authentic personality. In the misery and destitution of his self-banishment he too learns to withold love from individuals and to train the intensity of his feeling on "God" himself, "but he almost forgot God over the hard work of drawing near him."

Here is another of Rilke's famous "reinterpretations" of a traditional myth. Obviously, he hopes like Malte that "there will come a day when my hand will be far from me, and when I bid it write, it will write words that I do not mean." But that mystical moment of conversion, "the time of that other interpretation" does not come. His diary ends indeterminately. Its last words are "noch nicht": not yet.

It is possible to date the beginning of Rilke's last poetic period with unusual precision: 1912. In that year his "vie des châteaux" led him to Duino, the castle of his friend Princess Marie von Thurn und Taxis in whose garden, leaning against a tree, he had a mystical experience, a widening of consciousness during which he was inspired to compose the beginnings of a number of poems the likes of which he had never written before. When he came to from this trancelike state he was incapable of finishing them. On his incessant travels to Italy, to Spain, to Egypt, the best he could do was to add a couple of lines here and there, the rest eluded him. World War I caught him in Germany where he had found a congenial publisher in Anton Kippenberg of the famous Insel Verlag. The war and the destruction it wrought on the world he knew drove Rilke to despair. He could not return to his apartment in Paris and the possessions he had left behind. Even though he was released from conscription at the behest of highly placed friends, he suffered intolerably from having been inducted at all. To Rilke's immense relief the war finally ended. He greeted the revolutionary movements of the first moment with approval and hope, but was soon disappointed. His financial situation became precarious because of the devaluation of the German currency. At last, an invitation enabled him to go to Switzerland where he resided for the rest of his life.

During all this time, the unfinished poems burdened his mind, to no avail. Finally, after moving from place to place for two years, Rilke found his permanent abode, which patrons first rented and then bought for his use. In this medieval castlelike tower, called Muzot (pronounced: "Muzotte"), ideally suited to his simple but aristocratic taste, Rilke's prediction came true that he would be able to write as soon as he had the proper roof over his head. These sentences occur in *Malte*, written more than a decade earlier: "Oh, what a happy fate, to sit in a quiet room of an ancestral house, among many calm, sedentary things . . . : in that I would have written." During a few weeks in the winter of 1922, in what he himself describes as a creative storm, Rilke finished the long awaited ten poems, called *Duino Elegies* after the place of their inspiration, and quite unexpectedly was able to add another cycle of poems which he titled *Sonnets to Orpheus*.

Traditionally, elegies are poems of lament which mourn the transitoriness of human life and the futility of all things. So do Rilke's. They begin with the famous question: "Who, if I cried, would hear me?" An 'I' struggles to express a solitude that has been intensified to the point of unbearable torture. But the outcry of protest remains hypothetical. A series of subjunctive clauses makes clear that the line has already been crossed and the creaturelike utterance of one's torment no longer provides solace. The other pole, the highest authority which the powerless 'I' of the *Elegies* faces, is the Angel, a fictional figure who has already overcome the world of concrete phenomena which causes the 'I' to suffer so. A great deal of speculation has gone into the attempts to illuminate the meaning of the angels. Rilke himself, who at this time no longer considered himself a Christian, warned against viewing them in the light of that religion. It is probably best to think of them as embodiments of perfection, the inhabitants of the realm of the "other interpretation," identical with absolute poetry which had eluded Malte. Suffice it to say that unlike in the *Notebooks* the quest for God has been given up in the *Elegies* as impossible, and even the angel remains infinitely distant from man, unreachable. So uncanny and overwhelming is the angel that closer contact with it could not even be wished for, indeed would lead to the destruction of the individual. Of necessity, then, the 'I' decides to suppress the cry he had hardly begun: "So I repress myself, and swallow the call-note of depth-dark sobbing."

The outcry can be suppressed, but not the despair. What follows next is a gripping account of human solitude, of a total estrangement in which man is gradually disowned by all creatures. All the various characters of the *Elegies,* the angels, the many plants and animals, indeed the lifeless doll seem to have an advantage over man. In an exploration of the possibilities of earthly life, he parades before the reader, in the form of near-mythic figures, various exemplary forms of human existence that have traditionally been considered especially meaningful or sublime. He questions each as to the purpose of life: the child, the hero, the saints. One after the other, they are summoned forth and are asked to show us how the terrible fragility and the oppressive loneliness of existence might be overcome. Even the lovers merely occlude from one another the true meaning of life. The answer however is always the same: although Rilke never tires in his praise of the earthly magnificence of these figures, not a single one of them is found to be sufficient to justify human existence and to break through man's abject solitude.

What aspects of contemporary civilization have driven Rilke to such desperation? Since one can find ample evidence that he was partial to the periods preceding his own, we must now ask what changes history had brought so that what Rilke was fond of seemed threatened and what he feared seemed about to triumph? Strewn throughout the cycle, the answers can be found in the *Elegies,* such as in the Seventh where the speaking voice laments: "Where once was a permanent house, up starts some invented structure across our vision. . . . Spacious garners of power are formed by the Time Spirit, formless as that tense urge he's extracting from everything else. Temples he knows no longer." An industrial site, an electrical plant, is presented here as a construction typical of the present. Modern civilization is antagonistic to art. It is without feeling, without a sense of respect and solely oriented toward the utilitarian subjugation of nature.

At this point, however, it is necessary to add mention of another mythical figure: that of the poet who, despite the fact that he never appears personally on the poems' stage, is nevertheless always present as the principal and most eloquent advocate of man. It is to him that Rilke entrusts the possible salvation of mankind from the clutches of industrial capitalism. Such silver-lining, such glimpses of affirmation are not unusual even in the classical elegy. They are all-important in Rilke's cycle. It is no doubt the Ninth in which the breakthrough occurs most potently, where the hymnic tone triumphantly overwhelms the elegiac. It is the poet's task to fulfill the purpose of life by experiencing, praising, and thereby preserving the remnants of an earlier civilization. He is exhorted by the voice to show the angel "some simple thing." The famous enumeration of "House, Bridge, Fountain, Gate, Jug, Fruit tree, Window," with the characteristic addendum "Pillar, Tower," evokes a bucolic landscape, a patriarchal world of creation and participation in which man was not yet alienated from things, where he and nature collaborated in the production of all artefacts. This much admired catalogue, however sublime it might be, in the final analysis glorifies a retreat into the precapitalist past.

Even more than in the *Elegies* a new myth is proclaimed in the *Sonnets* that does away with the destructive dualisms of Western thought and replaces them with a monistic vision that restores the lost universal unity. Its prophet is Orpheus, the singer and lover of all things. If in the *Elegies,* despite an occasional upsurge of consent, lamentation predominates, the *Sonnets* are the opposite: poems of jubilant affirmation and glorification. It is not difficult to infer what it was in the Orphic mythology that attracted Rilke. First and foremost, he was a poet of such power that even the animals in the forest listened rapturously and the stones were moved. He had lost his young wife, Eurydice, to an early death and thereby became one of those deprived lovers that were compelled to disperse the strength of their feeling in all directions. Furthermore he was the only mortal allowed into Hades, the land of the dead, in an unsuccessful attempt at regaining Eurydice, and thus familiar with both realms, a monist and unifier. The legend of his own death is equally significant: because of his total absorption in his music he rejected the sexual advances of the maenads, excited followers of Dionysos, who killed him in revenge. In this manner he radically exemplifies the poet who will give up his life for his art. Finally, the legend has it that Orpheus was dismembered and the parts of his body distributed all over Greece. Wherever one was buried, poetry sprang up spontaneously. This corresponds to Rilke's cherished belief that in the end the true poet must have spent himself so completely that nothing remains of him except the substance of his art in everybody's consciousness.

With the publication of these two cycles Rilke felt he had done his life's work. Some critics like to think that the serene poems of his last years, his dedicated translations of Paul Valéry, and the cycles of poems he composed in French merit consideration as a separate "epoch" in his life. Be this as it may, Rilke died of leukemia, only fifty-one years old, in 1926. He is buried in the idyllic cemetery of Raron at the edge of the Rhône valley, the landscape he had loved more than any other.

E. S.

THE
NOTEBOOKS OF
MALTE LAURIDS
BRIGGE

Book One

S o, then people do come here in order to live; I would sooner
have thought one died here. I have been out. I saw: hospitals.
I saw a man who swayed and sank to the ground. People gathered
round him, so I was spared the rest. I saw a pregnant woman. She
was pushing herself cumbrously along a high, warm wall, groping
for it now and again as if to convince herself it was still there. Yes,
it was still there. And behind it? I looked on my map: Maison
d'Accouchement. Good. They will deliver her—they know how.
Further on, rue Saint-Jacques, a big building with a cupola. The
map said: Val-de-Grâce, Hôpital militaire. I didn't really need this
information, but it can't do any harm. The street began to smell
from all sides. A smell, so far as one could distinguish, of iodo-
form, of the grease of pommes frites, of fear. All cities smell in
summer. Then I saw a curiously purblind house; it was not to be
found on the map, but above the door there stood, still fairly legible:
Asyle de nuit. Beside the entrance were the prices. I read them. The
place was not expensive.

And what else? A child in a standing baby-carriage. It was fat,
greenish, and had a distinct eruption on its forehead. This was ev-
idently peeling as it healed and did not hurt. The child slept, its
mouth was open, breathing iodoform, pommes frites and fear. It
was simply like that. The main thing was, being alive. That was
the main thing.

To think that I cannot give up sleeping with the window open. Electric street-cars rage ringing through my room. Automobiles run their way over me. A door slams. Somewhere a window-pane falls clattering; I hear its big splinters laugh, its little ones snicker. Then suddenly a dull, muffled noise from the other side, within the house. Someone is climbing the stairs. Coming, coming incessantly. Is there, there for a long time, then passes by. And again the street. A girl screams: Ah tais-toi, je ne veux plus. An electric car races up excitedly, then away, away over everything. Someone calls. People are running, overtake each other. A dog barks. What a relief: a dog. Toward morning a cock even crows, and that is boundless comfort. Then I suddenly fall asleep.

These are the noises. But there is something here that is more terrible: the stillness. I believe that in great conflagrations there sometimes occurs such a moment of extreme tension: the jets of water fall back, the firemen no longer climb their ladders, no one stirs. Noiselessly a black cornice thrusts itself forward overhead, and a high wall, behind which the fire shoots up, leans forward, noiselessly. All stand and wait, with shoulders raised and faces puckered over the eyes, for the terrific crash. The stillness here is like that.

I am learning to see. I don't know why it is, but everything penetrates more deeply into me and does not stop at the place where until now it always used to finish. I have an inner self of which I was ignorant. Everything goes thither now. What happens there I do not know.

Writing a letter today, I was struck by the fact that I had been here only three weeks. Three weeks elsewhere, in the country for example, would be like a day; here they seem like years. And I mean to write no more letters. What's the use of telling anyone that I am changing? If I am changing, then surely I am no longer the person I was, and if I am something else than heretofore, then it is clear that I have no acquaintances. And to strange people, to people who do not know me, I cannot possibly write.

Have I said it before? I am learning to see. Yes, I am beginning. It still goes badly. But I intend to make the most of my time.

To think, for instance, that I have never been aware before how many faces there are. There are quantities of human beings, but there are many more faces, for each person has several. There are people who wear the same face for years; naturally it wears out, it gets dirty, it splits at the folds, it stretches, like gloves one has worn on a journey. These are thrifty, simple people; they do not change their face, they never even have it cleaned. It is good enough, they say, and who can prove to them the contrary? The question of course arises, since they have several faces, what do they do with the others? They store them up. Their children will wear them. But sometimes, too, if happens that their dogs go out with them on. And why not? A face is a face.

Other people put their faces on, one after the other, with uncanny rapidity and wear them out. At first it seems to them they are provided for always; but they scarcely reach forty—and they have come to the last. This naturally has something tragic. They are not accustomed to taking care of faces, their last is worn through in a week, has holes, and in many places is thin as paper; and then little by little the under layer, the noface, comes through, and they go about with that.

But the woman, the woman; she had completely collapsed into herself, forward into her hands. It was at the corner of rue Notre-Dame-des-Champs. I began to walk softly as soon as I saw her. When poor people are reflecting they should not be disturbed. Perhaps their idea will yet occur to them.

The street was too empty; its emptiness was bored; it caught my step from under my feet and clattered about with it hither and yon, as with a wooden clog. The woman startled and pulled away too quickly out of herself, too violently, so that her face remained in her two hands. I could see it lying in them, its hollow form. It cost me indescribable effort to stay with those hands and not to look at what had torn itself out of them. I shuddered to see a face from the inside, but still I was much more afraid of the naked flayed head without a face.

I am afraid. One has to take some action against fear, once one has it. It would be very nasty to fall ill here, and if it occurred to anyone to get me into the Hôtel-Dieu I should certainly die there. This hôtel is a pleasant hôtel, enormously frequented. One can scarcely examine the façade of the Cathedral of Paris without danger of being run over by one of the many vehicles that must cross the open space as quickly as possible to get in yonder. They are small omnibuses that sound their bells incessantly, and the Duke of Sagan himself would be obliged to have his equipage halted if some small dying person had taken it into his head to go straight into God's Hôtel. Dying people are headstrong, and all Paris is at a standstill when Madame Legrand, brocanteuse from the rue des Martyrs, comes driving toward a certain square in the Cité. It is to be noted that these fiendish little carriages are provided with uncommonly intriguing windows of opaque glass, behind which one can picture the most magnificent agonies; the phantasy of a concierge suffices for that. If one has even more power of imagination and it runs in other directions, conjecture becomes simply boundless. But I have also seen open cabs arriving, hired cabs with their hoods folded back, plying for the usual fare: two francs for the hour of agony.

This excellent hôtel is very ancient. Even in King Clovis' time people died in it in a number of beds. Now they are dying there in 559 beds. Factory-like, of course. Where production is so enormous an individual death is not so nicely carried out; but then that doesn't matter. It is quantity that counts. Who cares anything today for a finely-finished death? No one. Even the rich, who could after all afford this luxury of dying in full detail, are beginning to be careless and indifferent; the wish to have a death of one's own is growing ever rarer. A while yet, and it will be just as rare as a life of one's own. Heavens, it's all there. One arrives, one finds a life, ready made, one has only to put it on. One wants to leave or one is compelled to: anyway, no effort: Voilà votre mort, monsieur. One dies just as it comes; one dies the death that belongs to the disease one has (for since one has come to know all diseases, one knows, too, that the different lethal terminations belong to the disease and not to the people; and the sick person has so to speak nothing to do).

In sanatoria, where people die so willingly and with so much gratitude to doctors and nurses, they die from one of the deaths attached to the institution; that is favorably regarded. But when one dies at home, it is natural to choose that polite death of genteel circles, with which a first-class funeral is so to say inaugurated, with the whole sequence of its delightful formalities. The poor then stand outside such a house and gaze their fill. Their death is, of course, banal, without any fuss. They are glad when they find one that fits approximately. Too large it may be: one always keeps growing a little. Only when it does not meet round the chest or when it strangles, then there is difficulty.

When I think back to my home, where there is nobody left now, I imagine that formerly this must have been otherwise. Formerly one knew (or perhaps one guessed it) that one had one's death within one, as a fruit its kernel. The children had a little death within them and the grown-ups a big one. The women had it in their womb and the men in their breast. One *had* it, and that gave one a singular dignity and a quiet pride.

My grandfather, old Chamberlain Brigge, still looked as if he carried a death within him. And what a death it was: two months long and so loud that it could be heard as far off as the manor farm.

The long, old manor house was too small for this death; it seemed as if wings would have to be added, for the chamberlain's body grew larger and larger, and he wanted continually to be carried out of one room into another, falling into a terrible rage when, though the day had not yet come to an end, there was no room left in which he had not already lain. Then the whole troop of men-servants, maids and dogs, that he always had about him, had to go upstairs with him, under the usherance of the major-domo, into the room in which his saintly mother had died, which had been kept exactly as she had left it twenty-three years before and in which no one else had ever been allowed to set foot. Now the whole pack burst in. The curtains were drawn back, and the robust light of a summer afternoon inspected all the shy, frightened objects and turned clumsily around in the suddenly opened-up mirrors. And the people did likewise. There were chamber-maids who, in their curiosity, did not know where their hands were loitering, young menservants who gaped at everything, and older retainers who went about trying to recollect all that had been told them about this close-locked room in which they now found themselves at last.

But the dogs especially seemed to find their sojourn in a room where everything had a smell uncommonly exciting. The tall, lean Russian wolfhounds ran busily back and forth behind the arm-chairs, crossed the apartment in long dance-steps with a swinging movement, reared like heraldic animals, and looked, resting their slender paws on the white-and-gold window-sill, with tense pointed faces and backdrawn foreheads, to right and left out into the courtyard. Small glove-yellow dachshunds sat in the large silk-up-holstered easy-chair near the window, looking as though every-thing were quite in order, and a sullen-looking rubican setter rubbed his back along the edge of a gilt-legged table, causing the Sèvres cups on its painted tray to tremble.

Yes, for these absent-minded, drowsy things it was a terrible time. From books that some hasty hand had clumsily opened rose-leaves would tumble, to be trampled underfoot; small fragile objects were seized, and, when they were immediately broken, quickly put back again; many hidden things, too, were thrust beneath curtains, or even flung behind the gilt net-work of the fire-screen and from time to time something fell, fell muffled on carpeting, fell clear on the hard parquetry, but here and there it smashed, shattering sharply or cracking apart almost inaudibly, for these things, pampered as they were, could not survive any sort of fall.

And had it occurred to anyone to ask what caused all this, what had called down upon this anxiously guarded room the full mea-sure of destruction,—there would have been but *one* answer: Death.

The death of Chamberlain Christoph Detlev Brigge at Ulsgaard. For he lay, welling large out of his dark blue uniform, in the mid-dle of the floor and never stirred. In his big, stranger's face, no longer familiar to anyone, the eyes had fallen shut: he did not see what was happening. They had tried at first to lay him on the bed, but this he had resisted, for he detested beds since those first nights in which his illness had grown. Besides, the bed up there had proved too small, so nothing else remained but to lay him thus upon the carpet; for downstairs again he had refused to go.

So now he lay there, and one might think that he had died. The dogs, as it slowly began to grow dark, had one after the other squeezed through the crack in the door. Only the rubican setter with the sullen face sat beside his master, and one of his broad, tufted forepaws lay on Christoph Detlev's big, grey hand. Most of the servants, too, were now standing outside in the white corridor, which was brighter than the room; those, however, who still remained within glanced furtively now and then at the great darkening heap in the middle, and they wished that it were nothing more than a large garment over some rotten thing.

But it was something more. It was a voice, that voice which seven weeks before no one had known yet: for it was not the voice of the chamberlain. It was not Christoph Detlev to whom this voice belonged, but Christoph Detlev's death.

Christoph Detlev's death had been living at Ulsgaard for many, many days now and had spoken to everyone and demanded: demanded to be carried, demanded the blue room, demanded the little salon, demanded the large hall. Demanded the dogs, demanded that people should laugh, talk, play and be quiet and all at the same time. Demanded to see friends, women, and people who were dead, and demanded to die itself: demanded. Demanded and shouted.

For when night had fallen and those of the overwearied domestics who were not on watch tried to go to sleep, then Christoph Detlev's death would shout, shout and groan, roar so long and so constantly that the dogs, at first howling along with him, were silent and did not dare lie down, but stood on their long, slender, trembling legs, and were afraid. And when they heard it in the village roaring through the spacious, silvery, Danish summer night, they rose from their beds as if there were a thunderstorm, put on their clothes and remained sitting round the lamp without a word until it was over. And women near their time were laid in the most remote rooms and in the most impenetrable closets; but they heard it, they heard it, as if it were in their own bodies, and they pled to be allowed to get up too, and came, white and wide, and sat among the others with their blurred faces. And the cows that were calving at that time were helpless and bound, and from the body of one they tore the dead fruit with all the entrails, as it would not come at all. And everyone did their daily work badly and forgot to bring in the hay, because they spent the day dreading the night and because they were so fagged out by all their continuous watchings and terrified arisings, that they could not remember anything. And when they went on Sundays to the white, peaceful church, they prayed that there might no longer be a master at Ulsgaard: for this was a dreadful master. And what they all thought and prayed the pastor said aloud from the height of his pulpit; for he also had no nights any more and could not understand God. And the bell said it, having found a terrible rival that boomed the whole night through, and against which, even though it took to sounding with all its metal, it could do nothing. Indeed, they all said it; and there was one among the young men who dreamed that he had gone to the manor-house and killed the master with his pitch-fork; and they were so exasperated, so done, so overwrought, that they all listened as he told his dream, and quite unconsciously, looked at him to see if he were really equal to such a deed. Thus did they feel and speak throughout the whole district where, only a few weeks before, the chamberlain had been loved and pitied. But though they talked thus, nothing changed. Christoph Detlev's death, which dwelt at Ulsgaard, was not to be hurried. It had come to stay for ten weeks, and for ten weeks it stayed. And during that time it was more master than ever Christoph Detlev Brigge had been; it was like a king who, afterward and forever, is called the Terrible.

That was not the death of just any dropsical person; it was the wicked, princely death which the chamberlain had carried within him and nourished on himself his whole life long. All excess of pride, will and lordly vigor that he himself had not been able to consume in his quiet days, had passed into his death, that death which now sat, dissipating, at Ulsgaard.

How the chamberlain would have looked at anyone who asked of him that he should die any other death than this. He was dying his own hard death.

And when I think of the others whom I have seen or about whom I have heard: it is always the same. They all have had a death of their own. Those men who carried theirs inside their armor, within, like a prisoner; those women who grew very old and small, and then on a huge bed, as on a stage, before the whole family, the household and the dogs, passed away in discreet and seigniorial dignity. Even the children, and the very little ones at that, did not die just any child's death; they pulled themselves together and died that which they already were, and that which they would have become.

And what a melancholy beauty it gave to women when they were pregnant and stood there, and in their big bodies, upon which their slender hands instinctively rested, were *two* fruits: a child and a death. Did not the dense, almost nourishing smile on their quite vacant faces come from their sometimes thinking that both were growing?

I have taken action against fear. I have sat all night and written; and now I am as agreeably tired as after a long walk over the fields of Ulsgaard. Still it is hard to think that all that is no more, that strangers live in the old long manor house. It may be that in the white room up in the gable the maids are sleeping now, sleeping their heavy, moist sleep from evening until morning.

And one has nothing and nobody, and one travels about the world with a trunk and a case of books and really without curiosity. What sort of a life is it really: without a house, without inherited things, without dogs? If only one had at least one's memories. But who has them? Were childhood there—it is as though buried. Perhaps one must be old to be able to reach all that. I think it must be good to be old.

Today we had a lovely autumn morning. I walked through the Tuileries. Everything that lay toward the East, before the sun, dazzled. Where the sun fell all was hung with the mist as with a grey curtain of light. Grey in the grey, the statues sunned themselves in the not yet unshrouded gardens. Single flowers in the long parterres stood up and said: "Red", with a frightened voice. Then a very tall, slim man came round the corner from the Champs Elysées; he carried a crutch, but no longer thrust under his shoulder,—he held it in front of him lightly, and from time to time set it down firm and loud like a herald's staff. He could not repress a smile of joy, and smiled, past everything, at the sun, at the trees. His step was bashful as a child's, but unusually light, full of re-membrance of earlier walking.

How much such a little moon can do. There are days when everything about one is bright, light, scarcely stated in the clear air and yet distinct. Even what lies nearest has tones of distance, has been taken away and is only shown, not proffered; and every-thing related to expanse—the river, the bridges, the long streets, and the squares that squander themselves—has taken that expanse in behind itself, is painted on it as on silk. It is not possible to say what a bright green wagon on the Pont-Neuf can then become, or some red that is not to be held in, or even a simple placard on the party wall of a pearl-grey group of houses. Everything is simpli-fied, brought into a few right, clear planes, like the face in a Ma-net portrait. And nothing is trivial and superfluous. The booksell-ers on the quai open their stalls, and the fresh or worn yellow of their books, the violet brown of the bindings, the bigger green of an album—everything harmonizes, counts, takes part, creating a fullness in which nothing lacks.

In the street below there is the following compositon: a small wheelbarrow, pushed by a woman; on the front of it, a handor-gan, lengthwise. Behind that, crossways, a baby-basket in which a very small child is standing on firm legs, happy in its bonnet, re-fusing to be made to sit. From time to time the woman turns the handle of the organ. At that the small child stands up again, stamping in its basket, and a little girl in a green Sunday dress dances and beats a tambourine up toward the windows.

I think I ought to begin to do some work, now that I am learning to see. I am twenty-eight years old, and almost nothing has been done. To recapitulate: I have written a study on Carpaccio which is bad, a drama entitled "Marriage", which sets out to demon-strate something false by equivocal means, and some verses. Ah!

but verses amount to so little when one writes them young. One ought to wait and gather sense and sweetness a whole life long, and a long life if possible, and then, quite at the end, one might perhaps be able to write ten lines that were good. For verses are not, as people imagine, simply feelings (those one has early enough),—they are experiences. For the sake of a single verse, one must see many cities, men and things, one must know the animals, one must feel how the birds fly and know the gesture with which the little flowers open in the morning. One must be able to think back to roads in unknown regions, to unexpected meetings and to partings one had long seen coming; to days of childhood that are still unexplained, to parents whom one had to hurt when they brought one some joy and one did not grasp it (it was a joy for someone else); to childhood illnesses that so strangely begin with such a number of profound and grave transformations, to days in rooms withdrawn and quiet and to mornings by the sea, to the sea itself, to seas, to nights of travel that rushed along on high and flew with all the stars—and it is not yet enough if one may think of all this. One must have memories of many nights of love, none of which was like the others, of the screams of women in labor, and of light, white, sleeping women in childbed, closing again. But one must also have been beside the dying, must have sat beside the dead in the room with the open window and the fitful noises. And still it is not yet enough to have memories. One must be able to forget them when they are many and one must have the great patience to wait until they come again. For it is not yet the memories themselves. Not till they have turned to blood within us, to glance and gesture, nameless and no longer to be distinguished from ourselves—not till then can it happen that in a most rare hour the first word of a verse arises in their midst and goes forth from them.

But all my verses had a different origin; so they are not verses. And when I wrote my drama, how I went astray. Was I an imitator and a fool that I needed a third person to tell of the fate of two human beings who were making things hard for each other? How easily I fell into the trap. And I ought to have known that this third person who pervades all lives and literatures, this ghost of a third person who never was, has no significance and must be disavowed. He is one of the pretexts of Nature who is always endeavoring to divert the attention of men from her deepest secrets.

He is the screen behind which a drama unfolds. He is the noise at the threshold of the voiceless silence of a real conflict. One is inclined to think that heretofore they have all found it too difficult to speak of the two concerned. The third, just because he is so unreal, is the easiest part of the undertaking; him they have all been able to manage. From the very beginning of their plays one notices their impatience to arrive at this third person; they can scarcely wait for him. The moment he appears all is well. But how tiresome when he is late. Absolutely nothing can happen without him; everything stops, stands, waits. Yes, and how if this damming and stagnation kept on? What, Sir Dramatist, and you, public that knows life, what if he were found missing, this popular man-about-town or this arrogant youth, who fits into every marriage like a master-key? What if, for example, the devil had taken him? Let's assume this. One suddenly observes the unnatural emptiness of the theaters; they are bricked up like dangerous holes; only the moths from the rims of the boxes tumble through the unsupported void. The dramatists no longer enjoy their villa quarter. All the public detective agencies search on their behalf in remote parts of the world for the irreplaceable third person who was the action itself.

And all the time they are living among people—not these "third" persons, but the two, about whom so incredibly much might be said, about whom nothing has ever been said yet, although they suffer and act and don't know how to help themselves.

It is ridiculous. Here I sit in my little room, I, Brigge, who have grown to be twenty-eight years old and of whom no one knows. I sit here and am nothing. And nevertheless this nothing begins to think and thinks, five flights up, on a grey Parisian afternoon, these thoughts:

Is it possible, it thinks, that one has not yet seen, known and said anything real or important? Is it possible that one has had millennia of time to observe, reflect and note down, and that one has let those millennia slip away like a recess interval at school in which one eats one's sandwich and an apple?

Yes, it is possible.

Is it possible that despite discoveries and progress, despite culture, religion and world-wisdom, one has remained on the surface of life? Is it possible that one has even covered this surface, which might still have been something, with an incredibly uninteresting stuff which makes it look like the drawing-room furniture during summer holidays?

Yes, it is possible.

Is it possible that the whole history of the world has been misunderstood? Is it possible that the past is false, because one has always spoken of its masses just as though one were telling of a coming together of many human beings, instead of speaking of the individual around whom they stood because he was a stranger and was dying?

Yes, it is possible.

Is it possible that one believed it necessary to retrieve what happened before one was born? Is it possible that one would have to remind every individual that he is indeed sprung from all who have gone before, has known this therefore and should not let himself be persuaded by others who knew otherwise?

Yes, it is possible.

Is it possible that all these people know with perfect accuracy a past that has never existed? Is it possible that all realities are nothing to them; that their life is running down, unconnected with anything, like a clock in an empty room—?

Yes, it is possible.

Is it possible that one knows nothing of young girls, who nevertheless live? Is it possible that one says "women", "children", "boys", not guessing (despite all one's culture, not guessing) that these words have long since had no plural, but only countless singulars?

Yes, it is possible.

Is it possible that there are people who say "God" and mean that this is something they have in common?—Just take a couple of schoolboys: one buys a pocket knife and his companion buys another exactly like it on the same day. And after a week they compare knives and it turns out that there is now only a very distant resemblance between the two—so differently have they developed in different hands. ("Well," says the mother of one, "if you always must wear everything out immediately—") Ah, so: Is it possible to believe one could have a God without using him?

Yes, it is possible.

But if all this is possible—has even no more than a semblance of possibility—then surely, for all the world's sake, something must happen. The first comer, he who has had this disturbing thought, must begin to do some of the things that have been neglected; even if he is just anybody, by no means the most suitable person: there is no one else at hand. This young, insignificant foreigner, Brigge, will have to sit down in his room five flights up and write, day and night: yes, he will have to write; that is how it will end.

Twelve years old, or at most thirteen, I must have been at the time. My father had taken me with him to Urnekloster. I do not know what occasion he had to look up his father-in-law. Since my mother's death many years before, the two men had not seen each other, and my father himself had never been in the old manor house to which Count Brahe had been late in retiring. Afterwards I never again saw that remarkable house, which at my grandfather's death passed into strange hands. As I recover it in recalling my child-wrought memories, it is no complete building; it is all broken up inside me; here a room, there a room, and here a piece of hallway that does not connect these two rooms but is preserved, as a fragment, by itself. In this way it is all dispersed within me—the rooms, the stairways that descended with such ceremonious deliberation, and other narrow, spiral stairs in the obscurity of which one moved as blood does in the veins; the tower rooms, the high-hung balconies, the unexpected galleries onto which one was thrust out through a little door—all that is still in me and will never cease to be in me. It is as though the picture of this house had fallen into me from an infinite height and had shattered against my very ground.

There remains whole in my heart, so it seems to me, only that large hall in which we used to gather for dinner every evening at seven o'clock. I never saw this room by day; I do not even remember whether it had windows or on what they looked out; always, whenever the family entered, the candles were burning in the ponderous branched candlesticks, and in a few minutes one forgot the time of day and all that one had seen outside. This lofty and, as I suspect, vaulted chamber was stronger than everything else. With its darkening height, with its never quite clarified corners, it sucked all images out of one without giving one any definite substitute for them. One sat there as if dissolved; entirely without will, without consciousness, without desire, without defence. One was like a vacant spot. I remember that at first this annihilating state almost caused me nausea; it brought on a kind of sea-sickness which I only overcame by stretching out my leg until I touched with my foot the knee of my father who sat opposite me. It did not strike me until afterwards that he seemed to understand, or at least to tolerate, this singular behavior, although there existed between us an almost cool relationship which would not account for such a gesture. Nevertheless it was this slight contact that gave me strength to support the long repasts. And after a few weeks of spasmodic endurance, I became, with the almost boundless adaptability of a child, so inured to the eeriness of these gatherings, that it no longer cost me effort to sit at table for two hours; now these hours even passed comparatively swiftly, for I occupied myself in observing those present.

My grandfather called them "the family", and I also heard the others use the same term, which was entirely arbitrary. For, although these four persons were distantly related to one another, they in no way belonged together. My uncle, who sat next me, was an old man, on whose hard, burned countenance there were some black spots, the result, as I learned, of an exploded powder-charge; morose and malcontent as he was, he had retired from the army with the rank of major, and now made alchemistic experiments in some region of the manor house unknown to me; was also, as I heard the servants say, in communication with a prison whence once or twice a year corpses were sent him with which he shut himself in night and day, and which he cut up and prepared in some mysterious fashion so that they withstood putrefaction. Opposite him was the place of Miss Mathilde Brahe. She was a person of uncertain age, a distant cousin of my mother's; nothing was known of her beyond the fact that she kept up a very lively correspondence with an Austrian spiritualist, who called himself Baron Nolde and to whom she was so completely submissive that she would not undertake the slightest thing without first soliciting his consent, or rather, something like his benediction. She was at that time exceptionally stout, of a soft, lazy amplitude that looked as if it had been carelessly poured into her loose, light dresses; her movements were tired and undecided, and her eyes watered continually. And yet there was something about her which reminded me of my frail and slender mother. The longer I looked at her, the more I found in her face all those delicate and gentle features which since my mother's death I had never been able rightly to recall; only now, since I was seeing Mathilde Brahe every day, did I know again how she had looked; indeed, perhaps I knew it for the first time. Only now did the hundreds and hundreds of details compose in me an image of this dead mother, that image which accompanies me everywhere. Later it became clear to me that all the details which determined my mother's features were actually present in Miss Brahe's face—only they were pushed apart, warped and no longer connected with each other, as if some strange face had thrust itself among them.

Beside this lady sat the little son of a female cousin, a boy about the same age as myself, but smaller and more delicate. His pale, lean neck rose out of a pleated ruff and disappeared under a long chin. His lips were thin and tightly shut, his nostrils trembled slightly, and of his fine dark-brown eyes only one was moveable. It often sent across to me a quiet and melancholy look, while the other always remained fixed in the same corner, as though it had been sold and no longer came into account.

At the head of the table stood my grandfather's huge armchair, which a man-servant who had nothing else to do pushed beneath him and in which the old man took up but very little room. There were people who called this deaf and masterful old gentleman "Excellency" or "Marshal", others gave him the title of "General". And he doubtless possessed all these dignities, but it was so long since he had held offices that such appellations were hardly intelligible any more. It seemed to me anyway as if no definite name could adhere to his personality, at certain moments so sharp and yet again and again without precise contour. I could not make up my mind to call him Grandfather, though he was occasionally quite friendly to me and sometimes even called me to him, endeavoring to give a playful intonation to my name. For the rest, the whole family showed toward the Count a behavior mingled of veneration and timidity; little Erik alone lived in any degree of intimacy with the old master of the house; his moveable eye at times shot him rapid glances of understanding, to which Grandfather responded with equal rapidity; and sometimes on the long afternoons one might see them appear at the end of the long gallery, and observe how they walked, hand in hand, past the sombre old portraits, without speaking, apparently understanding one another in some other way.

I spent nearly the whole day in the park and outside in the beech-woods or on the heath; and luckily there were dogs at Urnekloster to accompany me; here and there I would come across a tenant's house, or a farmsteading, where I could get milk and bread and fruit, and I believe I enjoyed my liberty, in a pretty carefree manner, without letting myself, at least in the weeks that followed, be scared at the thought of the evening gatherings. I spoke to almost no one, for it was my joy to be alone; only with the dogs I had short conversations now and again: we understood each other admirably. Taciturnity was moreover a kind of family characteristic; I was accustomed to it in my father, and it did not surprise me that almost nothing was said during the evening meal.

In the early days after our arrival, Mathilde Brahe did indeed show herself extremely talkative. She asked my father about old acquaintances in foreign cities; she recalled remote impressions, she moved herself to tears by evoking the memory of departed friends and of a certain young man, who, she hinted, had been in love with her though she had not cared to respond to his pressing and hopeless passion. My father listened politely, bending his head now and again in agreement and answering only when necessary. The Count, at the head of the table, smiled continually with down-drawn lips, his face seeming larger than usual, as though he wore a mask. He also sometimes joined in the conversation himself, and then his voice would refer to no one in particular, but, though very low, could nevertheless be heard all over the room; it had something of the regular, indifferent movement of a clock; the silence round it seemed to have a strange empty resonance, the same for every syllable.

Count Brahe held it an especial courtesy toward my father to speak of his deceased wife, my mother. He called her Countess Sibylle, and all his sentences finished as if he were inquiring after her. Indeed it appeared to me, I don't know why, as though there were question of a very young girl in white who might appear among us at any moment. I heard him speak, too, in the same tone of "our little Anna Sophie". And when one day I asked about this young lady, who seemed particularly dear to my grandfather, I learned that he meant the daughter of the High Chancellor Conrad Reventlov, the whilom morganatic wife of Frederick the Fourth, who for nearly a century and a half had been reposing at Roskilde. Chronological sequence played no role whatever for him, death was a trifling incident which he utterly ignored, persons whom he had once received into his memory continued to exist, and their dying off could not alter that in the least. Several years later, after the old gentleman's death, they told how with the same obstinacy he would also take future events as present. He was said to have spoken on one occasion to a certain young married woman about her sons, about the travels of one of them in particular, while the young lady, just in the third month of her first pregnancy, sat almost insensible with horror and fright beside the incessantly talking old man.

But it began with my laughing. Indeed, I laughed out loud, and I could not stop myself. One evening, namely, Mathilde Brahe was not present. The aged, almost stone-blind servitor nevertheless held out the dish when he came to her seat. He remained in that attitude for a little; then, content and dignified and as if all were in order, he went on. I had watched this scene, and for the instant in which I saw it, it did not seem at all funny. But a while later, as I was just taking a bite, a fit of laughter rose to my head so speedily that I swallowed the wrong way and caused a great to-do. And though the situation was painful to myself, though I made every possible effort to be serious, the impulse to laugh kept spasmodically recurring and completely dominated me.

My father, as if to screen my bad manners, asked in his broad undertones: "Is Mathilde ill?" Grandfather smiled in his own way and replied with a phrase to which, taken up with myself as I was, I paid no attention, but which sounded something like: No, she merely does not wish to meet Christine. Neither did I see, therefore, that it was the effect of these words which made my neighbor, the brown major, rise and, with an indistinctly muttered apology and a bow in the Count's direction, leave the room. It only struck me that he turned once more at the door, behind the back of the master of the house, and made nodding and beckoning signs to little Erik and suddenly, to my greatest astonishment, to me as well, as though he were urging us to follow him. I was so surprised that my laughter ceased to press upon me. Beyond that I paid no further attention to the major; I thought him unpleasant, and I observed, too, that little Erik took no notice of him.

The meal dragged along as usual, and we had just reached the dessert when my eye was caught and carried along by a movement going on, in the half-darkness, at the back of the room. In that quarter a door which I thought was always kept shut, and which I had been told led to the mezzanine floor, had opened little by little, and now, as I looked on with a feeling entirely new to me of curiosity and consternation, there stepped into the darkness of the doorway a slender lady in a light-colored dress, who came slowly toward us. I do not know whether I made any movement or any sound; the noise of a chair being overturned forced me to tear my eyes from that strange figure, and I caught sight of my father, who had jumped up and now, his face pale as death, his hands clenched by his sides, was going toward the lady. She, meantime, quite untouched by this scene, moved toward us, step by step, and was already not far from the Count's place, when he rose brusquely and, seizing my father by the arm, drew him back to the table and held him fast, while the strange lady, slowly and indifferently, traversed the space now left clear, step by step, through an indescribable stillness in which only a glass clinked trembling somewhere, and disappeared through a door in the opposite wall of the dining-hall. At that moment I observed that it was little Erik who, with a profound obeisance, closed this door behind the stranger.

I was the only one who had remained seated at the table; I had made myself so heavy in my chair, it seemed to me I could never get up again by myself. For a while I saw without seeing. Then I thought of my father, and became aware that the old man still held him by the arm. My father's face was now angry, suffused with blood, but Grandfather, whose fingers clutched his arm like a white claw, was smiling his mask-like smile. Then I heard him say something, syllable by syllable, without being able to understand the meaning of his words. They must nevertheless have fallen deep into my hearing, for about two years ago I discovered them down in my memory one day, and I have known them ever since. He said: "You are violent, chamberlain, and uncivil. Why don't you let people go about their business?"

"Who is that?" broke in my father with a cry.

"Someone who has every right to be here. No stranger. Christine Brahe."

And again there was that same curiously attenuated silence, and once more the glass began to tremble. But then my father broke away with a gesture and rushed from the hall.

I heard him pacing to and fro in his room all night long; for I, too, could not sleep. But suddenly, toward morning, I did wake out of something like sleep and saw, with a terror that paralyzed me to the very heart, something white seated on my bed. Despair finally gave me strength to thrust my head under the covers, and there from fear and helplessness I began to cry. Suddenly it became cool and bright above my weeping eyes; I pressed them shut over my tears so as not to have to see anything. But the voice that now appealed to me from quite near came tepid and sweetish upon my face, and I recognized it: it was Miss Mathilde's voice. I was instantly reassured and yet continued, even when I had become quite quiet, to let myself be comforted; I did feel that this kindness was too effeminate, but I enjoyed it nevertheless and felt I had somehow deserved it.

"Auntie," I said at last, trying to assemble in her blurred countenance the features of my mother: "Auntie, who was the lady?"

"Ah," answered Miss Brahe with a sigh that seemed to me ludicrous, "an unfortunate woman, my child, an unfortunate woman."

That morning I noticed in one of the rooms several servants busy packing. I thought we were going to leave; it seemed to me quite natural that we should do so. Perhaps that was also my father's intention. I never learned what induced him to remain at Urnekloster after that evening. But we did not leave. We stayed on in that house eight or nine weeks longer, we endured the oppression of its strangeness, and we saw Christine Brahe three times more.

At that time I knew nothing of her story. I did not know that she had died a long, long time before, at the birth of her second child, a boy who grew up to a fearful and cruel fate,—I did not know she was a dead woman. But my father knew it. Had he sought to force himself, passionate as he was, yet with a clear and logical turn of mind, to endure this adventure calmly and without questioning? I saw, without comprehending, how he struggled with himself; I witnessed, without understanding, how he finally mastered himself.

That was when we saw Christine Brahe for the last time. On this occasion Miss Mathilde had also appeared at table; but she was in an unusual mood. As in the first days after our arrival, she talked incessantly with no definite connection and continually mixing herself up, while some physical restlessness compelled her constantly to adjust something about her hair or her dress,—till she unexpectedly jumped up with a shrill wailing cry and disappeared.

At the same moment my glance turned involuntarily to that particular door, and, in fact: Christine Brahe was entering. My neighbor, the major, made a short, violent movement that transmitted itself into my own body, but evidently he no longer had the strength to rise. His brown, old, spotted visage turned from one to another, his mouth hung open and his tongue writhed behind his decayed teeth; then all at once this face was gone, and his grey head lay on the table, and his arms lay over it and under it as if in pieces, and from somewhere a withered, speckled hand emerged and trembled.

And then Christine Brahe passed by, slowly, like a sick person, step by step, through indescribable silence, into which there rang only a single whimpering sound as of an old dog. But at that, to the left of the huge silver swan filled with narcissus, the old man's great mask thrust forward with its grey smile. He raised his wineglass to my father. And then I saw how my father, just as Christine Brahe passed behind his chair, reached for his glass and lifted it, like something very heavy, a handsbreadth above the table.

And that same night we left.

Bibliothèque Nationale.

I sit here reading a poet. There are a lot of people in the reading-room; but one is not aware of them. They are in the books. Sometimes they move in the pages, like sleepers who turn over between two dreams. Ah, how good it is to be among reading people. Why are they not always like that? You can go up to one of them and touch him lightly; he feels nothing. And if in rising, you chance to bump lightly against a neighbor and excuse yourself, he nods toward the side from which he hears your voice, his face turns toward you and does not see you, and his hair is like that of a man asleep. How comforting that is. And I sit, and have a poet. What a destiny. There are perhaps three hundred people in the room now, reading; but it is impossible that each single one of them should have a poet. (Heaven knows what they have.) There aren't three hundred poets. But just see, what a destiny: I, the poorest, perhaps, of all these readers, a foreigner: I have a poet. Though I am poor. Though the suit I wear every day is beginning to show certain places, and though my shoes in some respects are not above reproach. True, my collar is clean, my linen too, and I could, just as I am, enter any pastry-shop I pleased, perhaps on the Grands Boulevards, and could calmly put my hand out to a plate of cakes and take some. No one would find that surprising, nor would they reprimand me and show me out, for it is still a hand that belongs in respectable circles, a hand that is washed four or five times a day. There is nothing under the nails, the forefinger has no ink-stains, and the wrists, particularly, are irreproachable. Poor people don't wash so far up; that is a known fact. So one may draw certain conclusions from the cleanness of these wrists. And they are drawn. They are drawn in the shops. But still there are one or two individuals, on the Boulevard Saint-Michel, for example, and in the rue Racine, who are not deceived, who don't care a hang about my wrists. They look at me and they know. They know that I am really one of themselves, and am only playing a little comedy. After all, it is carnival-time. And they don't want to spoil my fun; they just grin a little and wink with their eyes. Not a soul has seen this. For the rest, they treat me as a gentleman. If someone happens to be near, they even act servile. Behave as if I had a fur coat on and my carriage following along behind. Sometimes I give them two sous, trembling lest they refuse them; but they accept them. And all would be well, had they not again grinned and winked a little. Who are these people? What do they want of me? Are they waiting for me? How do they recognize me? It is true, my beard looks somewhat neglected, and very, very slightly resembles their own sickly, aged, faded beards that have always impressed me. But haven't I the right to neglect my beard? Many busy men do that, and it never occurs to anyone promptly to reckon them on that account among the outcast. For it is clear to me that these are the outcast, not simply beggars; no, they are really not beggars; one must make distinctions. They are refuse, husks of humanity that fate has spewed out. Moist with the spittle of destiny they are stuck to a wall, a lamp-post, an advertisement-pillar, or they trickle slowly down the alley, with a dark, dirty track behind them. What in the world did that old woman want with me, who had crawled out of some hole, carrying the drawer of a night-stand with a few buttons and needles rolling about in it? Why did she keep walking beside me and watching me? As if she were trying to recognize me with her bleared eyes, that looked as though some diseased person had spat green slime into the bloody lids? And how came that little grey woman to stand that time for a whole quarter of an hour by my side before a shop-window, showing me an old, long pencil, that came pushing infinitely slowly out of her miserable, clenched hands? I pretended to look at the display in the window and not notice anything. But she knew I had seen her, she knew I stood there wondering what she was really doing. For I understood quite well that the pencil in itself was of no consequence: I felt it was a sign, a sign for the initiated, a sign the outcast know; I guessed she was indicating to me that I should go somewhere or do something. And the strangest part was that I could not rid myself of the feeling that there actually existed a certain compact to which this sign belonged, and that this scene was in truth something I should have expected.

That was two weeks ago. But scarcely a day passes now without such an encounter. Not only in the twilight; it happens at midday in the most crowded streets, that a little man or an old woman is suddenly there, nods to me, shows me something, and then vanishes, as though all the necessary were now done. It is possible that one day it may occur to them to come as far as my room; they certainly know where I live, and they will take care that the concierge does not stop them. But here, my dears, here I am safe from you. One must have a special card in order to get into this room. In this card I have the advantage of you. I go a little shyly, as one may imagine, through the streets, but finally I stand before a glass door, open it as if I were at home, show my card at the next door (just exactly as you show me your things, only with the difference that people understand me and know what I mean—), and then I am among these books, and taken away from you as though I had died, and sit and read a poet.

You do not know what that is, a poet?—Verlaine . . . Nothing? No recollection? No. You did not distinguish him among those you knew? You make no distinctions, I know. But it is another poet I am reading, one who does not live in Paris, quite another. One who has a quiet home in the mountains. Who rings like a bell in clear air. A happy poet who tells of his window and the glass doors of his book-case, that pensively reflect a dear, lonely distance. Just this poet it is that I would have liked to become. He knows so much about girls, and I too would have known a lot about them. He knows about girls who lived a hundred years ago; it no longer matters that they are dead, for he knows everything. And that is the main thing. He pronounces their names—those gentle, slender-written names with old-fashioned loops in the long letters and the grown-up names of their older girl-friends, in the sound of which one already hears a little bit of destiny, a little bit of disillusion and death. Perhaps their faded letters and the loosened leaves of their diaries, recording birthdays, summer parties, birthdays, are lying in a compartment of his mahogany desk. Or it may be that in the full-bellied commode at the back of his bedroom there is a drawer, in which their spring dresses are kept—white dresses that were worn for the first time at Easter, dresses of dotted tulle which properly belong in the summer, for which one could not wait. Oh, what a happy fate, to sit in the quiet room of an ancestral house, among many calm, sedentary things, and, outside in the airy, light-green garden, to hear the first wrens trying their skill, and in the distance the village clock. To sit and watch a warm streak of afternoon sun and know many things about girls of bygone days and be a poet. And to think that I too would have become such a poet, had I been allowed to live somewhere, anywhere in the world, in one of those many closed-up country houses about which no one troubles. I would have used only one room (the light room in the gable). There I would have lived with my old things, the family portraits, the books. And I would have had an armchair and flowers and dogs and a stout stick for the stony roads. And nothing more. Only a book bound in yellowish, ivory-colored leather, with an old flowery design on the fly-leaf: in that I would have written. I would have written a great deal, for I would have had many thoughts and many people's memories.

But things have fallen out otherwise, God will know why. My old furniture is rotting in a barn where I have been allowed to put it, while I myself—yes, my God—have no roof over me, and the rain rains into my eyes.

Occasionally I pass by little shops—in the rue de Seine, for example. Dealers in antiques or small second-hand booksellers or vendors of engravings with overcrowded windows. No one ever enters their shops; they apparently do no business. But if one looks in, they are sitting there, sitting and reading, without a care; they take no thought for the morrow, are not anxious about any success, have a dog that sits before them, all good-nature, or a cat that makes the silence still greater by gliding along the rows of books, as if it were rubbing the names off their backs.

Ah, if that were enough: sometimes I would like to buy such a full shop-window for myself and to sit down behind it with a dog for twenty years.

It is good to say it out aloud: "Nothing has happened." Once more: "Nothing has happened." Does that help?

That my stove began to smoke again and I had to go out, is really no misfortune. That I feel weary and chilled is of no consequence. That I have been running about the streets all day is my own fault. I might just as well have sat in the Louvre. But no, I could not have done that. There are certain people who go there to warm themselves. They sit on the velvet benches, and their feet stand like big empty boots side by side on the gratings of the hot air registers. They are extremely modest men who are thankful when the attendants in their dark-blue uniforms studded with medals suffer their presence. But when I enter, they grimace. They grimace and nod slightly. And then, when I go back and forth before the pictures, they keep me in view, always in view, always within that scrambled, blurry gaze. So it was well I did not go into the Louvre. I kept on the move incessantly. Heaven knows through how many towns, districts, cemeteries, bridges, and passage-ways. Somewhere or other I saw a man pushing a vegetable cart before him. He was shouting: "Chou-fleur, chou-fleur," pronouncing the "fleur" with a strangely muffled "eu." Beside him walked an angular, ugly woman who nudged him from time to time. And when she nudged him, he shouted. Sometimes he shouted of his own accord too, but that would prove useless, and he had to shout again immediately after, because they were in front of a house that would buy. Have I already said that the man was blind? No? Well, he was blind. He was blind and he shouted. I misrepresent when I say that, suppressing the barrow he was shoving, pretending I did not notice he was shouting "cauliflower." But is that essential? And even if it were essential, isn't the main thing what the whole business was for me? I saw an old man who was blind and shouted. That I saw. Saw.

Will anyone believe that there are such houses? No, they will say I am misrepresenting. This time it is the truth, nothing omitted, and naturally nothing added. Where should I get it from? Everyone knows I am poor. Everyone knows it. Houses? But, to be precise, they were houses that were no longer there. Houses that had been pulled down from top to bottom. What *was* there was the other houses, those that had stood alongside of them, tall neighboring houses. Apparently these were in danger of falling down, since everything alongside had been taken away; for a whole scaffolding of long, tarred timbers had been rammed slantwise between the rubbish-strewn ground and the bared wall. I don't know whether I have already said that it is this wall I mean. But it was, so to speak, not the first wall of the existing houses (as one would have supposed), but the last of those that had been there. One saw its inner side. One saw at the different storeys the walls of rooms to which the paper still clung, and here and there the join of floor or ceiling. Beside these room-walls there still remained, along the whole length of the wall, a dirty-white area, and through this crept in unspeakably disgusting motions, worm-soft and as if digesting, the open, rust-spotted channel of the water-closet pipe. Grey, dusty traces of the paths the lighting-gas had taken remained at the ceiling edges, and here and there, quite unexpectedly, they bent sharp around and came running into the colored wall and into a hole that had been torn out black and ruthless. But most unforgettable of all were the walls themselves. The stubborn life of these rooms had not let itself be trampled out. It was still there; it clung to the nails that had been left, it stood on the remaining handsbreadth of flooring, it crouched under the corner joints where there was still a little bit of interior. One could see that it was in the paint, which, year by year, it had slowly altered: blue into moldy green, green into grey, and yellow into an old, stale rotting white. But it was also in the spots that had kept fresher, behind mirrors, pictures, and wardrobes; for it had drawn and redrawn their contours, and had been with spiders and dust even in these hidden places that now lay bared. It was in every flayed strip, it was in the damp blisters at the lower edges of the wallpapers; it wavered in the torn-off shreds, and sweated out of the foul patches that had come into being long ago. And from these walls once blue and green and yellow, which were framed by the fracture-tracks of the demolished partitions, the breath of these lives stood out—the clammy, sluggish, musty breath, which no wind had yet scattered. There stood the middays and the sicknesses and the exhaled breath and the smoke of years, and the sweat that breaks out under armpits and makes clothes heavy, and the stale breath of mouths, and the fusel odor of sweltering feet. There stood the tang of urine and the burn of soot and the grey reek of potatoes, and the heavy, smooth stench of ageing grease. The sweet, lingering smell of neglected infants was there, and the fear-smell of children who go to school, and the sultriness out of the beds of nubile youths. To these was added much that had come from below, from the abyss of the street, which reeked, and more that had oozed down from above with the rain, which over cities is not clean. And much the feeble, tamed domestic winds, that always stay in the same street, had brought along; and much more was there, the source of which one did not know. I said, did I not, that all the walls had been demolished except the last—? It is of this wall I have been speaking all along. One would think I had stood a long time before it; but I'm willing to swear that I began to run as soon as I had recognized that wall. For that is the terrible thing, that I did recognize it. I recognize everything here, and that is why it goes right into me: it is at home in me.

I was somewhat worn out after all this, one might even say exhausted, and that is why it was too much for me that he too had to be waiting for me. He was waiting in the little crêmerie where I intended to eat two poached eggs; I was hungry, I had not managed to eat the whole day. But even then I could not take anything; before the eggs were ready something drove me out again into the streets, which ran toward me viscid with humanity. For it was carnival and evening, and the people all had time and roved about, rubbing against each other. And their faces were full of the light that came from the show-booths, and laughter bubbled from their mouths like matter from open sores. The more impatiently I tried to force my way forward, the more they laughed and the more closely they crowded together. Somehow a woman's shawl hooked itself to me; I dragged her after me, and people stopped me and laughed, and I felt I should laugh too, but I could not. Someone threw a handful of confetti into my eyes, and it burned like a whip. At the crossings people were wedged fast, shoved one into the other, and there was no forward movement in them, only a quiet, gentle swaying back and forth, as if they copulated standing. But although they stood, and I ran like a madman along the edge of the pavement where there were gaps in the crowd, yet in truth it was they who moved while I never stirred. For nothing changed; when I looked up I was still aware of the same houses on the one side and on the other the booths. Perhaps everything indeed stood fast, and it was simply a dizziness in me and in them which seemed to whirl everything around. I had no time to reflect on this; I was heavy with sweat, and a stupefying pain circled in me, as if something too large were driving along in my blood, distending the veins wherever it passed. And in addition I felt that the air had long been exhausted, and that I was now breathing only exhaled breath, which my lungs refused.

But it is over now; I have survived it. I am sitting in my room by the lamp; it is a little cold, for I do not venture to try the stove: what if it smoked, and I had to go out again? I am sitting and thinking: if I were not poor I would rent another room with furniture not so worn out, not so full of former occupants, as the furniture here. At first it really cost me an effort to lean my head on this arm-chair; for there is a certain greasy-grey hollow in its green covering, into which all heads seem to fit. For some time I took the precaution of putting a handkerchief under my hair, but now I am too tired to do that; I discovered that it is all right the way it is, and that the slight hollow is made exactly for the back of my head, as if to measure. But I would, if I were not poor, first of all buy a good stove, and burn the clean, strong wood that comes from the mountains, and not these miserable têtes de moineau, the fumes of which scare one's breathing so and make one's head so confused. And then someone would have to tidy up without coarse noises, and keep the fire the way I need it; for often when I have to kneel before the stove and poke for a quarter of an hour, the skin on my forehead tense with the close glow and with heat in my open eyes, I expend all the strength I have for the day, and then when I get among people they naturally have it easy. I would sometimes, when the crush is great, take a carriage and drive by; I would eat every day in a Duval . . . and no longer slink into crêmeries. . . Would he too have been in a Duval? No. He would not have been allowed to wait for me there. They don't allow the dying in. The dying? I am now sitting in my room; so I can try to reflect quietly on what happened to me. It is well to leave nothing in uncertainty. I went in, then, and at first only noticed that the table at which I usually sat was occupied by someone else. I bowed in the direction of the little counter, ordered, and sat down at the next table. But then I felt him, although he did not stir. It was precisely this immobility of his that I felt, and I understood it all at once. The connection between us was established, and I knew that he was stiff with terror. I knew that terror had paralyzed him, terror at something that was happening inside him. Perhaps one of his blood-vessels had burst; perhaps, just at this moment, some poison that he had long dreaded was penetrating the ventricle of his heart; perhaps a great abscess had risen in his brain like a sun that was changing the world for him. With an indescribable effort I compelled myself to look in his direction, for I still hoped it was all imagination. But then I sprang up and rushed out; for I had made no mistake. He sat there in a thick, black winter coat, his grey, strained face plunged deep into a woollen neckcloth. His mouth was closed as if it had fallen shut with great force, but it was not possible to say whether his eyes still saw: misty, smoke-grey spectacle lenses covered them, trembling slightly. His nostrils were distended, and the long hair over his wasted temples, out of which everything had been taken, wilted as if in too intense a heat. His ears were long, yellow, with large shadows behind them. Yes, he knew that he was now withdrawing from everything; not merely from human beings. A moment more and everything will have lost its meaning, and that table and the cup, and the chair to which he clings, all the near and the commonplace, will have become unintelligible, strange and heavy. So he sat there and waited until it should have happened. And defended himself no longer.

And I still defend myself. I defend myself, although I know my heart is already hanging out and that I cannot live any longer, even if my tormentors were to leave me alone now. I say to myself: "Nothing has happened," and yet I was only able to understand that man because within me too something is happening, that is beginning to draw me away and separate me from everything. How it always horrified me to hear said of a dying person: he could no longer recognize anybody. Then I would imagine to myself a lonely face that raised itself from pillows and sought, sought for some familiar thing, sought for something once seen, but there was nothing there. If my fear were not so great, I should console myself with the fact that it is not impossible to see everything differently and yet to live. But I am afraid, I am namelessly afraid of this change. I have, indeed, hardly got used yet to this world, which seems good to me. What should I do in another? I would so gladly stay among the significations that have become dear to me; and if anything has to change at all, I would like at least to be allowed to live among dogs, who possess a world akin to our own and the same things.

For a while yet I can write all this down and express it. But there will come a day when my hand will be far from me, and when I bid it write, it will write words I do not mean. The time of that other interpretation will dawn, when not one word will remain upon another, and all meaning will dissolve like clouds and fall down like rain. Despite my fear I am yet like one standing before something great, and I remember that it was often like that in me before I began to write. But this time I shall be written. I am the impression that will change. Ah, but a little more, and I could understand all this and approve it. Only a step, and my deep misery would be beatitude. But I cannot take that step; I have fallen and cannot pick myself up again, because I am broken. I still believed some help might come. There it lies before me in my own handwriting, what I have prayed, evening after evening. I transcribed it from the books in which I found it, so that it might be very near me, sprung from my hand like something of my own. And now I want to write it once again, kneeling here before my table I want to write it; for in this way I have it longer than when I read it, and every word is sustained and has time to die away.

"Mécontent de tous et mécontent de moi, je voudrais bien me racheter et m'enorgueillir un peu dans le silence et la solitude de la nuit. Ames de ceux que j'ai aimés, âmes de ceux que j'ai chantés, fortifiez-moi, soutenez-moi, éloignez de moi le mensonge et les vapeurs corruptrices du monde; et vous, Seigneur mon Dieu! accordez-moi la grâce de produire quelques beaux vers qui me prouvent à moi-même que je ne suis pas le dernier des hommes, que je ne suis pas inférieur à ceux que je méprise."

"They were children of fools, yea, children of base men: they were viler than the earth.

And now I am their song, yea, I am their byword. . . . They raise up against me the ways of their destruction.

They mar my path, they set forward my calamity, they have no helper . . .

And now my soul is poured out upon me; the days of affliction have taken hold upon me.

My bones are pierced in me in the night seasons: and my sinews take no rest.

By the great force *of my disease* is my garment changed: it bindeth me about as the collar of my coat . . .

My bowels boiled and rested not: the days of affliction prevented me . . .

My harp also is turned to mourning, and my organ into the voice of them that weep."

The doctor did not understand me. Nothing. And certainly it was difficult to describe. They wanted to try electric treatment. Good. I received a slip of paper: I had to be at the Salpêtrière at one o'clock. I was there. I had to pass a long row of barracks and traverse a number of courtyards, where people in white bonnets stood here and there under the bare trees like convicts. Finally I entered a long, gloomy, corridor-like room, that had on one side four windows of dim, greenish glass, one separated from the other by a broad, black partition. In front of them a wooden bench ran along, past everything, and on this bench they who knew me sat and waited. Yes, they were all there. When I became accustomed to the twilight of the place, I noticed that among them, as they sat shoulder to shoulder in an endless row, there could also be other people, little people, artisans, char-women, truckmen. Down at the narrow end of this corridor, on special chairs, two stout women had spread themselves out and were conversing, concierges probably. I looked at the clock; it was five minutes to one. In five minutes, or say ten, my turn would come; so it was not so bad. The air was foul, heavy, impregnated with clothes and breaths. At a certain spot the strong, intensifying coolness of ether came through a crack in a door. I began to walk up and down. It crossed my mind that I have been directed here, among these people, to this overcrowded, general consultation. It was, so to speak, the first public confirmation of the fact that I belonged among the outcast; had the doctor known by my appearance? Yet I had paid my visit in a tolerably decent suit; I had sent in my card. Despite that he must have learned it somehow; perhaps I had betrayed myself. However, now that it was a fact I did not find it so bad after all; the people sat quietly and took no notice of me. Some were in pain and swung one leg a little, the better to endure it. Various men had laid their heads in the palms of their hands; others were sleeping deeply, with heavy, fatigue-crushed faces. A stout man with a red, swollen neck sat bending forward, staring at the floor, and from time to time spat with a smack at a spot he seemed to find suitable for the purpose. A child was sobbing in a corner; it had drawn its long thin legs close up on the bench, and now clasped and held them tightly to its body, as though it must bid them farewell. A small, pale woman on whose head a crape hat adorned with round, black flowers, sat awry, wore the grimace of a smile about her meager lips, but her sore eyes were constantly overflowing. Not far from her had been placed a girl with a round, smooth face and protruding eyes that were without expression; her mouth hung open, so that one saw her white, slimy gums with their old stunted teeth. And there were many bandages. Bandages that swathed a whole head layer upon layer, until only a single eye remained that no longer belonged to anyone. Bandages that hid, and bandages that revealed, what was beneath them. Bandages that had been undone, in which, as in a dirty bed, a hand now lay that was a hand no longer; and a bandaged leg that protruded from the row on the bench, as large as a whole man. I walked up and down, and endeavored to be calm. I occupied myself a good deal with the wall facing me. I noticed that it contained a number of single doors, and did not reach up to the ceiling, so that this corridor was not completely separated from the rooms that must adjoin it. I looked at the clock; I had been pacing up and down for an hour. A while later the doctors arrived. First a couple of young fellows who passed by with indifferent faces, and finally the one I had consulted, in light gloves, chapeau à huit reflets, impeccable overcoat. When he saw me he lifted his hat a little and smiled absent-mindedly. I now hoped to be called immediately, but another hour passed. I cannot remember how I spent it. It passed. An old man wearing a soiled apron, a sort of attendant, came and touched me on the shoulder. I entered one of the adjoining rooms. The doctor and the young fellows sat round a table and looked at me, someone gave me a chair. So far so good. And now I had to describe what it was that was the matter with me. As briefly as possible, s'il vous plaît. For much time these gentlemen had not. I felt very odd. The young fellows sat and looked at me with that superior, professional curiosity they had learned. The doctor I knew stroked his pointed black beard and smiled absently. I thought I should burst into tears, but I heard myself saying in French: "I have already had the honor, monsieur, of giving you all the details that I can give. If you consider it indispensable that these gentlemen should be initiated, you are certainly able, after our conversation, to do this in a few words, while I find it very difficult." The doctor rose, smiling politely, and going toward the window with his assistants said a few words, which he accompanied with a horizontal, wavering movement of his hands. Three minutes later one of the young men, short-sighted and jerky, came back to the table, and said, trying to look at me severely, "You sleep well, sir?" "No, badly." Whereupon he sprang back again to the group at the window. There they discussed a while longer, then the doctor turned to me and informed me that I would be summoned again. I reminded him that my appointment had been for one o'clock. He smiled and made a few swift, abrupt movements with his small white hands, which were meant to signify that he was uncommonly busy. So I returned to my hallway, where the air had become much more oppressive, and began again to pace up and down, although I felt mortally tired. Finally the moist, accumulated smell made me dizzy; I stopped at the entrance door and opened it a little. I saw that outside it was still afternoon, with some sun, and that did me ever so much good. But I had hardly stood a minute thus when I heard someone calling me. A female sitting at a table two or three steps away hissed something to me. Who had told me to open the door? I said I could not stand the atmosphere. Well, that was my own affair, but the door had to be kept shut. Was it not permissible, then, to open a window? No, that was forbidden. I decided to resume my walking up and down, for after all that was a kind of anodyne and it hurt nobody. But now this too displeased the woman sitting at the little table. Did I not have a seat? No, I hadn't. Walking about was not allowed; I would have to find a seat. There ought to be one. The woman was right. In fact, a place was promptly found next the girl with the protruding eyes. There I now sat with the feeling that this state must certainly be the preparation for something dreadful. On my left, then, was this girl with the decaying gums; what was on my right I could not make out till after some time. It was a huge, immovable mass, having a face and a large, heavy, inert hand. The side of the face that I saw was empty, quite without features and without memories; and it was gruesome that the clothes were like that of a corpse dressed for the coffin. The narrow, black cravat had been buckled in the same loose, impersonal way around the collar, and the coat showed that it had been put on the will-less body by other hands. The hand had been placed on the trousers exactly where it lay, and even the hair looked as if it had been combed by those women who lay out the dead, and was stiffly arranged, like the hair of stuffed animals. I observed all these things with attention, and it occurred to me that this must be the place that had been destined for me; for I now believed I had at last arrived at that point of my life at which I would remain. Yes, fate goes wonderful ways.

Suddenly there rose quite nearby in quick succession the frightened, defensive cries of a child, followed by a low, hushed weeping. While I was straining to discover where this could have come from, a little, suppressed cry quavered away again, and I heard voices, questioning, a voice giving orders in a subdued tone, and then some sort of machine started up and hummed indifferently along. Now I recalled that half wall, and it was clear to me that all this came from the other side of the doors and that work was going on in there. Actually, the attendant with the soiled apron appeared from time to time and made a sign. I had given up thinking that he might mean me. Was it intended for me? No. Two men appeared with a wheelchair; they lifted the mass beside me into it, and I now saw that it was an old paralytic who had another, smaller side to him, worn out by life, and an open, dim and melancholy eye. They wheeled him inside, and now there was lots of room beside me. And I sat and wondered what they were likely to do to the imbecile girl and whether she too would scream. The machines back there kept up such an agreeable mechanical whirring, there was nothing disturbing about it.

But suddenly everything was still, and in the stillness a superior, self-complacent voice, which I thought I knew, said: "Riez!" A pause. "Riez! Mais riez, riez!" I was already laughing. It was inexplicable that the man on the other side of the partition didn't want to laugh. A machine rattle, but was immediately silent again, words were exchanged, then the same energetic voice rose again and ordered: "Dites-nous le mot: avant." And spelling it: "A-v-a-n-t." Silence. "On n'entend rien. Encore une fois . . ."

And then, as I listened to the hot, flaccid stuttering on the other side of the partition, then for the first time in many, many years it was there again. That which had struck into me my first, profound terror, when as a child I lay ill with fever: the Big Thing. Yes, that was what I had always called it, when they all stood around my bed and felt my pulse and asked me what had frightened me: the Big Thing. And when they got the doctor and he came and spoke to me, I begged him only to make the Big Thing go away, nothing else mattered. But he was like the rest. He could not take it away, though I was so small then and might so easily have been helped. And now it was there again. Later it had simply stayed away; it had not come back even on nights when I had fever; but now it was there, although I had no fever. Now it was there. Now it grew out of me like a tumor, like a second head, and was a part of me, though it could not belong to me at all, because it was so big. It was there like a huge, dead beast, that had once, when it was still alive, been my hand or my arm. And my blood flowed both through me and through it, as if through one and the same body. And my heart had to make a great effort to drive the blood into the Big Thing; there was hardly enough blood. And the blood entered the Big Thing unwillingly and came back sick and tainted. But the Big Thing swelled and grew over my face like a warm bluish boil and grew over my mouth, and already the shadow of its edge lay upon my remaining eye.

I cannot recall how I got out through the numerous courtyards. It was evening, and I lost my way in this strange neighborhood and went up boulevards with interminable walls in one direction and, when there was no end to them, returned in the opposite direction until I reached some square or other. Thence I began to walk along a street, and other streets came that I had never seen before, and still other streets. Electric cars would come racing up and past, too brilliantly lit and with harsh, beating clang of bells. But on their signboards stood names I did not know. I did not know in what city I was or whether I had a lodging somewhere here or what I must do in order not to have to go on walking.

And now this illness too, which has always affected me so strangely. I am sure it is underestimated. Just as the importance of other diseases is exaggerated. This disease has no particular characteristics; it takes on those of the person it attacks. With a somnambulic certainty it drags out of each his deepest danger, that seemed passed, and sets it before him again, quite near, imminent. Men, who once in their school-days attempted the helpless vice that has for its duped intimate the poor, hard hands of boys, find themselves at it again; or an illness they had conquered in childhood begins in them again; or a lost habit reappears, a certain hesitant turn of the head that had been peculiar to them years before. And with whatever comes there rises a whole tangle of insane memories, which hangs about it like wet seaweed on some sunken thing. Lives of which one would never have known mount to the surface and mingle with what has actually been, and push aside past matters that one had thought to know: for in that which ascends is a rested, new strength, but that which has always been there is wearied by too frequent remembrance.

I am lying in my bed, five flights up, and my day, which nothing interrupts, is like a dial without hands. As a thing long lost lies one morning in its old place, safe and well, fresher almost than at the time of its loss, quite as though someone had cared for it—: so here and there on my coverlet lie lost things out of my childhood and are as new. All forgotten fears are there again.

The fear that a small, woollen thread that sticks out of the hem of my blanket may be hard, hard and sharp like a steel needle; the fear that this little button on my night-shirt may be bigger than my head, big and heavy; the fear that this crumb of bread now falling from my bed may arrive glassy and shattered on the floor, and the burdensome worry lest at that really everything will be broken, everything for ever; the fear that the torn border of an opened letter may be something forbidden that no one ought to see, something indescribably precious for which no place in the room is secure enough; the fear that if I fell asleep I might swallow the piece of coal lying in front of the stove; the fear that some number may begin to grow in my brain until there is no more room for it inside me; the fear that it may be granite I am lying on, grey granite; the fear that I may shout, and that people may come running to my door and finally break it open; the fear that I may betray myself and tell all that I dread; and the fear that I might not be able to say anything, because everything is beyond utterance,—and the other fears . . . the fears.

I asked for my childhood and it has come back, and I feel that it is just as difficult as it was before, and that it has been useless to grow older.

Yesterday my fever was better, and today the day is beginning like spring, like spring in pictures. I will try to go out to the Bibliothèque Nationale, to my poet whom I have not read for so long, and perhaps later I can walk slowly through the gardens. Perhaps there will be wind over the big pond that has such real water, and children will come to launch their boats with the red sails and watch them.

Today I really did not expect it; I went out so bravely, as though that were the simplest and most natural thing in the world. And yet, again there was something, which took me like paper, crumpled me up and threw me away, something unheard-of.

The Boulevard Saint-Michel lay deserted and vast, and it was easy to walk along its gentle decline. Window-casements overhead opened with a glassy ring, and the flash of them flew across the street like a white bird. A carriage with bright red wheels rolled past, and further down someone was carrying something light green. Horses in gleaming harness trotted on the dark-sprinkled carriageway, which was clean. The wind was lively, fresh, mild, and everything rose upward: odors, cries, bells.

I passed in front of one of those cafés where sham gypsies in red jackets usually play of an evening. From the open windows the air that had not slept last night crept out with a bad conscience. Sleek-haired waiters were busy sweeping in front of the door. One of them was bending over, throwing handful after handful of yellow sand under the tables. A passer-by nudged him and pointed down the boulevard. The waiter, who was all red in the face, looked sharply for a little in that direction, and then a laugh spread over his beardless cheeks, as though it had been spilled across them. He beckoned to the other waiters, turned his laughing face rapidly several times from right to left, so as to call everyone while missing nothing of the scene himself. Now they all stood gazing or searching down the street, smiling or annoyed that they had not yet discovered what was so absurd.

I felt a little fear beginning in me. Something urged me across to the other side of the street; but I only began to walk faster and glanced involuntarily over the few people in front of me, about whom I noticed nothing unusual. Yet I saw that one of them, an errand-boy with a blue apron and an empty basket slung over one shoulder, was staring after someone. When he had had enough, he wheeled round where he stood toward the houses and signaled across the street to a laughing clerk with that wavering gesture of the hand before the forehead which is familiar to everyone. Then his black eyes flashed and he came toward me with a satisfied swagger.

I expected, as soon as my eye had room, to see some unusual and striking figure; but it turned out there was no one walking ahead of me save a tall, emaciated man in a dark overcoat and with a soft black hat on his short, faded blond hair. I made sure there was nothing laughable about this man's clothing or behavior, and I was already trying to look beyond him down the boulevard, when he stumbled over something. As I was following close behind him, I was on my guard, but when the place came there was nothing there, absolutely nothing. We both walked on, he and I, the distance between us remaining the same. Now came a street-crossing, and there the man ahead of me hopped down from the sidewalk with uneven legs, somewhat as children walking now and again hop or skip, when they are happy. On the other side of the crossing he simply made one long step up. But no sooner was he there than he drew up one leg a little and hopped on the other, once, high, and immediately again and again. This time too one could quite well have taken this abrupt movement for a stumble, had one persuaded oneself that some small object lay there, a pip, a slippery fruitpeel, anything; and the strange thing was that the man himself appeared to believe in the presence of an obstacle, for he turned round every time and looked at the offending spot with that half-annoyed, half-reproachful air people have at such moments. Once again something warned me to take the other side of the street, but I did not obey and continued to follow this man, fixing my whole attention on his legs. I must admit I felt singularly relieved when for some twenty steps this hopping did not recur, but when I then raised my eyes I noticed that something else had begun to annoy the man. The collar of his overcoat had stood up, and try as he would to put it down again, fussing now with one hand, now with both at once, he did not succeed. That happens. It didn't bother me. But then I perceived with boundless astonishment that in this person's busy hands there were two movements: one a rapid, secret movement, with which he covertly flipped the collar up, and that other movement, elaborate, prolonged, as if exaggeratedly spelled out, which was meant to put it down. This observation disconcerted me so much that two minutes passed before I realized that in the man's neck, behind his hunched-up overcoat and the nervous activity of his hands, was the same horrible, bisyllabic hopping which had just left his legs. From that moment I was bound to him. I understood that this hopping impulse was wandering about his body, trying to break out here and there. I understood why he was afraid of people, and I myself began cautiously to test whether passers-by noticed anything. A cold stab went through my back when his legs suddenly made a slight, jerking spring, but no one saw it, and I thought out the plan of myself stumbling a little in case anyone began to notice. That would certainly be one way of making the curious believe that some small, inconspicuous obstacle really had been lying in the road, on which both of us had happened to tread. But, while I thus reflected on helping, he had himself discovered a new and excellent expedient. I forgot to mention that he carried a stick; well, it was an ordinary stick, made of dark wood with a smooth, curved handle. And in his searching anxiety, the idea had occurred to him of holding this stick against his back, at first with one of his hands (for who knew what the other might yet be needed for?) right along his spine, pressing it firmly into the small of his back, and thrusting the curved end under his collar, so that one felt it hard and like a support behind the cervical and the first dorsal vertebra. This attitude was not striking, at most a little cocky; the unexpected spring day might excuse that. No one thought of turning round to look, and now all went well. Wonderfully well. It is true that at the next crossing two hops got out, two little, half-suppressed hops, but they didn't amount to anything; and the only really visible leap was so cleverly managed (a hose-line lay right across the street) that there was nothing to be afraid of. Yes, things were still going well; from time to time the other hand also seized the stick and pressed it in more firmly, and at once the danger was again overcome. I could do nothing to keep my anxiety from growing nevertheless. I knew that as he walked and made ceaseless efforts to appear indifferent and absentminded, that awful jerking was accumulating in his body; in me, too, was the anxiety with which he felt it growing and growing, and I saw how he clung to his stick, when the jolting began inside him. The expression of his hands then became so severe and unrelenting that I placed all my hope in his will, which was bound to be strong. But what could a will do here. The moment must come when the man's strength would be exhausted; it could not be long now. And I, walking behind him with quickly-beating heart, I put my little strength together like money, and, gazing at his hands, I besought him to take it if he needed it.

I believe that he took it; how could I help the fact that it was not more.

At the Place Saint-Michel there were many vehicles and people hurrying hither and thither, we were several times held up between two carriages, and then he would take a breath and let himself go a little, by way of rest, and there would be a slight hopping and a little nodding. Perhaps that was the ruse by which the imprisoned malady sought to get the better of him. His will had given way at two points, and the concession had left behind in the obsessed muscles a gentle, enticing stimulation and this compelling two-beat rhythm. But the stick was still in its place, and the hands looked annoyed and angry. In this fashion we set foot on the bridge, and all was well. All was well. But now his gait became noticeably uncertain; sometimes he ran two steps, sometimes he stood still.

Stood still. His left hand gently let go the stick and rose, rose, so slowly that I saw it tremble against the air; he thrust his hat back a little, and drew his hands across his brow. He turned his head slightly, and his gaze wavered over sky, houses and water, without grasping anything. And then he gave in. His stick had gone, he stretched out his arms as if to take off and fly, and there broke out of him a sort of elemental force that bent him forward and dragged him back and made him nod and bow, flinging dance-force out of him in among the crowd. For already many people were around him, and I saw him no more.

What sense would there have been in my going anywhere else. I was empty. Like a blank sheet of paper I drifted along past the houses, up the boulevard again.

✳ I am attempting to write to you, although there is really nothing to say after a necessary leave-taking. I am attempting it nevertheless; I think I must, because I have seen the saint in the Panthéon, the solitary, saintly woman and the roof and the door and the lamp inside with its modest circle of light, and the sleeping city beyond and the river and the moon-lit distance. The saint watches over the sleeping city. I wept. I wept, because it was all suddenly so unexpectedly there. I wept as I looked; I could not help myself.

I am in Paris; those who learn this are glad, most of them envy me. They are right. It is a great city; great and full of strange temptations. As concerns myself, I must admit that I have in certain respects succumbed to them. I believe there is no other way of saying it. I have succumbed to these temptations, and this has brought about certain changes, if not in my character, at least in my outlook on the world, and, in any case, in my life. An entirely different conception of all things has developed in me under these influences; certain differences have appeared that separate me from other men, more than anything heretofore. A world transformed. A new life filled with new meanings. For the moment I find it a little hard because everything is too new. I am a beginner in my own circumstances.

---

* A rough draft of a letter.

Wouldn't it be possible for once to get a glimpse of the sea? Yes, but only think, I imagined you might come. Could you perhaps have told me if there was a doctor? I forgot to ask about that. Besides, I no longer need the information.

Do you remember Baudelaire's incredible poem, "Une Charogne"? Perhaps I understand it now. Except for the last verse he was in the right. What should he have done after that happened to him? It was his task to see in this terrible thing, seeming to be only repulsive, that existence which is valid among all that exists. Choice or refusal there is none. Do you imagine it was by chance that Flaubert wrote his Saint-Julien-l'Hospitalier? This, it seems to me, is decisive: whether a man can bring himself to lie beside a leper and warm him with the heart-warmth of nights of love,— that could not end otherwise than well.

But do not imagine I am suffering disappointments here—quite the contrary. I marvel sometimes how readily I give up everything I expected for the reality, even when the reality is bad.

My God, if any of it could be shared! But would it *be* then, would it *be*? No, it *is* only at the price of solitude.

The existence of the horrible in every particle of air! You breathe it in with what is transparent; but inside you it precipitates, hardens, takes on pointed, geometrical forms between your organs; for whatever of torment and horror has happened on places of execution, in torture-chambers, madhouses, operating-theatres, under the vaults of bridges in late autumn: all this has a tough imperishability, all this subsists in its own right and, jealous of all that is, clings to its own frightful reality. People would like to be allowed to forget much of this; sleep gently files over such grooves in their brains, but dreams drive sleep away and trace the designs again. And they wake up gasping and let the gleam of a candle melt into the darkness, and drink, like sugared water, the half-light solace. But, alas, on what a ledge this security rests! Only the slightest movement, and once again vision stands out beyond the known and friendly, and the contour but now so consoling grows clearer as an outline of terror. Beware of the light that makes space more hollow; do not look around to see whether perchance, behind you as you sit up, a shadow has arisen as your master. Better perhaps to have remained in the darkness, and your unconfined heart would have sought to be the heavy heart of all that is indistinguishable. Now you have gathered yourself together into yourself, see yourself ending ahead of you in your own hands; you trace from time to time with an uncertain gesture the outline of your face. And there is scarcely any room inside you; and it almost calms you to think that nothing very large can possibly abide in this narrowness; that even the stupendous must become an inward thing and must restrict itself to fit the surroundings. But outside, outside is beyond calculation. And when it rises out there, it fills up inside you as well, not in your bloodvessels, which are partly under your own control, nor in the phlegm of your more impassive organs: in the capillaries it rises, drawn up by tubular suction into the outermost branches of your infinitely ramified being. There it mounts, there it overflows you, rising higher than your breath, up which you flee as to your last stand. Ah, whither then, whither then? Your heart drives you out of yourself, your heart pursues you, and you stand almost outside yourself and cannot get back again. Like a beetle that has been trodden on you gush out of yourself, and your little bit of surface hardness and adaptability go for nothing.

O night without objects. O obtuse window outward, o carefully closed doors; arrangements from long ago, taken over, accredited, never quite understood. O stillness in the staircase, stillness from adjoining rooms, stillness high up against the ceiling. O mother: o you only one, who shut out all this stillness, long ago in childhood. Who take it upon yourself, saying: Don't be afraid, it is I. Who has the courage all in the night yourself to be this stillness for that which is afraid and perishing with fear. You strike a light, and already the noise is you. And you hold the light before you and say: It is I; don't be afraid. And you put it down, slowly, and there is no doubt: it is you; you are the light around these familiar intimate things, that are there without afterthought, good, simple, unambiguous. And when there is restlessness somewhere in the wall, or a step on the floor: you only smile, smile, smile transparent against a light background into the fearsome face that looks searchingly at you, as if you were one and in the secret with every half-sound, in concert and agreement with it. Does any power equal your power among the rulers of the earth? See, kings lie and stare, and the teller of tales cannot distract them. On the blissful breasts of their favorite mistress terror creeps over them and makes them shaky and lifeless. But you, you come and hold the monstrous thing behind you, and are in front of it altogether; not like a curtain it can throw open here or there. No, as if you had overtaken it at the call that needed you. As if you had come far ahead of anything that may yet happen, and had behind you only your hasting hither, your eternal path, the flight of your love.

The mouleur, whose shop I pass every day, has hung two masks beside his door. The face of the young drowned woman, a cast of which was taken in the Morgue because it was beautiful, because it smiled, smiled so deceptively, as though it knew. And beneath it, *his* face, which did know. That hard knot of senses tightly drawn together. That relentless self-condensing of a music continually seeking to evaporate. The countenance of one whose ear a god had closed so that there might be no tones but his own. So that he might not be led astray through the turbid and ephemeral in noises. He, in whom were their clarity and duration; so that only the silent senses might carry the world in to him, soundless, an expectant, waiting world, unfinished, before the creation of tone.

Consummator of the world: as that which falls down in rain over the earth and upon the waters, falling down carelessly, falling haphazard,—rises again out of all things, more invisible, and joyous in its law, and ascends and floats and forms the heavens: so the ascent of our precipitations rose out of you and domed the world about with music.

Your music: that it might have been about the universe; not about us. That a hammerclavier had been built for you in the Thebais; and an angel had led you to that solitary instrument, through the ranges of the desert mountains in which kings repose and hetairæ and anchorites. And he would have flung himself up and away, fearful lest you begin.

And then you would have streamed forth, streaming one, unheard; giving back to the All that which only the All can endure. Bedouins would have raced past in the distance, superstitious; but merchants would have flung themselves to the ground at the borders of your music, as if you were the tempest. Only a few solitary lions would have prowled a wide circle round you by night, afraid of themselves, menaced by their stirring blood.

For who will now fetch you out again from ears that are covetous? Who will drive them from the concert halls, the venal ones with their sterile hearing that fornicates and never conceives? The seed radiates, and they stand under it like sluts and play with it, or it falls, while they lie there in their abortive satisfactions, like the seed of Onan amongst them.

But, Master, were a virginal spirit to lie with innocent ear beside your sound: he would die of blessedness, or he would gestate infinite things and his impregnated brain would burst with so much birth.

I do not underestimate it. I know it takes courage. But let us assume for a moment that someone had it, this courage de luxe to follow them, in order to know for always (for who would forget it again, or mistake it?) into what holes they creep afterwards and what they do with the rest of their long day and whether they sleep at night. That especially should be ascertained: whether they sleep. But it will take more than courage. For they do not come and go like the other people, whom it would be a small matter to follow. They are here and away again, set down and removed like lead soldiers. The places where one finds them are somewhat remote, but by no means hidden. The bushes recede, the path curves slightly round the grass-plot: there they are, with a quantity of transparent space around them, as if they were standing under a glass dome. You might take them for pensive pedestrians, these inconspicuous men of slight, in every respect modest build. But you would be wrong. Do you see the left hand, how it grasps for something in the slanting pocket of the old overcoat; how it finds it and takes it out and holds the small object into the air, awkwardly attracting attention? In less than a minute two or three birds appear, sparrows, that come hopping up inquisitively. And if the man succeeds in conforming to their very exact idea of immobility, there is no reason why they should not come still nearer. At last the first one flies up, and flutters nervously a while about the level of that hand which (God knows) holds out a little piece of worn-down sweet bread with unpretentious, expressly renunciatory fingers. And the more people collect around him—at a suitable distance, of course— the less has he in common with them. He stands there like a candle that is burning out and sheds light with its remnant of wick and is all warm with it and has never stirred. And how he attracts, how he allures them, all those little, stupid birds cannot tell at all. If there were no spectators and one let him stand there long enough, I am sure an angel would suddenly appear and, overcoming his repulsion, eat the old sweetish morsel from that stunted hand. But now, as always, people are in the way. They take care that only birds come; they find that ample, and they assert that he expects nothing else. What else could it expect, this old, rainbattered doll, sticking slightly awry in the earth like the figureheads of ships in the little gardens at home; does its posture too come from its once having stood forward somewhere on its life, where the motion is greatest? Is it now so washed out because it was once many-colored? Will you ask it?

Only don't ask the women anything when you see one feeding the birds. Them one could even follow; they do it just in passing; it would be easy. But let them be. They do not know how it happened. All at once they have a quantity of bread in their handbags, and hold out large pieces from under their flimsy mantillas, pieces that are a little chewed and moist. It does them good to think that their spittle will get out into the world a little, that the little birds will fly about with this aftertaste, even if they do, naturally, at once forget it again.

There I sat before your books, obstinate man, trying to understand them the way those others do who do not leave you intact, but have taken their portion and are satisfied. For as yet I did not understand fame, that public destruction of one in process of becoming, into whose building-ground the mob breaks, displacing his stones.

Young man anywhere, in whom something stirs that makes you shiver, profit by the fact that no one knows you. And if they contradict you who hold you of no account, and if they give you up entirely whom you frequent, and if they would extirpate you because of your precious thoughts—what is this obvious danger, which holds you concentrated within yourself, against the subtle enmity of fame, later, which renders you innocuous by scattering you?

Ask no one to speak of you, not even contemptuously. And when time passes and you find your name getting about among people, take it no more seriously than anything else you find in their mouth. Think rather that it has grown rank, and discard it. Take another, any other, so that God may call you in the night. And conceal it from everyone.

Most lonely one, holding aloof, how they have caught up with you by reason of your fame. But lately they were against you from the very root, and now they deal with you as with their equal. And they carry your words about with them in the cages of their presumption and exhibit them in the squares and tease them a little from their own safe distance. All your terrible wild beasts.

Only then did I read you, when for me they broke out and fell upon me in my wilderness, desperate as they are. Desperate, as you yourself became in the end, you whose course is wrongly entered on every chart. Like a fissure it crosses the heavens, this hopeless hyperbola of your path, that only once curves toward us and draws off again in terror. What did it matter to you whether a woman stays or goes and whether someone is seized with dizziness and someone else with madness and whether the dead live and the living appear to be dead: what did it matter to you? It was all so natural for you; you passed through it, as one crosses a vestibule, and did not stop. But yonder you lingered, stooping; where our becoming seethes and precipitates and changes color, inside. Farther in than anyone has yet been; a door had sprung open before you, and now you were among the alembics in the firelight. Yonder where, mistrustful, you took no one with you, yonder you sat discerning transitions. And there, since it was in your blood to show and not to fashion or to say, there you took the enormous decision at once and single-handed so to magnify these minutiæ, which you yourself first became aware of only through glasses, that they should be seen of thousands, immense, before all eyes. Your theater came into being. You could not wait until this life almost without dimension, condensed into drops by the centuries, should be discovered by the other arts and gradually made visible for single individuals, who little by little meet together in their insight and at last demand to see in common these august rumors confirmed in the parable of the scene thrown open before them. This you could not wait for; you were there, and that which is scarcely measurable—a feeling that mounted by half a degree; the angle of refraction, which you read off at close quarters, of a will burdened by almost nothing, the slight cloudiness in a drop of longing and that barely perceptible color-change in an atom of confidence—all this you had to determine and preserve; for in such processes life itself now was, our life, which had slipped into us, had withdrawn inward, so deeply that it was scarcely possible even to conjecture about it any more.

Given as you were to showing, a timelessly tragic poet, you had to translate this capillary action all at once into the most convincing gestures, into the most present things. Then you set about that unexampled act of violence in your work, which ever more impatiently, ever more desperately, sought equivalents among the visible for the inwardly seen. There was a rabbit, a garret, a room where someone paces to and fro; there was a clatter of glass in the next room, a fire outside the windows, there was the sun. There was a church and a rocky valley that was like a church. But that did not suffice; towers had ultimately to enter and whole mountain ranges; and the avalanches that bury landscapes overwhelmed the stage with its surfeit of tangible things, for the sake of the impalpable. Then you could do no more. The two extremities you had bent together sprang apart; your mad strength escaped from the flexible shaft, and your work was as nothing.

Who should understand, otherwise, why in the end you would not leave the window, obstinate as you always were? You wanted to see the people passing by; for the thought had occurred to you whether some day one might not make something out of them, if one decided to begin.

Then for the first time did it strike me that one cannot say anything about a woman; I noticed when they spoke of her, how much they left blank, how they named and described other people, surroundings, localities, objects, up to a certain point where all that stopped, gently and as it were cautiously stopped, just at the light contour, never traced over, that enclosed her. "What was she like?" I would then ask. "Fair, somewhat like you," they would say, and would enumerate all sorts of other points they knew; but at that she became quite indistinct again, and I could picture nothing more to myself. I was able really to see her only when Maman told me the story, which I asked for again and again—.

—And every time she came to the scene with the dog, she used to close her eyes, and somehow fervently to keep her face, quite covered but everywhere shining through, between her hands which touched it, cold, at the temples. "I saw it, Malte", she adjured me, "I saw it." It was during her last years that I heard her tell this. At the time when she no longer wanted to see anyone and when she always, even on a journey, carried with her the small fine, silver sieve, through which she filtered everything she drank. Solid food she no longer took, save for some biscuit or bread, which, when she was alone, she broke into bits and ate crumb by crumb, as children eat crumbs. Her fear of needles already dominated her completely at that time. To others she simply said by way of excuse, "I really cannot digest anything any more, but don't let that trouble you, I feel very well indeed." But to me she would suddenly turn (for I was already a little bit grown-up) and say, with a smile that cost her a severe effort, "What a lot of needles there are, Malte, and how they lie about everywhere, and when you think how easily they fall out . . ." She tried to say this playfully; but terror shook her at the thought of all the insecurely fastened needles that might at any instant, anywhere, fall into something.

But when she told about Ingeborg, then nothing could happen to her; then she did not spare herself; then she spoke louder, then she laughed at the memory of Ingeborg's laugh, then everyone should see how lovely Ingeborg had been.

"She made us all happy," she said, "your father, too, Malte, literally happy. But afterwards, when we were told she was going to die, though she seemed to be ailing only a little, and we all went about hiding the truth, she sat up in bed one day and said, as if to herself, like a person who wants to hear how something sounds: 'You mustn't put such a strain on yourselves; we all know it, and I can set your minds at rest; it will be all right just as it comes; I don't want any more.' Just imagine, she said 'I don't want any more'; she, who made us all happy. Will you understand that some day, Malte, when you are grown up? Think about it later on, perhaps it will come to you. It would be good if there were someone who understood such things."

"Such things" occupied Maman when she was alone, and she was always alone in these last years.

"I shall never really hit upon it, Malte," she sometimes said with her strangely daring smile, which was not meant to be seen by anyone and fulfilled its whole purpose in being smiled. "But that no one is tempted to find it out! If I were a man, yes, just if I were a man, I would ponder over it, in the proper order and sequence and from the beginning. For there must surely be a beginning, and if one could only lay hold on that, it would at least be something. Ah, Malte, we pass away like that, and it seems to me people are all distracted and preoccupied and pay no real attention when we pass away. As if a shooting-star fell and no one saw it and no one had made a wish. Never forget to wish something for yourself, Malte. One should never give up wishing. I believe there is no fulfilment, but there are wishes that last a long time, all one's life, so that anyhow one could not wait for their fulfilment."

Maman had had Ingeborg's small desk brought up and put in her own room. I often found her at it, for I was allowed to go in whenever I pleased. My step was completely lost in the carpet, but she felt my presence, and stretched out one of her hands to me over the other shoulder. This hand had no weight whatever, and to kiss it was like kissing the ivory crucifix that was held out to me before I went to sleep. At this low writing desk, which opened with a drop-leaf before her, she would sit as at some instrument. "There is so much sun in it," she said, and in truth the interior was remarkably bright, with its old yellow lacquer on which flowers were painted, alternately red and blue. And where there were three together, a violet one between separated the other two. These colors and the green of the narrow, horizontal border of arabesques, had sunk in as dim as the background, without being really distinct, was luminous. This resulted in a strangely muted relationship of tones that had an intimate bearing upon each other, without expressing themselves about it.

Maman drew out the little drawers, which were all empty.

"Ah, roses," she said, bending forward a little into the dim odor that had never quite vanished. She always imagined that something might yet be suddenly discovered in some secret drawer which no one had thought of and which would yield only at the pressing of some hidden spring. "It will jump forward all of a sudden, you shall see," she said gravely and anxiously, and pulled hastily at all the drawers. But any papers that had actually been left in the drawers she had carefully folded and locked away without read-

ing. "I should not understand it in any case, Malte; it would cer-
tainly be too difficult for me." She was convinced that everything
was too complicated for her. "There are no classes in life for be-
ginners; it is always the most difficult that is asked of one right
away." They assured me that she had become like this only after
the terrible end of her sister, the Countess Ollegaard Skeel, who
was burned to death as she sought to rearrange the flowers in her
hair before a ball, in front of a candle-lit mirror. But more recently
it had been Ingeborg that after all seemed to her the most difficult
to understand.

And now I shall write down the story as Maman told it when I
asked for it.

"It was in the middle of summer, on the Thursday after Inge-
borg's funeral. From the place on the terrace where we were hav-
ing tea, one could see through the giant elms to the gable of the
family vault. The table had been set as if there had never been one
more person sitting at it, and we had also spread ourselves out
around it. And we had each brought something, a book or a work-
basket, so that we were even a little crowded. Abelone (Maman's
youngest sister) was dispensing the tea, and we were all occupied
handing things round; only your grandfather was looking from his
armchair toward the house. It was the hour when the mail was
expected, and it usually happened that Ingeborg brought it, as she
was detained longer in the house over the arrangements for din-
ner. Now during the weeks of her illness we had had plenty of
time to get accustomed to her not coming; for we knew, of course,
that she could not come. But that afternoon, Malte, when she ac-
tually could not come any more—: she came. Perhaps it was our
fault; perhaps we called her. For I remember that all at once I was
sitting there trying to think what it really was that was now dif-
ferent. Suddenly it became impossible for me to say *what;* I had
quite forgotten. I looked up and saw all the others turned toward
the house, not in any special, striking way, but just calm and as
usual in their expectancy. And I was just on the point—(I go quite
cold, Malte, when I think about it) but, God help me, I was just
on the point of saying: 'Wherever is—?' When Cavalier shot from
under the table, as he always did, and ran to meet her. I saw it,
Malte; I saw it. He ran toward her, although she was not coming;
for him she was coming. We understood that he was running to

meet her. Twice he looked round at us, as if questioning. Then he rushed at her as he always did, Malte, just as he always did, and he reached her, for he began to jump round and round, Malte, round something that was not there, and then he leaped up on her, right up to lick her. We heard him whining for joy, and by the way he bounded into the air several times in quick succession, you might have imagined he was hiding her from us with his gambols. But suddenly there was a howl, and whirling in mid air from his own momentum, he pitched back with unaccustomed clumsiness, and lay there quite strangely flat and never moved. From the other wing of the house the man-servant came out with the letters. He hesitated for a little; evidently it was not easy to walk toward our faces. Besides, your father had already motioned to him to stop. Your father, Malte, did not like animals; but for all that he now went up, slowly, as it seemed to me, and bent over the dog. He said something to the servant, something brief, monosyllabic. I saw the servant spring forward to lift Cavalier up; but your father took the dog himself, and carried it, as if he knew exactly where to take it, into the house."

Once when it had grown almost dark during this story, I was on the point of telling Maman about the hand: at that moment I could have done it. I had taken a long breath in order to begin; but then it occurred to me how well I had understood the servant's not being able to approach their faces. And in spite of the waning light I feared what Maman's face would be like when it should see what I had seen. I quickly took another breath, to make it appear that that was all I had meant to do. A few years later, after the remarkable night in the gallery at Urnekloster, I went about for days with the intention of taking little Erik into my confidence. But after our nocturnal conversation he had once more closed himself completely to me, avoided me; I believe that he despised me. And just for this reason I wanted to tell him about "the hand". I imagined I would rise in his estimation (and I wanted that keenly for some reason) if I could make him understand that I had really had that experience. But Erik was so clever at evasion that I never got to it. And then we did leave right afterward. So, strangely enough, this is the first time I am relating (and after all only for myself) an occurence that now lies far back in the days of my childhood. How small I must still have been I see from the fact that I was kneeling on the armchair in order to reach comfortably up to the table on which I was drawing. It was an evening, in winter, in our apartment in town, if I am not mistaken. The table stood in my room, between the windows, and there was no lamp in the room save that which shone on my papers and on Mademoiselle's book; for Mademoiselle sat next me, her chair pushed back a little, and was reading. She was far away when she read, and I don't know whether she was in her book; she could read for hours, she seldom turned the leaves, and I had the impression that the pages became steadily fuller under her eyes, as though she looked words into them, certain words that she needed and that were not there. So it seemed to me as I went on drawing. I was drawing slowly, without any very decided intention, and when I didn't know what to do next, I would survey the whole with head bent a little to the right; in that position it always came to me soonest what was lacking. They were officers on horseback, who were riding into battle, or they were in the midst of it, and that was far simpler, for in that case, almost all one needed to draw was the smoke that enveloped everything. Maman, it is true, always insists that they were islands I was painting; islands with large trees and a castle and a flight of steps and flowers along the edge that were supposed to be reflected in the water. But I think she is making that up, or it must have been later.

It is certain that on that particular evening I was drawing a knight, a solitary, easily recognizable knight, on a strikingly caparisoned horse. He became so gaily-colored that I had to change crayons frequently, but the red was most in demand and for it I reached again and again. Now I needed it once more, when it rolled (I can see it yet) right across the lighted sheet to the edge of the table and, before I could stop it, fell past me and disappeared. I needed it really urgently, and it was very annoying to clamber down after it. Awkward as I was, I had to make all sorts of preparations to get down; my legs seemed to me far too long, I could not pull them out from under me; the too-prolonged kneeling posture had numbed my limbs; I could not tell what belonged to me, and what to the chair. At last I did arrive down there, somewhat bewildered, and found myself on a fur rug that stretched from under the table as far as the wall. But here a fresh difficulty arose. My eyes, accustomed to the brightness above and all inspired with the colors on the white paper, were unable to distinguish anything at all beneath the table, where the blackness seemed to me so dense that I was afraid I should knock against it. I therefore relied on my sense of touch, and kneeling, supported on my left hand, I combed around with my other hand in the cool, long-haired rug, which felt quite friendly; only that no pencil was to be found. I imagined I must be losing a lot of time, and was about to call to Mademoiselle and ask her to hold the lamp for me, when I noticed that to my involuntarily strained eyes the darkness was gradually growing more penetrable. I could already distinguish the wall at the back, which ended in a light-colored molding; I oriented myself with regard to the legs of the table; above all I recognized my own outspread hand moving down there all alone, a little like an aquatic animal, examining the ground. I watched it, as I remember still, almost with curiosity; it seemed as if it knew things I had never taught it, groping down there so independently, with movements I had never noticed in it before. I followed it up as it pressed forward, I was interested in it, ready for all sorts of things. But how should I have been prepared to see suddenly come to meet it out of the wall another hand, a larger, extraordinarily thin hand, such as I had never seen before. It came groping in similar fashion from the other side, and the two outspread hands moved blindly toward one another. My curiosity was not yet used up but suddenly it came to an end, and there was only terror. I felt that one of the hands belonged to me, and that it was committing itself to something irreparable. With all the authority I had over it, I checked it and drew it back flat and slowly, without taking my eyes off the other, which went on groping. I realized that it would not leave off; I cannot tell how I got up again. I sat deep in the armchair, my teeth chattered, and I had so little blood in my face that it seemed to me there could be no more blue in my eyes. Mademoiselle—, I wanted to say and could not, but at that she took fright of her own accord, and, flinging her book away, knelt beside the chair and cried out my name; I believe she shook me. But I was perfectly conscious. I swallowed a couple of times; for now I wanted to tell about it.

But how? I made an indescribable effort to master myself, but it was not to be expressed so that anyone could understand. If there were words for this occurrence, I was too little to find them. And suddenly the fear seized me that nevertheless they might suddenly be there, beyond my years, these words, and it seemed to me more terrible than anything else that I should then have to say them. To live through once again the reality down there, differently, conjugated, from the beginning; to hear myself admitting it—for that I had no strength left.

It is of course imagination on my part to declare now that I already at that time felt that something had entered into my life, directly into mine, with which I alone should have to go about, always and always. I see myself lying in my little crib and not sleeping and somehow vaguely foreseeing that life would be like this: full of many special things that are meant for *one* person alone and that cannot be told. Certain it is that a sad and heavy pride gradually arose in me. I pictured to myself how one would go about, full of what is inside one, and silent. I felt an impetuous sympathy for grown-ups; I admired them, and proposed to tell them that I admired them. I proposed to tell it to Mademoiselle at the next opportunity.

And then came one of those illnesses that set themselves to prove to me that this was not my first private experience. The fever rummaged in me and brought up from way down adventures, pictures, facts, of which I had been ignorant: I lay there overloaded with myself, awaiting the moment when I should be bidden to stow all this back into myself again, properly and in order. I began, but it grew under my hands, it resisted, it was much too much. Then rage seized me, and I flung everything into myself pell-mell and squeezed it together; but I couldn't shut over it again. And then I yelled, half open as I was, I yelled and yelled. And when I began to see out from myself, they had been standing for a long time around my bed and holding my hands, and a candle was there, and their great shadows moved behind them. And my father commanded me to say what was the matter. It was a friendly, subdued order, but an order nevertheless. And he became impatient when I did not reply.

Maman never came at night—, or rather, she did come once. I

had cried and cried, and Mademoiselle had come and Sieversen, the housekeeper, and Georg, the coachman; but that had been of no avail. And then finally they had sent the carriage for my parents, who were at a great ball, at the Crown Prince's, I think. And all at once I heard the carriage driving into the courtyard, and I became quiet, sat up and watched the door. There was a slight rustling in the adjoining rooms, and Maman came in in her grand court dress, of which she took no care—almost ran in, and let her white fur fall behind her and took me in her bare arms. And I, astonished and enchanted as never before, touched her hair, her well-tended little face, the cool jewels at her ears, and the silk at the curve of her shoulders, fragrant of flowers. And we remained like this, weeping tenderly and kissing one another, until we felt that Father was there and that we must separate. "He has high fever," I heard Maman say timidly, and my father took my hand and counted my pulse. He wore the uniform of the Master-of-the-Hunt with its lovely, broad, watered blue ribbon of the Order of the Elephant. "What nonsense to send for us," he said, speaking into the room without looking at me. They had promised to go back if it was nothing serious. And it certainly was nothing serious. But on my bedspread I found Maman's dancecard and white camellias, which I had never seen before and which I laid on my eyes when I felt how cool they were.

B ut it was the afternoons that were long in such illnesses. In the morning after a bad night one always fell asleep, and when one wakened and thought, now it was morning again, it was really afternoon and remained afternoon and never ceased to be afternoon. So one lay there in one's tidied bed, and grew a little at the joints perhaps, and was far too tired to imagine anything to oneself. The taste of apple-sauce lasted a long time, and it was even quite an achievement somehow involuntarily to interpret this flavor and let the clean acid circulate in one instead of thoughts. Later on, as strength returned, the pillows were propped up behind one, and one could sit up and play with soldiers; but they fell so easily on the sloping bed-tray and always the whole row at once; and as yet one was not so thoroughly back in life as always to begin over again from the beginning. Suddenly it was too much, and one begged to have everything taken away quickly, and it was good once more to see only one's two hands, a little further off on the empty bedspread.

When Maman sometimes came for half an hour and read me fairy tales (Sieversen came for the proper, long reading), it was not for the sake of the fairy tales. For we agreed that we did not like fairy tales. We had a different conception of the marvelous. We found that if everything happened naturally that would always be the most marvelous. We set no great store on flying through the air, fairies disappointed us, and from transformations into something else we expected but a very superficial change. But we did read a little, so as to appear occupied; we didn't like, when anyone came in, having to explain first what we were doing; especially toward Father were we exaggeratedly explicit.

Only when we were quite sure of not being disturbed, and darkness was gathering outside, it might happen that we abandoned ourselves to memories, common memories, which seemed old to both of us and over which we smiled; for we had both grown up since then. It occurred to us that there was a time when Maman wished I had been a little girl, and not this boy that once and for all I was. I had somehow guessed this, and I had hit upon the notion of sometimes knocking in the afternoon at Maman's door. Then when she asked who was there, I took delight in answering from outside, "Sophie," making my small voice so dainty that it tickled my throat. And when I entered then (in the little, girlish housedress I wore anyway, with sleeves rolled all the way up), I was simply Sophie, Maman's little Sophie, busy about household duties, whose hair Maman had to braid so that she should not be mistaken for the wicked Malte, if he ever returned. This was by no means to be desired; his absence was as agreeable to Maman as to Sophie, and their conversations (which Sophie always carried on in the same high-pitched voice) consisted mostly in enumerating Malte's naughtinesses and complaining about him. "Ah yes, that Malte," Maman would sigh. And Sophie knew a lot about the mischievousness of boys in general, as though she were acquainted with a whole heap of them.

"I should like very much to know what has become of Sophie," Maman would suddenly say in the midst of these recollections. On that point Malte could of course provide no information. But when

Maman suggested that she must certainly be dead, he would stubbornly contradict and adjure her not to believe that, however little proof there might be to the contrary.

When I reflect on it now, I marvel that I nevertheless always managed wholly to return from the world of these fevers and to adjust myself to that thorough community of life, where each wanted support in the feeling that he was among people he knew, and where one so carefully got on together in the comprehensible. If one expected something, it came or it did not come; there was no third possibility. There were things that were sad, once and for all, and there were pleasant things and a whole quantity of incidental things. But when a joy was arranged for one, it was a joy, and one had to behave accordingly. All this was essentially very simple, and once one understood that, it took care of itself. For into these appointed boundaries everything fitted: the long monotonous lesson-hours, when it was summer outside; the walks that had afterward to be described in French; the visitors into whose presence one was summoned and who found one amusing just when one was sad, and who made merry over one as at the melancholy visage of certain birds that have no other. And of course the birthdays, to which one had children invited whom one scarcely knew, embarrassed children who made one embarrassed, or impudent children who scratched one's face and broke what one had just received, and who then suddenly drove away when everything had been pulled out of boxes and drawers and lay about in heaps. But when one played alone, as usual, one might happen inadvertently to trespass beyond this prearranged, on the whole harmless world and find oneself among circumstances that were entirely different and by no means to be foreseen.

At times Mademoiselle had her migraine, which was unusually violent; and these were the days when I was hard to find. I know that on these occasions the coachman was sent to the park, when it occurred to Father to ask for me and I was not there. From one of the upper guest-rooms I could see him run out and call for me at the entrance to the long drive. These guest-rooms were side by side in the gable of Ulsgaard and, as we very seldom had visitors in those days, were almost always empty. But adjoining them was that great corner room that had so strong an attraction for me. There was nothing to be seen in it save an old bust which, I believe, represented Admiral Juel; but the walls were panelled all around with deep, grey closets, in such a way that even the window had been placed above the closets in the bare, white-washed wall. I had found the key in one of the closet doors, and it opened all the others. So in a short time I had examined everything: eighteenth-century chamberlains' dress-coats, all cold with their inwoven silver threads, and the beautifully embroidered vests that went with them; uniforms of the Orders of the Dannebrog and the Elephant, so rich and fussy and with linings so soft to the touch, one at first mistook them for women's dresses. Then real gowns, which, held out by their panniers, hung there stiffly like the marionettes from some too grand play now so conclusively out-moded that their heads had been used for some other purpose. But alongside these were closets in which it was dark when one opened them, dark because of high-buttoning uniforms, which looked much more worn than all the other things, and which really wished they were not being preserved.

No one will find it to be wondered at that I pulled all this out and tilted it into the light; that I held now this, now that, against me or flung it about me; that I hastily donned some costume that might fit and, arrayed in it, ran, curious and excited, to the nearest guest-room, before the narrow pier-glass which was composed of bits of irregularly green glass. Ah, how one trembled to be in there, and how ravishing when one was. When out of the dimness something drew near, more slowly than oneself, for the mirror did not, so to speak, believe it, and did not want, sleepy as it was, to repeat promptly what had been said to it. But naturally it had to in the end. And now it was something very surprising, strange, altogether different from one's expectation, something sudden, independent, which one rapidly surveyed, only in the next instant to recognize oneself after all, not without a certain irony which came within a hairsbreadth of spoiling all the fun. But if one promptly began to talk, to bow, if one nodded to oneself, walked away, constantly looking round, and then came back, brisk and determined—one had imagination siding with one as long as one liked.

It was then that I first learned to know the influence that can emanate directly from a particular costume itself. Hardly had I donned one of these suits, when I had to admit that it got me in its power; that it prescribed my movements, my facial expression, yes, even my ideas. My hand, over which the lace cuff fell and fell again, was anything but my usual hand; it moved like a person acting; I might even say that it was watching itself, exaggerated though that sounds. These disguises never, indeed, went so far as to make me feel a stranger to myself: on the contrary, the more varied my transformations, the more convinced did I become of myself. I grew bolder and bolder; I flung myself higher and higher; for my dexterity in recapture was beyond all doubt. I did not notice the temptation in this rapidly growing security. To my undoing, the last closet, which I had heretofore thought I could not open, yielded one day, to surrender to me, not specific costumes, but all kinds of random paraphernalia for masquerades, the fantastic peradventures of which drove the blood to my cheeks. It is impossible to recount all I found there. In addition to a baútta that I remember, there were dominos in various colors, there were women's dresses that tinkled brightly with the coins with which they were sewn; there were pierrot-costumes that looked silly to me, and braided Turkish trousers, all folds, and Persian fezzes from which little camphor sacks slipped out, and coronets with stupid, expressionless stones. All these I rather despised; they were of such a shabby unreality and hung there so peeled-off and miserable and collapsed so will-lessly when one dragged them out into the light. But what transported me into a sort of intoxication were the capacious mantles, the wraps, the shawls, the veils, all those yielding, wide, unused fabrics, that were so soft and caressing, or so slithery that one could scarcely take hold of them, or so light that they flew by one like a wind, or simply heavy with all their own weight. In them I first discerned really free and infinitely mobile possibilities: being a slave-girl about to be sold, or being Jeanne d'Arc or an old king or a wizard; all this lay to hand, especially as there were also masks, large, threatening or astonished faces with real beards and full or high-drawn eyebrows. I had never seen masks before, but I understood at once that masks ought to be. I had to laugh when it occurred to me that we had a dog who looked as if he wore one. I recalled his affectionate eyes, that always seemed to be looking as from behind into his hirsute visage. I was still laughing as I dressed up, and in the process I completely forgot what I had intended to represent. No matter; it was novel and exciting not to decide till afterward before the mirror. The face I fastened on had a singularly hollow smell; it lay tight over my own face, but I was able to see through it comfortably, and not till the mask sat firm did I select all sorts of materials, which I wound about my head like a turban, in such a way that the edge of the mask, which reached downward into an immense yellow cloak, was almost entirely hidden also on top and at the sides. At length, when I could do no more, I considered myself sufficiently disguised. I seized in addition a large staff, which I made walk along beside me at arm's length, and in this fashion, not without difficulty, but, as it seemed to me, full of dignity, I trailed into the guest-room toward the mirror.

It was really grandiose, beyond all expectation. And the mirror gave it back instantly, it was too convincing. It would not have been at all necessary to move much; this apparition was perfect, even though it did nothing. But I wanted to discover what I actually was, so I turned a little and finally raised both arms: large, almost conjuring gestures were, I saw immediately, the only fitting ones. But just as this solemn moment I heard quite near me, muffled by my disguise, a very complicated noise; much frightened, I lost sight of the presence in the mirror and was badly upset to perceive that I had overturned a small round table with heaven knows what, probably very fragile objects. I bent down as well as I could and found my worst fears confirmed: it looked as though everything were in pieces. The two useless green-violet porcelain parrots were of course shattered, each in a different malign fashion. A box, from which rolled bonbons that looked like insects in silken cocoons, had cast its cover far away; only half of it was to be seen, the other had totally disappeared. But most annoying of all was a scent-bottle that had been shivered into a thousand tiny fragments, from which the remainder of some sort of old essence had spurted that now formed a spot of very repulsive profile on the clear parquet. I wiped it up quickly with something or other that was hanging down about me, but it only became blacker and more unpleasant. I was indeed desperate. I picked myself up and tried to find something with which to repair the damage. But nothing was to be found. Besides I was so hampered in my vision and in every movement, that wrath rose in me against my absurd situation, which I no longer understood. I pulled at all my garments, but they clung only the tighter. The cords of the mantle strangled. me, and the stuff on my head pressed as though more and more were being added to it. Furthermore the atmosphere had become dim and as though misty with the oldish fume of the spilled liquid.

Hot and angry, I rushed to the mirror and with difficulty watched through the mask the working of my hands. But for this the mirror had just been waiting. Its moment of retaliation had come. While I strove in boundlessly increasing anguish to squeeze somehow out of my disguise, it forced me, by what means I do not know, to lift my eyes and imposed on me an image, no, a reality, a strange, unbelievable and monstrous reality, with which, against my will, I became permeated: for now the mirror was the stronger, and I was the mirror. I stared at this great, terrifying unknown before me, and it seemed to me appalling to be alone with him. But at the very moment I thought this, the worst befell: I lost all sense, I simply ceased to exit. For one second I had an indescribable, painful. and futile longing for myself, then there was only he: there was nothing but he.

I ran away, but now it was he that ran. He knocked against everything, he did not know the house, he had no idea where to go; he managed to get down a stairway, and in his course stumbled over someone who shouted in struggling free. A door opened, several persons came out: Oh, oh, what a relief it was to know them! There were Sieversen, the good Sieversen, and the housemaid and the butler: now for a decision. But they did not spring forward to the rescue; their cruelty knew no bounds. They stood there and laughed; my God, they could stand there and laugh. I wept, but the mask did not let the tears escape; they ran down inside over my cheeks and dried at once and ran again and dried. And at last I knelt before them, as no human being ever knelt; I knelt, and lifted up my hands, and implored them: "Take me out, if you still can, and keep me", but they did not hear; I had no longer any voice.

Sieversen used to tell to the day of her death how I sank down and how they went on laughing, thinking that was part of it. They were used to that from me. But then I had continued to lie there and had not answered. And their fright when they finally discovered that I was unconscious and lay there like a piece of something among all those wrappings, just like a piece of something.

Time passed with incalculable rapidity, and all at once it had got to the point again when the minister, Dr. Jespersen, had to be invited. This meant a luncheon, tiresome and interminable for all parties. Accustomed to the very pious neighborhood which always went into a state of dissolution on his account, Dr. Jespersen was entirely out of his element with us; he was, so to speak, lying on dry land and gasping. The gills he had developed for himself worked with difficulty; bubbles formed, and the whole thing was not without danger. Of material for conversation there was, to be exact, none whatever; remainders were being disposed of at unbelievable prices, it was a liquidiation of all stocks. In our house Dr. Jespersen had to content himself with being a sort of private person; but that was exactly what he had never been. As far back as he could think, his profession had been the soul. For him the soul was a public institution which he represented, and he saw to it that he was never off duty, not even in his relations with his wife, "his modest, faithful Rebecca, being sanctified by the bearing of children," as Lavater expressed it in another case.

*(As for my father, his attitude to God was perfectly correct and of a faultless courtesy. At church it sometimes seemed to me as though he were positively Master-of-the-Hunt to God himself, when he stood there and waited and bowed his head. To Maman, on the contrary, it seemed almost offensive that anyone could stand in a polite relationship to God. Had she chanced upon a religion with expressive and detailed observances, it would have been bliss for her to kneel for hours, to prostrate herself and to make the sign of the cross with great gestures before her breast and about her shoulders. She did not actually teach me to pray, but it was a comfort to her to know that I kneeled willingly and clasped my hands, with fingers now bent, now upright, whichever seemed to me more expressive. Left a good deal to myself, I passed early through a series of developments which I did not until much later, in a period of despair, connect with God; and then, indeed, with such

---

* Written on the margin of the MS.

violence that God took shape and was shattered for me almost in the same moment. It is plain that after this I had to start all over again from the beginning. And for that beginning I sometimes thought I needed Maman, though naturally it was the right thing to live through it alone. And of course she had long been dead by that time.)

With Dr. Jespersen Maman could be almost exuberant. She would embark on conversations with him which he took seriously, and then when he heard himself talking she thought that was enough, and forgot him suddenly, as though he were already gone. "However can he," she sometimes said, "drive about and go in to see people, just when they are dying!"

He came to her also on that occasion, but she certainly no longer saw him. Her senses were fading, one after the other, and the first to go was sight. It was in the autumn, and we should have been leaving for the city, but just then she fell ill, or rather she began at once to die, slowly and hopelessly to die off over her whole surface. The doctors came, and on a certain day they were all present together and took possession of the whole house. For a few hours it seemed to belong to the Geheimrat and his assistants, as though we had no longer any say. But immediately after that they lost all interest, came only one at a time, as if from pure politeness, to accept a cigar and a glass of port. And meanwhile Maman died.

There was yet to be expected only Maman's sole brother, Count Christian Brahe, who, as will be remembered, had been for a time in the Turkish service, where he was always said to have gained great distinction. He arrived one morning, accompanied by a singular servant, and I was surprised to see that he was taller than my father and apparently older as well. The two gentlemen at once exchanged a few words which, as I surmised, referred to Maman. A pause ensued. Then my father said: "She is very much disfigured." I did not understand this expression, but I shivered when I heard it. I had the impression that my father, too, had had to master himself before he uttered it. But it was probably above all his pride that suffered in making this admission.

Not until several years later did I hear further mention of Count Christian. That was at Urnekloster, and it was Mathilde Brahe who especially liked to talk about him. I am sure, however, that she embellished the various episodes of his career in a rather arbitrary fashion; for my uncle's life, of which only rumors ever penetrated to the public and even to the family, rumors that he never took the trouble to contradict, offered boundless opportunities for interpretation. Urnekloster is now in his possession. But no one knows whether he is living there. Perhaps he is still traveling, as his habit was; perhaps the news of his death is on its way from some remotest part of the earth, written by his foreign servant in bad English or in some unknown tongue. Or perhaps this man will give no sign of life when one day he is left alone. Perhaps they have both disappeared long ago, remaining only on the passenger list of some missing ship under names that were not their own.

I will confess that when in those days a carriage drove into the courtyard of Urnekloster, I always expected to see *him* enter, and my heart began to beat in a peculiar manner. Mathilde Brahe declared that that was how he would come, that was one of his odd ways, suddenly to turn up when one least thought it possible. He never came; but for weeks my imagination busied itself with him. I had the feeling as if we owed each other some contact, and I would have liked to know something real about him.

When shortly after this, however, my interest veered round and as a result of certain events went over entirely to Christine Brahe, I did not, strangely enough, make any attempt to learn anything about the circumstances of her life. On the other hand, I was troubled by the thought of whether her portrait really was among the paintings in the gallery. And the wish to make certain of this grew so exclusive and tormenting that for several nights I could not sleep, until, quite unexpectedly, there came that night on which, heaven help me, I rose and went upstairs with my light, which seemed to be afraid.

For my own part, I had no thought of fear. I had no thought of anything; I went. The tall doors yielded so lightly before me and above me, the rooms through which I passed kept very still. And at last I noticed by the depth that came wafting toward me, that I had entered the gallery. On my right I felt the windows with the night, and the pictures should be on my left. I lifted my light as high as I could. Yes: there were the pictures.

At first I meant to look at the women only, but I soon recognized one portrait and then another, similar to the ones at Ulsgaard, and when I lit them up thus from below, they moved and wanted to come into the light, and it seemed heartless of me not to wait for that at least. There was Christian IV, again and again, with his beautifully braided lovelock along his broad, slowly rounded cheek. There were presumably his wives, of whom I knew only Christine Munk; and suddenly Mrs. Ellen Marsvin looked at me, suspicious in her widow's weeds and with the same string of pearls on the brim of her high hat. There were King Christian's children: always fresh ones by new wives, the "incomparable" Eleonore, on a white pacing palfrey, in her heyday, before the ordeal. The Gyldenlöves: Hans Ulrik, of whom the women in Spain thought that he painted his face, so full-blooded was he, and Ulrik Christian, whom one never again forgot. And nearly all the Ulfelds. And that one there, with one eye painted over black, might well be Henrik Holck, who came to be Count of the Empire and Field Marshal at the age of thirty-three, and that had happened this way: On his way to the damsel Hilleborg Krafse, he dreamed he was given a naked sword instead of his bride; and he took it to heart and turned back and began his brief and foolhardy life, which ended with the plague. I knew them all. We also had at Ulsgaard the ambassadors to the Congress of Nimwegen, who all slightly resembled one another because they had all been painted at the same time, each with a slim, cropped eyebrow-like moustache over the sensual, almost seeing mouth. That I recognized Duke Ulrik goes without saying, and Otto Brahe and Claus Daa and Sten Rosensparre, the last of his race; for of them all I had seen portraits in the dining-room at Ulsgaard, or I had found in old portfolios copper-plate engravings that represented them.

But then there were also many whom I had never seen; few women, but there were children. My arm had been tired for some time and was shaking, yet I raised the light again and again in order to see the children. I understood them, those little girls that carried a bird on their hand and forgot about it. Sometimes a little dog sat at their feet, a ball lay there, and on a table nearby there were fruit and flowers; and on the pillar behind there hung, small and preliminary, the coat-of-arms of the Grubbes, or the Billes, or the Rosenkrantzes. So much had been collected round them, as though a lot had to be made good. But they stood there simply in their dresses and waited; one saw they were waiting. And that made me think of the women again and of Christine Brahe, and whether I should recognize her.

I wanted to run quickly to the end of the gallery and returning thence to look for her, when I knocked against something. I turned so abruptly round that little Erik leaped back, whispering:

"Take care with your light!"

"You here?" I said breathless, and I was not sure whether this was a good, or a thoroughly bad, omen. He only laughed and I didn't know what next. My light was flickering, and I could not very well see the expression of his face. Probably it was unfortunate that he was there. But then, drawing nearer, he said:

"*Her* portrait is not there; we are still looking for it upstairs."

With his low voice and his one moving eye he made a kind of upward gesture. And I realized that he meant the attic. But suddenly a singular thought occurred to me.

"We?" I asked. "Is she upstairs then?"

"Yes," he nodded, standing very close to me.

"She is looking too, herself?"

"Yes, we are looking."

"So the picture has been put away, has it?"

"Yes, just imagine," he said indignantly. But I did not quite grasp what she wanted with the picture.

"She wants to see herself," he whispered quite close.

"Ah, yes," I replied, as if I understood. At that he blew out my candle. I saw him straining forward, into the light, with eyebrows raised high. Then it was dark. I stepped back involuntarily.

"What are you doing?" I cried, stifled and quite dry in the throat. He sprang after me and hung on my arm, tittering.

"But what?" I rebuked him and tried to shake him off, but he clung fast. I could not prevent him from putting his arm round my neck.

"Shall I tell you?" he hissed, and a little saliva sprayed against my ear.

"Yes, yes, quick."

I didn't know what I was saying. He had got his arms fully round me now, stretching as he did so.

"I brought her a looking glass," he said and tittered again.

"A looking-glass?"

"Yes, because after all her portrait isn't there."

"No, no," I murmured.

He suddenly drew me somewhat further toward the window and pinched my upper arm so sharply that I cried out.

"She is not in there," he breathed into my ear.

Involuntarily I pushed him away, something about him cracked, I thought I had broken him.

"Go on, go on—" and now I had to laugh myself. "Not in there? How so, not in there?"

"You are stupid," he countered angrily, whispering no longer. His voice had changed register, as though he were beginning a new and as yet unused part of it. "Either one is in there", he pronounced with a severity beyond his years, "and in that case one is not here: or one is here, and cannot be in there."

"Of course," I answered quickly, without reflecting. I feared he might otherwise go away and leave me alone. I even grabbed at him.

"Shall we be friends?" I proposed. He wanted to be urged.

"It's all the same to me," he said curtly.

I attempted to inaugurate our friendship, but did not dare embrace him. "Dear Erik," was all I could manage, and touched him lightly somewhere. I felt very tired all at once. I looked round; I no longer understood how I had come here and my not having been afraid. I did not rightly know where the windows were and where the pictures. And as we left he had to lead me.

"They won't do anything to you," he assured me magnanimously and tittered again.

D ear, dear Erik; perhaps you were after all my only friend. For I have never had one. It is a pity you set no store by friendship. I should have liked to tell you so many things. Perhaps we would have got on together. One can never know. I remember your portrait was being painted at that time. Grandfather had got someone to come and paint you. An hour every morning. I cannot recall what the painter looked like; his name has slipped my memory, though Mathilde Brahe used to repeat it every minute.

Did he see you as I see you? You wore a suit of heliotrope-colored velvet. Mathilde Brahe adored that suit. But that doesn't matter now. I should only like to know whether he saw you. Let us assume that he was a real painter. Let us assume that it did not occur to him you might die before he should be done; that he did not look at the matter at all sentimentally; that he simply worked. That the dissimilarity of your two brown eyes fascinated him; that he was not for one moment ashamed of the immoveable one; that he had the tact not to place anything on the table beside your hand, which leaned perhaps a little bit—. Let us assume whatever else is necessary and approve it: then we have a portrait, your portrait, the last in the gallery at Urnekloster.

(And when one goes, having seen them all, there is still that boy there. One moment: who is it? A Brahe. Do you see the pale argent on the sable field and the peacock feathers? There is the name, too: Erik Brahe. Wasn't that an Erik Brahe who was executed? Yes, of course, that is well enough known. But this cannot be the same. This boy died when he was quite young, no matter when. Can't you see that?)

When visitors came and Erik was summoned, Miss Mathilde Brahe always asserted that it was absolutely incredible how much he resembled the old Countess Brahe, my grandmother. She was said to have been a very great lady. I did not know her. I remember very well, on the other hand, my father's mother, the real mistress of Ulsgaard. This she must always have remained, however strongly she resented Maman's entering the house as the wife of the Master-of-the-Hunt. After that she constantly acted as though she were effacing herself, and referred the servants to Maman for every trivial detail, while in important matters she calmly made decisions herself and had them carried out without accounting to anyone. Maman, I imagine, did not wish it otherwise. She was so little fitted to oversee a large house; she entirely lacked the faculty of distinguishing between subordinate and important things. Everything about which one spoke to her always seemed to be the whole matter, and over it she forgot other things which after all were there too. She never complained about her mother-in-law. And to whom should she have complained? Father was an extremely respectful son, and Grandfather had little to say.

Mrs. Margarete Brigge had always been, as far as my recollection of her goes, a tall and unapproachable old lady. I cannot picture her except as much older than the chamberlain. She lived her life in our midst without consideration for anyone. She was dependent upon none of us; she had always about her a sort of lady-companion, the ageing Countess Oxe, whom by some benefaction she had put under a boundless obligation. This must have been a single exception in her life, for she was not given to good deeds. She did not like children, and animals were not allowed to come near her. I do not know whether there was anything else she did like. It was said that as a very young girl, she had been engaged to the handsome Felix Lichnowski, who came to so cruel an end at Frankfort. And in fact, after her death a portrait of the prince was found, which, if I am not mistaken, was returned to his family. I now believe that perhaps, through the retired country life which existence at Ulsgaard more and more became with the passing years, she had missed another, a brilliant life, her natural one. It is hard to say whether she lamented this. Perhaps she despised it, because it had never come to her, because it had failed the opportunity of being lived with skill and talent. She had taken all this so deeply into herself, and had grown crusts over it, many hard, brittle, slightly metal-sheened crusts, of which that for the time uppermost appeared cool and new. Now and again she nevertheless betrayed by a naïve impatience that she was not getting sufficient attention; in my time she could suddenly choke at table in some obvious and complicated fashion which assured her of the sympathy of all, and made her appear, for the moment at least, as sensational and exciting as she would have liked to be in the larger sense. I suspect, however, that my father was the only one who took these much too frequent accidents seriously. He would look at her, bending politely forward, and one could see how he was in thought offering her, so to speak, his own perfectly good windpipe, placing it entirely at her disposal. The chamberlain had naturally stopped eating, too; he took a little sip of wine and refrained from comment.

At table he had on one single occasion upheld his own opinion against his spouse. That had been long ago; yet the story was still retailed maliciously and in secret; almost everywhere there was someone who had never heard it. It was to the effect that there had been a time when the chamberlain's wife would fly into a passion about wine-stains that had been made on the table-cloth through clumsiness; that any such stain, on whatever occasion it might happen, was always noted by her and, one might say, exposed, under the severest rebuke. It had even come to this once when several distinguished guests were present. A few innocent stains, of which she made far too much, formed the subject of her sarcastic accusations, and though Grandfather tried his best to warn her by little signs and jocular apostrophes, she would still have persisted obstinately in her reproaches, which in fact she had to cut short in the middle of a sentence. For something unprecedented and absolutely incomprehensible occurred. The chamberlain had asked for the red wine, which had just been passed around, and was now most attentively absorbed in filling his own glass. Only, strangely enough, he did not cease pouring although the glass had long been full, but amid growing stillness continued to pour slowly and carefully, until Maman, who could never restrain herself, burst out laughing, and thus set right the whole affairs by turning it to laughter. For everyone joined in, relieved, and the chamberlain looked up and handed the bottle to the servant.

Later another peculiarity got the upper hand of my grandmother. She could not bear having anyone in the house fall ill. Once when the cook had cut herself and she happened to see her with her bandaged hand, she maintained that the whole house reeked of iodoform, and it was difficult to convince her that the woman could not be dismissed for that reason. She did not wish to be reminded of sickness. If anyone was imprudent enough to manifest some slight discomfort in her presence, she considered it nothing less than a personal affront, and long bore the offender a grudge.

In that autumn of Maman's death, the chamberlain's wife shut herself up completely in her apartments with Sophie Oxe and broke off all intercourse with us. Even her son was no longer admitted. It is true this dying fell most unfittingly. The rooms were cold, the stoves smoked, and the mice had thronged into the house—no place was safe from them. But it was not only that: Mrs. Margarete Brigge was indignant that Maman was dying; that there should stand on the order of the day a subject about which she declined to speak; that the young wife presumed to take precedence of herself, who intended to die sometime at a date that was by no means fixed yet.

For on the fact that she would have to die she often reflected. But she didn't want to be hurried. She would die, of course, when it pleased her, and then all the others could go and die, after her, if they were in such haste.

She never quite forgave us Maman's death. Moreover, she aged very rapidly during the following winter. When she walked she was as tall as ever, but she drooped in her armchair, and her hearing grew harder. One could sit and stare at her, for hours, she did not feel it. She was somewhere within herself; she returned only rarely and for moments to her senses, which were empty, which she no longer inhabited. Then she would say something to the Countess, who adjusted her shawl, and with her large, freshly-washed hands would draw in her dress, as if water had been spilled or as if we were not quite clean.

She died on the approach of spring, in the city, one night. Sophie Oxe, whose door stood open, had heard nothing. When they found Margarete Brigge in the morning she was as cold as glass.

Immediately after that the chamberlain's great and terrible sickness set in. It was as if he had awaited her end, that he might die as inconsiderately as he had to.

It was in the year after Maman's death that I first noticed Abelone. Abelone was always there. This was most disparaging to her. And then Abelone was not sympathetic, as I had decided a good while before on some occasion, and I had since never seriously reviewed that opinion. To inquire what might be the state of affairs with Abelone, would until now have seemed almost ludicrous to me. Abelone was there, and one used her up as best one could. But all at once I asked myself: Why is Abelone here? Everyone in our house had a reason to be there, even if it was not always as obvious as, for example, the utility of Sophie Oxe. But why was Abelone there? For a while there had been talk of her needing diversion. But that had passed into oblivion. No one contributed anything to Abelone's diversion, and she certainly did not give one the impression of being diverted.

Besides, Abelone had one good point: she sang. That is to say, there were times when she sang. There was a strong, unswerving music in her. If it is true that angels are masculine, then one may well say there was something masculine in her voice: a radiant, celestial masculinity. I, who even as a child had been so distrustful of music (not because it lifted me out of myself more violently than anything else, but because I had noticed that it never dropped me again where it had found me, but lower down, somewhere deep in the unfinished), I endured this music, on which one could ascend upright, higher and higher, until one imagined that for a while this must just about have been heaven. I did not suspect that Abelone was to open yet other heavens for me.

At first our relationship consisted in her telling me of the days of Maman's girlhood. She set great store by convincing me how valiant and young Maman had been. There was no one at that time, she assured me, to compare with Maman in dancing or riding. "She was the most daring girl and quite tireless, and then she suddenly married," said Abelone, still amazed after so many years. "It happened so unexpectedly, no one could really understand it."

I was interested in knowing why Abelone had not married. She appeared to me old comparatively, and that she might still do so never occurred to me.

"There wasn't anybody," she answered simply and in so doing became really beautiful. Is Abelone beautiful? I asked myself in surprise. Then I left home to go to the Academy for Young Noblemen, and an odious and painful time began. But there at Sorö, when I stood in the embrasure of a window, apart from the others, left a little in peace by them, I would look out into the trees, and at such moments, and at night, there grew in me the certainty that Abelone was beautiful. And I began to write her all those letters, long and short, many secret letters, in which I thought I was speaking of Ulsgaard and of my being unhappy. But, as I see it now, they must after all have been love-letters. For the holidays came at last, which began by not wanting to come at all, and then it was as if by pre-arrangement that we did not meet in the presence of the others.

Nothing whatever had been agreed upon between us, but when the carriage turned into the park I could not refrain from getting out, perhaps simply because I did not want to drive up to the house like any stranger. Summer was already at its height. I headed into one of the side paths and toward a laburnum tree. And there was Abelone. Beautiful, beautiful Abelone.

I shall never forget how it was when you looked at me. How you wore that gaze of yours, holding it up, like something that was not fixed, upon your back-tilted face.

Ah, did not the climate change at all, did it not grow milder round about Ulsgaard with all our warmth? Do not certain roses bloom longer in the park now, even into December?

I shall tell nothing about you, Abelone. Not because we deluded one another: since you loved someone, even then, whom you have never forgotten, you lover, and I loved all women; but because only wrong is done in the telling.

There are tapestries, Abelone, wall tapestries. I am imagining that you are here; there are six tapestries: come, let us pass slowly before them. But first step back and see them all together. How quiet they are, are they not? There is little variety in them. There is always that oval blue island, floating in the subdued red background, which is all flowery and inhabited by little animals busy with their own affairs. Only yonder, in the last hanging, the island rises a little, as if it had grown lighter. It has always one figure on it, a lady, in various costumes, but always the same. Sometimes there is a smaller figure beside her, a maid-servant; and always there are the heraldic animals, large, also on the island, also taking part in the action. On the left a lion, and, on the right, so clear, the unicorn. They carry the same pennants, which show high above them: three silver moons ascendant in a blue chevron on a red field. Have you looked? Will you begin with the first?

She is feeding the falcon. How sumptuous her raiment is. The bird is on her gloved hand and it stirs. She is watching it and at the same time dipping into the bowl the maid-servant brings, to offer it something. Below, on the right, a little silken-haired dog is lying on the train of her dress, looking up and hoping it will be remembered. And, did you notice, a low rose-trellis shuts off the island at the back. The blazoned animals rear with heraldic arrogance. Once more the coat-of-arms envelops each as a mantle. A handsome clasp holds it together. It waves.

Does one not involuntarily approach the next tapestry more softly, as soon as one sees how profoundly the lady is absorbed: she is weaving a garland, a small, round crown of flowers. Thoughtfully she chooses the color of the next carnation in the flat basin the maid-servant holds for her, while she strings the one just selected. Behind her on a bench stands unused a basket full of roses, which a monkey has discovered. This time they must be carnations. The lion no longer takes part; but on the right the unicorn understands.

Should not music come into this stillness, is it not already there, subdued? Gravely and quietly adorned, she has gone forward (how slowly, has she not?) to the portable organ, and stands there, playing, separated by the row of pipes from the maid-servant, who is blowing the bellows on the other side. So lovely she has never yet been. Strangely her hair is brought forward in two plaits, fastened together over the head-dress in such a way that its ends rise out of the knot like a short helmet-crest. Out of humor, the lion endures the sounds, unwillingly, biting back a howl. But the unicorn is beautiful, as in undulating motion.

The island grows broader. A tent has been set up. Of blue damask and shot with golden flames. The animals hold it open, and, simple almost in her princely dress, she steps forth. For what are her pearls compared with herself. The maid has opened a small casket, and the lady now lifts from it a chain, a heavy, magnificent ornament that has always been locked away. The little dog sits beside her, on a high place prepared for it, and looks on. And have you discovered the motto up on the rim of the tent? It is: A mon seul désir.

What has happened? Why is the little rabbit running down there, why does one see at once that it is running? Everything is so restrained. The lion has nothing to do. She herself holds the banner. Or is she holding to it? With her other hand she has reached for the horn of the unicorn. Is this mourning, can mourning be so erect, and a mourning-dress so mute as this velvet, green-black, and faded in places?

But here is yet another festival; no one is invited to it. Expectation plays no part in it. Everything is here. Everything for ever. The lion looks round almost threateningly: no one may come. We have never yet seen her weary; is she weary? Or has she only seated herself because she is holding something heavy? A monstrance, one might think. But she curves her other arm toward the unicorn, and the creature bridles, flattered, and rears and leans upon her lap. It is a mirror, the thing she holds. See: she is showing the unicorn its image—.

Abelone, I am imagining that you are here. Do you understand, Abelone? I think you must understand.

Book Two

Even the tapestries of the Dame à la Licorne are now no longer in the old château of Boussac. The time has come when everything is disappearing out of houses, they can no longer keep anything. Danger has become safer than security. No one of the lineage of the Delle Viste walks beside one having that in his blood. They are all gone. No one speaks your name, Pierre d'Aubusson, grand Grand Master of an ancient house, at whose behest perhaps these pictures were woven that praise everything and part with nothing. (Ah, that the poets should ever have written differently about women, more literally, as they thought. Certain it is, we were to know only this.) Now one comes before them by chance among chance comers and is almost frightened to be uninvited. But there are others who pass by, even though they are never many. The young people scarcely linger, unless it somehow belongs in their line of study to have seen these things once, with a view to this or that characteristic.

Young girls one does occasionally find before them. For there are lots of young girls in museums, who somewhere have gone away out of the houses that no longer keep anything. They find themselves before these tapestries and forget themselves a little. They have always felt that this existed, a subdued life like this, of leisurely gestures never quite explained; and they remember dimly that for a time they even believed this life would be their own. But then they quickly bring out a sketchbook and begin to draw, whatever it may be: one of the flowers or a little, happy animal. Exactly what, they have been informed, would not matter. And it really does not matter. Only to draw, that is the main thing; for with this intent they one day left home, rather violently. They are of good family. But when they lift their arms as they sketch, it appears that their dress has not been fastened at the back or at any rate not entirely. There are a couple of buttons that can't be reached. For when the dress was made there had not yet been any question of their suddenly going away alone. In the family there is always someone for such buttons. But here, good heavens, who is going to bother about it in so large a city? Unless perhaps one has a friend; but friends are in the same quandary, and that would end in their buttoning each other's dresses. That is ridiculous and reminds one of the family, of which one does not want to be reminded.

But inevitably one wonders sometimes as one draws, whether it would not have been possible after all to remain at home. If only one could have been religious, sincerely religious, in tempo with the others. But it seemed so absurd, to try doing that in common. The path has somehow grown narrower: families can no longer approach God. So there remained only various other things one might manage to share. But then, if one divided honestly, so little came to each person that it was a shame. And if one cheated in the dividing, disputes arose. No, it is really better to draw, no matter what. In time some resemblance will appear. And Art, when one gets it gradually like this, is after all something truly enviable.

And in their strenuous absorption with what they have undertaken, these young women, they never manage any more to raise their eyes. They do not notice that with all their drawing they still do nothing save suppress within themselves the unalterable life that is radiantly opened up before them, endlessly ineffable, in these woven pictures. They do not want to believe it. Now that so many things are changing, they too want to change. They are very close to abandoning themselves and thinking about themselves as men might speak of them when they are not present. That seems to them to be their progress. They are already nearly convinced that one seeks one enjoyment and then another and again another that is yet stronger: That life consists in this, if one would not lose it in a silly way. They have already begun to look about, to search; they, whose strength has always lain in being found.

That comes, I believe, of their weariness. For centuries now, they have performed the whole of love; they have always played the full dialogue, both parts. For the man has only imitated them, and badly. And has made their learning difficult with his inattentiveness, with his negligence, with his jealousy, which was also a sort of negligence. And they have nevertheless persevered day and night, and have increased in love and misery. And from among them, under the stress of endless needs, have gone forth those powerful lovers, who, while they called him, surpassed their man; who grew beyond him when he did not return, like Gaspara Stampa or like the Portuguese nun, who never desisted until their torture turned into a bitter, icy splendor that was no longer to be restrained. We know about one and another because of letters that have been preserved as by a miracle, or books of poems written in accusation or lament, or portraits that look at us in some gallery through a weeping which the painter caught because he did not know what it was. But there have been innumerably many more: those who burned their letters, and others who had no strength left to write them. Aged women, grown hard, but with a kernel of savoriness which they kept hidden. Uncouth, strong-grown women, who, grown strong through exhaustion, let themselves become like their husbands and who were yet entirely different inwardly, there where their love had labored, in the dark. Child-bearing women who never wanted to bear children, and who, when they finally died after their eighth child, had the gestures and the lightness of girls looking forward to love. And those women who remained beside bullies and drunkards because they had found the means for being, within themselves, further from them than anywhere else; and they could not suppress this, when they came among people, but shimmered as though they consorted always with the blessed. Who can say how many they were, or who they were. It is as if they had destroyed before-hand the words with which one might grasp them.

But now that so much is changing, is it not up to us to change ourselves? Could we not try to develop ourselves a little, and slowly take upon ourselves our share of work in love, little by little. We have been spared all its toil, and so for us it has slipped in among the diversions, the way sometimes a piece of real lace will fall into a child's drawer and please and no longer please and finally lie there among torn and dismembered things, worse than any of them. We have been spoiled by easy enjoyment like all dilettanti and stand in the odor of mastery. But what if we were to despise our successes, what if we were to start from the very outset to learn the work of love, which has always been done for us? What if we were to go ahead and become beginners, now that much is changing?

Now I know too how it was when Maman unrolled the little pieces of lace. For she had taken for her own use a single one of the drawers in Ingeborg's desk.

"Shall we look at them, Malte?" she would say, and was as joyful as if she were about to be given a present of everything there was in the little yellow-lacquered drawer. And then out of sheer expectation she couldn't even open up the tissue-paper. I had to do that every time. But I too was greatly excited when the laces made their appearance. They were wound on a wooden spindle which was not to be seen for all the laces. Then we would unroll them slowly and watch the designs as they opened out, and were a little scared every time one of them came to an end. They stopped suddenly.

First came bands of Italian work, tough pieces with drawn threads, in which everything was repeated over and over, as distinctly as in a cottage garden. Then all at once a whole succession of our glances would be barred with Venetian needle-point, as though we had been cloisters or prisons. But the view was freed again, and one saw deep into gardens more and more artful, until everything was dense and warm against the eyes as in a hot-house: gorgeous plants we did not know opened gigantic leaves, tendrils groped for one another as though they were dizzy, and the great open blossoms of the point d'Alençon dimmed everything with their pollen. Suddenly, all weary and confused, one stepped out into the long track of the Valenciennes, and it was winter and early morning, with hoar frost. And one pushed through the snowcovered bushes of the Binche, and came to places where nobody had been yet; the branches hung so strangely downward, there might well have been a grave beneath them, but that we concealed from each other. The cold pressed ever closer upon us, and at last, when the very fine pillow-laces came, Maman said: "Oh, now we shall get frostflowers on our eyes", and so it was too, for inside ourselves it was very warm.

Over the rolling up again we both sighed; it was a lengthy task, but we were not willing to entrust it to anyone else. "Just think, if we had had to make them", said Maman, looking really frightened. I could not imagine that at all. I caught myself having thought of little insects incessantly spinning these things and which on that account are left in peace. No, of course, they were women.

"They surely got to heaven, whoever made this", I said admiringly. I remember it occurred to me that for a long time I had not asked about heaven. Maman drew a long breath, the laces were assembled again.

After a while, when I had already forgotten about it, she said quite slowly: "To heaven? I believe they are completely in all this. If one sees it so, that may well be an eternal beatitude. One does know so little about it."

Often, when visitors came, it was said that the Schulins were retrenching. Their large, old manor-house had burned down a few years before, and they were now living in the two narrow side wings and retrenching. But having guests was in their blood once and for all. They could not give it up. If someone arrived at our house unexpectedly, he probably came from the Schulins; and if someone suddenly looked at the clock and hastened away in alarm, he was surely expected at Lystager.

By that time Maman really never went out any more, but the Schulins could not comprehend anything of the sort: there was nothing for it but one day to drive over and see them. It was in December, after some early snowfalls; the sleigh was ordered for three o'clock, I was to go along. But nobody in our house ever started punctually. Maman, who did not like having the carriage announced, usually came down much too soon, and when she found no one, something always occurred to her that ought to have been done long ago, and she would begin hunting or arranging somewhere upstairs, so that she could hardly be got at again. Finally we would all stand waiting. And when at last she was seated and tucked in, it appeared that something had been forgotten, and Sieversen would have to be fetched; for only Sieversen knew where it was. But then we would suddenly drive off, before Sieversen returned.

It had never really quite cleared off that day. The trees stood as though they could not find their way in the mist, and there was something presumptuous about driving into it. At intervals it began to snow quietly on, and now it was as though even the last traces were being erased and we were driving into a white sheet. There was nothing but the sound of the sleighbells, and one could not say where it actually came from. At one moment it ceased, as if the last bell had been spent; but then it gathered itself up again and was all together and scattered forth again lavishly. The church tower on the left might have been imaginary. But the outline of the park wall was suddenly there, high, almost on top of one, and we found ourselves in the long avenue. The tinkling of the bells no longer dropped off entirely; it seemed to hang itself in clusters right and left on the trees. Then we swung in and drove around something, past something else on the right, and came to a halt in the center.

Georg had quite forgotten that the house was no longer there, and for all of us at that moment it was there. We ascended the front steps that led up to the old terrace, and only wondered that all was quite dark. Suddenly a door opened, below and behind us on the left, and someone cried, "This way!" and lifted and swung a misty light. My father laughed: "We are climbing around here like ghosts", and he helped us down the steps again.

"But still there was a house there just now", said Maman, and could not accustom herself so quickly to Viera Schulin, who had come running out, all warm and laughing. So naturally one had to go in quickly, and the house was not to be thought of any longer. Wraps were taken off in a small anteroom, and then one was right in among the lamps and facing the warmth.

These Schulins were a powerful race of independent women. I do not know if there were any sons. I only remember three sisters; the eldest had been married to a Marchese in Naples, from whom she was at that time slowly divorcing herself amid many lawsuits. Then came Zoë, about whom it was said that there was nothing she did not know. And above all there was Viera, this warm Viera;

God knows what has become of her. The Countess, a Narishkin, was really a fourth sister and in certain respects the youngest. She knew about nothing and had to be continuously instructed by her children. And the good Count Schulin felt as though he were married to all these ladies, and he went about and kissed them, at random.

Just then he was laughing loudly and greeted us in detailed fashion. I was passed around among the ladies and pawed and questioned. But I had firmly resolved, when that should be over, to slip out somehow and look around for the house. I was convinced it was there today. The getting out was not so difficult; down among all the skirts one could creep along like a dog, and the door of the ante-room was still on the latch. But outside the house-door would not yield. There were several contrivances on it, chains and locks, which I did not handle properly in my hurry. Yet it did suddenly open, but with a loud noise, and before I could get outside I was seized and pulled back.

"Hold on, one can't decamp like that here", said Viera Schulin in amusement. She bent over me, and I resolved to reveal nothing to this warm person. But she, as I said nothing, took it for granted that a natural need had driven me to the door; she seized my hand, and had already started to walk, intending, half confidentially, half pompously, to take me somewhere. This intimate misunderstanding mortified me beyond all bounds. I tore myself loose and looked angrily at her. "It is the house I want to see", I said proudly. She did not understand.

"The large house outside by the stairs."

"Goose," she said, snatching at me, "there is no house there any more." I insisted that there was.

"We'll go sometime by day," she proposed, to meet me half-way. "One can't go crawling around there at this hour. There are holes there, and right behind are father's fish-ponds which aren't allowed to freeze over. You'll fall in and be turned into a fish."

Therewith she pushed me before her, back again into the bright rooms. There they all sat and talked, and I contemplated them one after the other: of course they only go when it isn't there, I thought contemptuously; if Maman and I lived here, it would always be there. Maman looked distraught, while the others were all talking at once. She was certainly thinking of the house.

Zoë sat down beside me and began to ask me questions. She had a well-regulated face in which comprehension renewed itself from time to time, as though she were continually comprehending something. My father sat leaning a little to the right, listening to the Marchioness, who was laughing. Count Schulin stood between Maman and his wife and was relating some incident. But the Countess, I saw, interrupted him in the middle of a sentence.

"No, child, you are imagining that," said the Count good-humoredly, but suddenly there was the same disquieted expression in his face, which he thrust forward over the two ladies. The Countess was not so easily to be diverted from her so-called imagination. She wore a very strained look, like someone who does not wish to be disturbed. She made slight, dissuasive gestures with her soft, beringed hands, somebody said "Sst!", and suddenly there was complete silence.

Behind the people in the room the immense pieces of furniture from the old house pressed against each other, much too close. The heavy family silver shone and bulged, as though one were looking at it through a magnifying glass. My father looked round in surprise.

"Mamma smells something", said Viera Schulin behind him, "and then we all always have to be quiet; she smells with her ears", but in saying it she herself stood, with high-drawn eyebrows, attentive and all nose.

The Schulins had become a little peculiar in this regard since the fire. In the close, over-heated rooms some odor would come up at any moment, and then everyone would analyze it and express his opinion. Zoë, practical and conscientious, did something at the stove; the Count went around, stopped for a little at each corner and waited: "It isn't here," he then said. The Countess had risen and did not know where she ought to search. My father turned slowly round on his heels, as if he had the smell behind him. The Marchioness, who had promptly assumed that it was a nasty smell, held her handkerchief over her mouth and looked at everyone in turn to see if it had gone. "Here, here", cried Viera, from time to time, as if she had it. And around each word there was a strange silence. As for me, I had busily smelled along too. But all at once (whether because of the heat of the room or the nearness of so many lights) I was overcome for the first time in my life by something akin to fear of ghosts. It became clear to me that all these well-defined grown people, who just a minute before had been talking and laughing, were going about, stooped and busy with something invisible; that they admitted something was there which they did not see. And it was frightful that this thing should be stronger than them all.

My fear increased. It seemed to me that what they were seeking might suddenly break out of me like an eruption; and then they would see it and point at me. Utterly desperate, I looked across to Maman. She sat there singularly erect; it seemed to me that she was waiting for me. Scarcely did I reach her side, and perceive that she was trembling inwardly, when I knew that the house was only now fading again.

"Malte, coward", came a laugh from somehere. It was Viera's voice. But we did not let go of one another and endured it together; and we remained like that, Maman and I, until the house had again quite vanished.

R ichest in almost incomprehensible experiences, however were the birthdays. One already knew, of course, that life took pleasure in making no distinctions; but on this day one got up with a right to joy that was not to be doubted. Probably the sense of this right had been very early developed in one, at the stage when one grasps at everything and gets simply everything, and when, with unerring power of imagination one enhances those objects one happens to retain with the primary-colored intensity of one's just then prevailing desire.

But suddenly come those curious birthdays when, fully established in the consciousness of this right, one sees others becoming uncertain. One would still like to have somebody dress one as in earlier years, and then take to oneself all that follows. But hardly is one awake when somebody shouts outside that the cake hasn't arrived yet; or one hears something break as the presents are being arranged on the table in the next room; or somebody comes in and leaves the door open, and one sees everything before one should have seen it. That is the moment when something like an operation is performed on one: a brief but atrociously painful incision. But the hand that does it is experienced and steady. It is quickly over. And scarcely has it been survived, when one no longer thinks about oneself; one must rescue the birthday, watch the others, anticipate their mistakes, and confirm them in the illusion that they are managing everything admirably. They do not make it easy for one. It appears they are of an unexampled clumsiness, almost stupid. They contrive to come in with parcels of some sort that are destined for other people; one runs to meet them and afterwards has to make it appear as if one had been running around in the room for exercise, not toward anything definite. They want to surprise one and with a very superficial pretense of expectation lift the bottom layer of the toy-boxes, where there is nothing more than cotton-wool; then one has to relieve them of their embarrassment. Or, if it was a mechanical toy they are giving one, they overwind it themselves the first time they wind it up. It is therefore well to practise betimes, pushing along an overwound mouse or the like surreptitiously with one's foot: in this way one can often deceive them and help them out of their shame.

One managed all these things as they were demanded of one; it required no special ability. Talent was really necessary only when someone had taken pains and, important and kind, brought one a joy, and one saw even at a distance that it was a joy for somebody quite different, a totally alien joy; one didn't even know anyone for whom it would have done: so alien was it.

The telling of stories, the real telling, must have been before my time. I never heard anyone tell stories. In the days when Abelone spoke to me of Maman's youth, it became apparent that she could not tell them. Old Count Brahe was supposed still to be able to do so. I will write down what Abelone knew about it.

As a very young girl Abelone must have had a time of peculiar and wide sensibility. The Brahes lived in town at the period, in the Bredgade, and entertained a good deal of company. When she came up to her room late in the evening she would think she was tired like the others. But then all at once she would feel the window, and, if I understood her aright, she could stand before the night for hours, thinking: this concerns me. "I stood there like a prisoner," she said, "and the stars were freedom." In those days she was able to fall asleep without growing heavy. The expression "falling asleep" is by no means appropriate to this girlhood year. Sleep was something that ascended with one, and from time to time one's eyes were open and one lay on a new surface, not yet by any means the highest. And then one was up before day; even in winter, when the others came in sleepy and late to the late breakfast. In the evenings, when darkness fell, there were of course only lights for the whole household, common lights. But the two candles, quite early in the new darkness, with which everything began again, those one had to oneself. They stood in their low double sconce, and shone peacefully through the small, oval shades of tulle painted with roses, which had to be slid down from time to time. There was nothing disturbing in that; for one thing, one was in absolutely no hurry, and then it would so happen that one had to look up occasionally and reflect, when one was writing at a letter or in the diary which had been begun once long ago in an entirely different hand, timorous and beautiful.

Count Brahe lived quite apart from his daughters. He considered it mere fancy when anyone purported to share his life with others. ("Hm, share—", he would say.) But he was not displeased when people spoke to him of his daughters; he would listen attentively, as though they were living in another town.

It was therefore something entirely out of the ordinary that one day after breakfast he signed to Abelone to come to him. "We have the same habits, it seems. I too write early in the morning. You can help me." Abelone still remembered as if it had been yesterday.

The very next morning she was led into her father's study, which was reputed to be inaccessible. She had no time to look about her, for she had to sit down at once opposite the Count at the writing-table, which seemed to her like a vast plain with books and piles of papers for villages.

The Count dictated. Those who asserted that Count Brahe was writing his memoirs were not altogether wrong. Only these were not the political and military memoirs that were so eagerly awaited. "I forget those," said the old gentleman curtly, when anyone broached facts of this sort to him. But what he did not wish to forget was his childhood. To this he clung. And it was quite in order, according to him, that this very distant time should win the upper hand in him now, that as he turned his gaze inward, it should

lie there, as in a clear northern summer night, ecstatic and un-
sleeping.

Sometimes he sprang up and talked into the candles so that they
flickered. Or whole sentences had to be scored out again, and then
he would pace violently to and fro, waving in his Nile-green silk
dressing-gown. During all this there was yet another person pre-
sent, Sten, the Count's old valet, a Jutlander, whose duty it was,
when my grandfather sprang up, to lay his hands quickly over the
loose single sheets covered with memoranda that lay about on the
table. His Grace had the notion that the paper of today was
worthless, that it was much too light and flew away at the slight-
est opportunity. And Sten, of whom one saw only the long upper
half, shared this distrust and seemed to squat on his hands, blind
in the daylight and grave as a nightbird.

This Sten spent his Sunday afternoons reading Swedenborg, and
none of the domestics would have dared enter his room because
he was supposed to be conjuring up spirits. Sten's family had al-
ways trafficked with spirits, and Sten was quite especially predes-
tined to this commerce. Something had appeared to his mother on
the night she bore him. Sten had large, round eyes, and the other
end of his gaze came to rest somewhere behind the person at whom
he was looking. Abelone's father often asked after the spirits, as
one would inquire about the health of someone's relatives. "Are
they coming, Sten?" he would ask benevolently. "It is good if they
come."

The dictating went its way for a few days. But then Abelone could
not write "Eckernförde." It was a proper name, and she had never
heard it before. The Count, who in truth had long been seeking a
pretext for giving up the writing, which was too slow for his rec-
ollections, pretended irritation.

"She cannot write it," he said sharply, "and others will not be
able to read it. And will they *see* at all, what I am saying?" he
went on angrily, keeping his eyes fixed on Abelone.

"Will they see him, this Saint-Germain?" he shrieked at her. "Did
we say Saint-Germain? Strike it out. Write: the Marquis de Bel-
mare."

Abelone struck out and wrote. But the Count continued to speak
so rapidly that one could not keep up with him.

"He could not endure children, this excellent Belmare, but he
took me on his knee, small as I was, and I had the idea of biting

his diamond studs. That pleased him. He laughed, and lifted my chin until we were looking into each other's eyes. 'You have splendid teeth," he said, 'teeth that are enterprising . . .'—But I remember his eyes. I have gone about a good deal since then. I have seen all kinds of eyes, but, believe me: such eyes never again. For those eyes a thing did not need to be present; they had it in them. You have heard of Venice? Very well, I tell you they would have looked Venice here into this room, so that it would have been there, like that table. I once sat in the corner of the room listening as he spoke to my father about Persia; sometimes I think my hands still smell of it. My father thought highly of him and his Highness the Landgrave was something like a disciple of his. But naturally there were enough who reproached him with believing in the past only when it was inside himself. They could not understand that the whole business has no meaning unless one has been born with it."

"Books are empty," cried the Count, turning toward the walls with a furious gesture, "it is blood that matters, it is in blood that we must be able to read. He had marvelous histories and curious illustrations in his blood, this Belmare; he could open it where he pleased, something was always described there; not a page in his blood had been skipped. And when he shut himself up from time to time and turned the leaves in solitude, he came to the passages about the alchemy and about precious stones and about colors. Why shouldn't all that have been there? It must surely be somewhere.

"He might easily have been able to live with a truth, this man, had he been alone. But it was no trifle to be alone with such a truth. And he was not so lacking in taste as to invite others to visit him when he was with her; she should not be gossiped about: he was far too much of an Oriental for that. "Adieu, Madame," he said to her in all veracity, "until another time. Perhaps in another thousand years we shall be somewhat stronger and more undisturbed. Your beauty is just in process of becoming, Madame," he said, and this was no mere polite speech. With that he went off and laid out his zoological garden for the people, a kind of Jardin d'Acclimatation for the larger kind of lies, which had never been seen in our latitudes, and a hot-house of exaggerations, and a small, well-tended figuerie of false secrets. Then people came from all sides, and he went about with diamond buckles on his shoes and was entirely at the disposal of his guests.

"A superficial existence, eh? Nevertheless it was essentially chivalrous toward his lady, and in the process he managed to conserve his years very well."

For some time now the old man had no longer been addressing Abelone, whom he had forgotten. He paced to and fro like a madman and threw provocative glances at Sten, as though Sten should transform himself at a given moment into the person about whom he was thinking. But Sten was not yet transforming himself.

"One ought to see him," the Count went on stubbornly. "There was a time when he was perfectly visible, although in many cities the letters he received were not addressed to anyone: they bore simply the name of the town, nothing else. But I saw him.

"He was not handsome." The Count gave a strangely hurried laugh. "Nor was he even what people would call important or distinguished: there were always more distinguished men about him. He was wealthy: but with him this was like a caprice, on which one couldn't rely. He was well grown, though others carried themselves better. Of course, I couldn't tell in those days whether he was brilliant or this and that to which we attach value: but he *was*."

The Count, trembling, stood still and made a movement as if to set something in space, which remained there.

At that instant he became aware of Abelone.

"Do you see him?" he asked her imperiously. And suddenly he seized one of the silver candlesticks and held the blinding light into her face.

Abelone remembered that she had seen him.

On the following days Abelone was summoned regularly, and after this incident the dictation proceeded much more quietly. The Count was putting together from all kinds of documents his earliest recollections of the Bernstorff circle, in which his father had played a certain role. Abelone had now adjusted herself so well to the peculiarities of her task that anyone seeing the two together might easily have mistaken their efficacious collaboration for real intimacy.

Once, when Abelone was about to retire, the old gentleman approached her as though he were holding a surprise in his hands behind his back. "Tomorrow we shall write about Julie Reventlow," he said, savoring his words, "she was a saint."

Probably Abelone looked at him incredulously.

"Yes, yes, such things are still possible", he insisted in a commanding tone, "all things are possible, Countess Abel."

He took Abelone's hands and opened them like a book. "She had the stigmata," he said, "here and here." And with his cold finger he tapped hard and sharp on both her palms. Abelone did not know the expression "stigmata." We'll see later, she thought; she was quite impatient to hear about the saint her father had actually seen. But she was not summoned again, neither the next morning nor later.—

"The Countess Reventlow has often been mentioned in your family since then," concluded Abelone briefly, when I asked her to tell me more. She looked tired; she maintained also that she had forgotten most of these events. "But I still feel the two marks sometimes," she said smiling and could not refrain from it and gazed almost with curiosity into her empty hands.

E ven before my father's death everything had changed. Uls-gaard was no longer in our possession. My father died in town, in a flat that seemed hostile and strange to me. I was already abroad at the time and returned too late.

They had laid him on a bier, between two rows of tall candles, in a room on the courtyard. The perfume of the flowers was un-intelligible, like many voices all sounding at once. His handsome face, in which the eyes had been closed, wore an expression of courteous recollection. He was clothed in his uniform of Master-of-the-Hunt; but for some reason or other the white ribbon had been put on instead of the blue. His hands were not folded; they lay obliquely crossed and looked imitation and meaningless. They had hurriedly told me that he had suffered a great deal: nothing of this was to be seen. His features were set in order like the furniture in a guestroom which some visitor has left. I had the feeling that I had already seen him dead several times: I knew it all so well.

The surroundings alone were new, unpleasantly so. New was this oppressive room, which had windows opposite, probably the win-dows of other people. It was new that Sieversen should come in from time to time and do nothing. Sieversen had grown old. Then I was bidden to breakfast. More than once the meal was an-nounced. I had no desire whatever for breakfast that day. I did not notice that they wanted to get me out of the room; finally, as I did not go, Sieversen somehow gave me to understand that the doctors were in the house. I did not see why. There was still something to be done, said Sieversen, looking at me intently with her reddened eyes. Then somewhat precipitately two gentlemen entered: they were the doctors. The first lowered his head with a jerk, as if he had horns and were going to butt, in order to look at us over his glasses: first at Sieversen, then at me.

He bowed with the stiff formality of a student. "The Master-of-the-Hunt had one other wish," he said, in the exact manner of his entering; again one felt his precipitancy. I somehow compelled him to direct his gaze through his spectacles. His colleague was a stoutish, thin-shelled, blonde man; I thought it would be easy to make him blush. Meanwhile a pause ensued. It was strange that the Master-of-the-Hunt still had wishes.

Involuntarily I looked again at the fine, regular countenance. And I knew then that he wanted certainty. Fundamentally he had always desired certainty. Now he was about to have it.

"You are here for the perforation of the heart: if you please."

I bowed and stepped back. The two doctors acknowledged my courtesy simultaneously and began at once to confer about their work. Someone was already pushing the candles aside. But the elder of the two again took a few paces toward me. From a certain distance he stretched forward, in order to spare himself the last part of the way, and looked at me angrily.

"It is not necessary," he said, "that is to say, I think it would perhaps be better, if you . . ."

He seemed to me neglected and shabby in his sparing and hurried attitude. I bowed once more; circumstances ordained that I should already be bowing again.

"Thanks," I said shortly, "I shall not disturb you."

I knew that I would endure this and that there was no reason for withdrawing from the business. It had to come this way. That was perhaps the meaning of the whole. Besides, I had never before seen how it is when someone's breast is pierced. It seemed to me in order not to reject so rare an experience, when it came easily and naturally. In disappointments I really no longer believed, even then; so there was nothing to fear.

No, no, nothing in the world can one imagine beforehand, not the least thing. Everything is made up of so many unique particulars that cannot be foreseen. In imagination one passes them over and does not notice that they are lacking, hasty as one is. But the realities are slow and indescribably detailed.

Who would have thought, for example, of that resistance? Scarcely had the broad, high breast been laid bare, when the hurried little man had picked out the spot in question. But the rapidly applied instrument did not penetrate. I had the feeling that suddenly all time had gone from the room. We were like a group in a picture. But then time caught up again with a slight, gliding sound, and there was more of it than could be used up. Suddenly there was knocking somewhere. I had never heard such knocking before: a warm, closed, double knocking. My ear transmitted it, and at the same time I saw that the doctor had struck bottom. But it took a little while before the two impressions coincided within me. So, so, I thought, it is through now. The knocking, as regards tempo, was almost malicious.

I looked at the man whom I had now known for so long. No, he was in complete command of himself: a gentleman working swiftly and objectively, who had to leave immediately. He showed no trace of enjoyment or satisfaction. Only on his left temple a few hairs had stood up, out of some ancient instinct. He carefully withdrew the instrument, and there was left something resembling a mouth, from which twice in succession blood escaped, as if it were pronouncing a word in two syllables. The young, blonde doctor quickly took it up with an elegant gesture on his piece of cotton. And now the wound remained still, like a closed eye.

It is to be assumed that I bowed once more, without this time paying much attention. At least, I was astonished to find myself alone. Someone had put the uniform in order again, and the white ribbon lay across it as before. But now the Master-of-the-Hunt was dead, and not he alone. Now the heart had been pierced, our heart, the heart of our race. Now it was all over. This, then, was the shattering of the helm: "Today Brigge and nevermore," something said within me.

Of my own heart I did not think. But when it occurred to me later, I knew for the first time quite certainly that for this purpose it did not come in question. It was an individual heart. It was already at its task of beginning from the beginning.

I know I imagined that I could not set out again at once. Everything must first be put in order, I repeated to myself. What wanted putting in order was not quite clear to me. There was almost nothing to be done. I walked about the town and noticed that it had changed. I found it pleasant to step out of the hotel in which I was staying, and to see that it was now a town for grown people, on its good behavior for one, almost as for a stranger. Everything had become a little small, and I walked out the Langelinie to the lighthouse and back again. When I came to the region of the Amaliengade it was not surprising that from somewhere something should emanate which one had acknowledged for years and which tried out its old power again. There were certain cornerwindows here or porches or lanterns which knew a great deal about one and threatened one with that knowledge. I looked them in the face and let them feel that I was staying at the Hotel "Phoenix" and could leave again at any moment. But my conscience was not at rest in so doing. The suspicion arose in me that as yet none of these influences and associations had really been mastered. One had one day secretly abandoned them, all unfinished as they were. So one's childhood also would still, in a way, have to be accomplished, if one did not want to give it up as forever lost. And while I understood how I had lost it, I felt at the same time that I would never have anything else I could appeal to.

I spent a few hours every day in the Dronningens Tvaergade, in those confined rooms that had the injured look of all rented apartments in which someone has died. I went to and fro between the writing-table and the big white porcelain stove, burning the Master-of-the-Hunt's papers. I had begun by throwing the letters into the fire in bundles, just as they were bound together; but the little packets were too firmly tied and only charred at the edges. I had to prevail over myself to loosen them. Most of them had a strong, convincing scent which assailed me as though it wanted to awaken memories in me too. I had none. Then some photographs, heavier than the rest, happened to slip out; these photographs burned incredibly slowly. I don't know how it was, but suddenly I imagined that Ingeborg's likeness might be among them. But each time I looked, I saw women, mature, magnificent, distinctly beautiful, who suggested a different train of thought to me. For it appeared that I was not altogether without memories after all. It was in just such eyes as these that I sometimes found myself when, as a growing boy, I used to accompany my father along the streets. Then from the interior of a passing carriage they could envelop me with a look from which it was scarcely possible to escape. Now I knew that in those days they had been comparing me with him and that the comparison did not turn out in my favor. Certainly not; the Master-of-the-Hunt has no need to fear comparisons.

It may be that I now know something that he did fear. Let me tell how I come to this assumption. Deep inside his wallet there was a paper that had been folded for a long time, friable, broken at the folds. I read it before I burned it. It was in his most careful hand, firmly and regularly written; but I noticed at once that it was only a copy.

"Three hours before his death", it began and it referred to Christian the Fourth. I cannot, of course, repeat the contents verbatim. Three hours before his death he demanded to get up. The doctor and Wormius, the valet, helped him to his feet. He stood somewhat unsteadily, but he stood, and they put on his quilted dressing gown. Then he sat down suddenly on the front end of the bed and said something. It was unintelligible. The doctor kept constant hold of his left hand to prevent him from sinking back on the bed. So they sat, and from time to time the king said, with difficulty and indistinctly, these unintelligible words. At length the doctor began to speak encouragingly to him; he hoped gradually to make out what the king was trying to say. After a little the king interrupted him and said, all at once quite distinctly, "O doctor, doctor, what is your name?" The doctor had difficulty in remembering.

"Sperling, most gracious majesty."

But this was really not the important thing. The king, as soon as he heard that they understood him, opened wide his right eye, the one that remained to him, and expressed with his whole face the single word his tongue had been forming for hours, the sole word that still existed: "Döden," he said, "Döden." *

There was no more on the sheet. I read it several times before I burned it. And it occurred to me that my father had suffered a great deal at the last. So they had told me.

---

* Death, death.

Since then I have reflected a good deal on the fear of death, not without taking into consideration certain personal experiences of my own. I believe I may well say that I have felt it. It has overtaken me in the busy town, in the midst of people, often without any reason. Often, indeed, there have been abundant reasons; when for example a person on a bench fainted and everybody stood around and looked at him, and he was already far beyond fear: then I had his fear. Or that time in Naples: that young creature sat there opposite me in the street car and died. At first it looked like a fainting spell; we even drove on for a while. But then there was no doubt that we had to stop. And behind us vehicles halted and piled up, as though there would never be any more moving in that direction. The pale, stout girl might have quietly died like that, leaning against the woman beside her. But her mother would not allow this. She contrived all possible difficulties for her. She disordered her clothes and poured something into her mouth which could no longer retain anything. She rubbed her forehead with a liquid someone had brought, and when the eyes, at that, rolled back a little, she began to shake her to make her gaze come forward again. She shouted into those eyes that heard nothing, she pushed and pulled the whole thing to and fro like a doll, and finally she raised her arm and struck the puffy face with all her might, so that it should not die. That time I was afraid.

But I had already been afraid before. For example, when my dog died. The one who laid the blame on me once and for all. He was very sick. I had been kneeling beside him the whole day, when he suddenly gave a bark, jerky and short, as he used to do when a stranger entered. A bark like that had been agreed on between us for such cases, and I glanced involuntarily at the door. But it was already in him. I anxiously sought his eyes, and he too sought mine; but not to bid me farewell. His look was hard and surprised. He reproached me with having allowed it to enter. He was convinced I could have prevented it. It was now clear that he had always overrated me. And there was no time left to explain to him. He continued to gaze at me surprised and solitary, until it was over.

Or I was afraid when in autumn, after the first night frosts, the flies came into the rooms and revived once again in the warmth. They were singularly dried up and took fright at their own buzzing; one could see they didn't quite know what they were doing.

They sat there for hours and let themselves be, until it occurred to them that they were still alive; then they flung themselves blindly in every direction and didn't know what to do when they got there, and one could hear them falling down again here and there and elsewhere. And finally they crawled about everywhere and slowly strewed death all over the room.

But even when I was alone I could be afraid. Why should I pretend that those nights had never been, when in fear of death I sat up, clinging to the fact that sitting at least was still something alive: that the dead did not sit. This always happened in one of those chance rooms which promptly left me in the lurch when things went badly with me, as if they feared to be cross-examined and become involved in my troubles. There I sat, probably looking so dreadful that nothing had the courage to stand by me; not even the candle, which I had just done the service of lighting it, would have anything to do with me. It burned away there by itself, as in an empty room. My last hope then was always the window. I imagined that outside there, there still might be something that belonged to me, even now, even in this sudden poverty of dying. But scarcely had I looked thither when I wished the window had been barricaded, blocked up, like the wall. For now I knew that things were going on out there in the same indifferent way, that out there, too, there was nothing but my loneliness. The loneliness I had brought upon myself and to the greatness of which my heart no longer stood in any sort of proportion. People came to my mind whom I had once left, and I did not understand how one could forsake people.

My God, my God, if any such nights await me in the future, leave me at least one of those thoughts that I have sometimes been able to pursue! It is not unreasonable, this that I ask; for I know that they were born on my very fear, because my fear was so great. When I was a boy, they struck me in the face and told me I was a coward. That was because I was still bad at being afraid. Since then, however, I have learned to be afraid with real fear, fear that increases only when the force that engenders it increases. We have no idea of this force, except in our fear. For it is so utterly inconceivable, so totally opposed to us, that our brain disintegrates at the point where we strain ourselves to think it. And yet, for some time now I have believed that it is *our own* force, all our own force that is still too great for us. It is true we do not know it; but is it not just that which is most our own of which we know the least? Sometimes I reflect on how heaven came to be and death: through our having distanced what is most precious to us, because there was still so much else to do beforehand and because it was not secure with us busy people. Now times have elapsed over this, and we have become accustomed to lesser things. We no longer recognize that which is our own and are terrified by its extreme greatness. May that not be?

M oreover I now well understand how one could carry with one, through all the years, way inside one's wallet, the description of a dying hour. It need not even be an especially selected one; they all have something almost extraordinary. Can one not, for example, imagine somebody copying out how Felix Arvers died? It was in a hospital. He was dying in a gentle and unruffled way, and the nun perhaps thought he had gone further with it than in reality he had. Quite loudly she called out an indication where such and such was to be found. She was a rather uneducated nun; the word "corridor", which at the moment was not to be avoided, she had never seen written; so it was that she said "collidor," thinking that was the word. At that Arvers postponed dying. It seemed to him necessary to put this right first. He became perfectly lucid and explained to her that it should be "corridor". Then he died. He was a poet and hated the approximate; or perhaps he was only concerned with the truth; or it annoyed him to carry away this last impression that the world would go on so carelessly. That can no longer be determined. Only let no one believe it was pedantry. Else the same reproach would fall on the saintly Jean-de-Dieu, who leapt up in the midst of his dying and arrived just in time to cut down the man who had hanged himself in the garden, tidings of whom had in some marvelous fashion penetrated the hermetic tension of his agony. He too was concerned only with the truth.

T here exists a creature which is perfectly harmless; when it passes before your eyes you scarcely notice it and forget it again immediately. But as soon as it invisibly gets somehow into your ears, it develops there, it hatches, as it were, and cases have been known where it has penetrated even into the brain and has thriven devastatingly in that organ, like those pneumococci in dogs that gain entrance through the nose.

This creature is one's neighbor.

Now since I have been drifting about alone like this, I have had innumerable neighbors; neighbors above me and beneath me, neighbors on the right and on the left, sometimes all four kinds at once. I could simply write the history of my neighbors; that would be the work of a lifetime. It is true that it would be, rather, the history of the symptoms of maladies they have generated in me; but this they share with all creatures of this kind, that their presence is demonstrable only through the disturbances they call forth in certain tissues.

I have had unpredictable neighbors and very regular ones. I have sat and endeavored to find out the law of the former; for it was clear that even they had a law. And if the punctual ones stayed out of an evening, I have tried to depict to myself what could have happened to them, and kept my light burning and been as anxious as a young wife. I have had neighbors who were just experiencing hatred, and neighbors who were involved in a passionate love; or I lived through the sudden change of one into the other in the middle of night, and then, of course, sleep was not to be thought of. Indeed, this led one to observe that sleep is much less frequent than is supposed. My two Petersburg neighbors for example attached little importance to sleep. One of them stood and played the fiddle, and I am sure that as he did so he looked across into the overwakeful houses which never ceased to be brightly lit during those improbable August nights. Of my other neighbor on the right I know at least that he lay in bed; during my time, indeed, he no longer got up at all. He even had his eyes shut, but it could not be said that he slept. He lay and recited long poems, poems by Pushkin and Nekrasov, with the cadence in which children recite when it is demanded of them. And despite the music of my neighbor on the left, it was this fellow with his poems who wove himself a cocoon in my brain, and God knows what would have hatched out of it had not the student who occasionally visited him one day mistaken the door. He told me the story of his acquaintance, and it turned out on the whole to be reassuring. At any rate, it was a literal, unambiguous tale that destroyed the teeming maggots of my conjectures.

This petty functionary next door there had one Sunday hit upon the idea of solving a singular problem. He assumed that he was going to live a considerable time, say another fifty years. The generosity he thus showed toward himself put him in a radiant humor. But now he sought to surpass himself. He reflected that one could change these years into days, hours, minutes, indeed, if one could stand it, into seconds; and he calculated and calculated, and a total resulted such as he has never seen before. It made him giddy. He had to recover a little. Time was precious, he had always heard, and he was amazed that a person possessing such a quantity was not continually being guarded. How easily he could be stolen. But then his good, almost exuberant humor came back again; he put on his fur coat, to look a little broader and more imposing, and presented to himself the whole of this fabulous capital, addressing himself a trifle condescendingly:

"Nikolai Kusmitch," he said benevolently and imagined himself also sitting without the fur coat, thin and miserable on the horsehair sofa, "I hope, Nikolai Kusmitch," he said, "that you will not pride yourself on your wealth. Always remember that that is not the chief thing; there are poor people who are thoroughly respectable; there are even impoverished members of the nobility and generals' daughters, who go about peddling things on the streets." And the benefactor cited a number of other cases known to the whole town.

The other Nikolai Kusmitch, the one on the horse-hair sofa, the recipient of this gift, did not, so far, look in the least overbearing; one might safely assume he would be reasonable. He in fact altered nothing in his modest, regular mode of living, and he now employed his Sundays in putting his accounts in order. But after a few weeks it struck him that he was spending an incredible amount. I will retrench, he thought. He rose earlier; he washed less thoroughly, he drank his tea standing, he ran to his office and arrived much too soon. He saved a little time everywhere. But when Sunday came there was nothing of all this saving. Then he realized that he had been duped. I should never have changed it, he said to himself. How long one can live on just one year. But then, this confounded small change, it disappears, one doesn't know how. And there came an ugly afternoon, which he passed sitting in the corner of the sofa and waiting for the gentleman in the fur coat, from whom he meant to demand the return of his time. He would bolt the door and not allow him to depart until he had produced the amount. In notes, he would say, of ten years if you prefer. Four notes of ten, and one of five, and the remainder he could keep, in the devil's name. Yes, he was ready to present him with the rest, just so that no difficulties should arise. Exasperated he sat in the horse-hair sofa and waited, but the gentleman never came. And he, Nikolai Kusmitch, who had so easily seen himself sitting there a few weeks before, was unable, now that he really sat there, to picture to himself the other Nikolai Kusmitch, the one in the fur coat, the generous one. Heaven knew what had become of him; probably his defalcations had been traced, and he was now sitting locked up somewhere. Surely he had not brought misfortune to him alone. Such swindlers always work on a large scale.

It occurred to him that there must be some state authority, a kind of Time Bank, where he might exchange part at least of his shabby seconds. After all, they were genuine. He had never heard of such an institution, but something of the sort was surely to be found in the directory under "T", or perhaps it was called "Bank for Time"; one could easily look under "B". As a last resort the letter "I" might be considered, too, for presumably it would be an imperial institution; that would accord with its importance.

Later Nikolai Kusmitch used always to assert that, although he was comprehensibly in a very depressed mood, he had not been drinking anything on that Sunday evening. He was therefore perfectly sober when the following incident occurred, so far as one can tell at all what did happen then. Perhaps he had taken a little nap in the corner of his sofa; that was always possible. This short sleep gave him at first the greatest relief. I've been meddling with figures, he said to himself. Now I have no head for figures. It is plain, however, that too great importance should not be attached to them; they are, after all, only an arrangement on the part of the state, so to speak, for the sake of order. No one had ever seen them anywhere except on paper. The possibility, for example, of meeting a Seven or a Twenty-five at a party was excluded. There simply weren't any there. And so, this slight confusion had taken place, out of pure absent-mindedness: Time and Money, as though the two could not be kept apart. Nikolai Kusmitch almost laughed. It was really excellent thus to have caught on to oneself, and in good

time, that was the important thing, in good time. Now it would
be different. Time, yes, that was an embarrassing matter. But had
this perhaps happened only to him? Didn't time go for others too,
the way he had found out, in seconds, even if they didn't know it?

Nikolai Kusmitch was not altogether free of malicious joy. Let
it—, he was just about to think, when something singular hap-
pened. He suddenly felt a breath on his face; it blew past his ears;
he felt it on his hands. He opened his eyes wide. The window was
securely shut. And as he sat there in the dark room with wide-
opened eyes, he began to realize that what he now sensed was ac-
tual time, passing by. He recognized them concretely, these tiny
seconds, all equally tepid, one like the other, but swift, but swift.
Heaven knew what else they were planning. That he should be the
one whom this befell, he who felt every sort of wind as an insult!
Now one would sit there, and the draught would always go on
like this, one's whole life long. He foresaw all the neuralgias one
would get from it; he was beside himself with rage. He leaped up;
but his surprises were not yet at an end. Beneath his feet as well
there was something like a movement, not one movement only, but
several, curiously interoscillating. He went stiff with terror: could
that be the earth? Certainly, it was the earth. And the earth moved,
after all. That had been spoken of in school; it had been passed
over rather rapidly and later was readily hushed up; it was not
held fitting to speak of it. But now that he had once become sen-
sitive, he was able to feel this too. Did others feel it? Perhaps, but
they did not show it. Probably it did not make any difference to
them, these sailor-folk. But Nikolai Kusmitch was unquestionably
rather delicate in this respect; he avoided even the street cars. He
staggered about in his room as if he were on deck and had to hold
on right and left. Unluckily something else occurred to him, about
the oblique position of the earth's axis. No, he could not stand all
these movements. He felt wretched. Lie down and keep quiet, he
had once read somewhere. And since that time Nikolai Kusmitch
had been lying down.

He lay and kept his eyes closed. And there were periods, days
of easier motion, so to speak, when it was quite bearable. And then
he had thought out this with the poems. One would scarcely have
believed how it helped. When one recited a poem slowly like this,
with even stressing of the rhymes, one had, to some degree, some-

thing stable on which to keep a steady gaze, inwardly, of course. Lucky, that he knew all these poems. But he had always been specially interested in literature. He did not complain about his state, the student, who had long known him, assured me. Only in course of time an exaggerated admiration had developed in him for those who, like the student, could go about and bear the motion of the earth. I remember this story so accurately because it reassured me uncommonly. I may well say I have never again had such an agreeable neighbor as this Nikolai Kusmitch, who surely would also have admired me.

After this experience I resolved in similar cases to go at once straight to the facts. I noticed how simple they were and what a relief compared with conjectures. As if I had not known that all our insights are added later, balances, nothing more. Right afterward a new page begins with something entirely different, nothing carried forward. Of what help in the present case were the few facts, which it was child's play to establish? I shall relate them immediately, when I have told what concerns me at the moment: that these facts tended rather to make my situation, which (as I now admit) was really difficult, still more embarrassing.

To my honor be it said that I wrote a great deal in these days; I wrote spasmodically. True, when I had gone out I did not look forward to coming home again. I even made short detours and in this way lost a half-hour during which I might have been writing. I admit that this was a weakness. Once in my room, however, I had nothing to reproach myself. I wrote; I had my own life, and the life next door there was quite another life, with which I shared nothing: the life of a medical student who was studying for his examination. I had nothing similar in prospect; that already constituted a decisive difference. And in other respects as well our circumstances were as different as could be. That was all evident to me. Until the moment, when I knew that it would come; then I forgot that there was nothing in common between us. I listened so, that my heart grew loud. I left everything and listened. And then it came: I was never mistaken.

Almost everyone knows the noise caused by any round, tin object, let us assume the lid of a canister, when it slips from one's grasp. As a rule such a lid doesn't even land on the floor very loudly; it falls abruptly, rolls along on its edge, and really becomes disagreeable only when its momentum runs down and it bumps, wobbling in every direction before it comes to rest. Now, that is the whole story: a tin object of the kind fell in the next room, rolled, lay still, and, in between, at certain intervals, stamping could be heard. Like all noises that impose themselves by repetition, this also had its internal organization; it ran its whole gamut, never exactly the same. But it was just this precisely which spoke for its lawfulness. It could be violent or mild or melancholy; it could pass by precipitately, as it were, or glide unendingly long before it came to rest. And the final oscillation was always surprising. On the other hand, the stamping that accompanied it seemed almost mechanical. But it punctuated the noise differently each time; that seemed to be its function. I can now review these details much more accurately; the room next me is empty. He has gone home, to the country. He needed to recover. I live on the top storey. On my right is another house, no one has moved into the room under me as yet: I have no neighbors.

In this condition it almost surprises me that I did not take the matter more lightly. Although I was warned in advance every time by my feeling. I should have profited by that. Don't be afraid, I ought to have said to myself, it's coming now; for I knew I was never mistaken. But that was perhaps due to the very facts I had had told me; since knowing them I was still more easily frightened. It affected me as almost ghostly that what released this noise was that small, slow, soundless movement with which the student's eyelid would of its own accord sink and close over his right eye as he read. This was the essential thing in his story, a trifle. He had already had to let his examinations lapse a few times; his ambition had become sensitive, and probably his people at home brought pressure to bear whenever they wrote. So what remained but to pull himself together. But several months before the decisive date, this weakness had supervened; this slight, impossible fatigue, that seemed so foolish, as when a windowblind refuses to stay up. I am sure that for weeks he felt one ought to be able to master it. Else I should never have hit upon the idea of offering him my own will. For one day I understood that he had come to the end of his.

And after that, whenever I felt the thing coming, I stood on my side of the wall and begged him to help himself to mine. And in time it became clear to me that he was accepting it. Perhaps he ought not to have done so, especially when one considers that it really did not help. Even supposing we managed to achieve a slight delay, it is still questionable whether he was actually in a position to make use of the moments we thus gained. And meantime my outlays were beginning to tell on me. I know I was wondering whether things could go on much longer in this fashion, on the very afternoon that someone came up to our floor. The staircase being narrow, this always caused considerable disturbance in the little hotel. After a while it seemed to me that someone entered my neighbor's room. Our two doors were the last in the passage, his being at an angle and close to mine. But I knew that he saw friends there occasionally, and, as I have said, I took absolutely no interest in his affairs. It is possible that his door was opened several times more, that there was coming and going outside. For that I was really not responsible.

Now on this same evening it was worse than ever. It was not yet very late, but being tired I had already gone to bed; I thought I should probably be able to sleep. Suddenly I sprang up as if someone had touched me. Immediately after, it began. It leaped and rolled and ran up against something, swaying and clattering. The stamping was frightful. In between someone on the floor below knocked distinctly and angrily against the ceiling. The new lodger, too, was naturally disturbed. Now: that must be his door. I was so wide awake that I thought I heard his door, although he was so astonishingly careful with it. It seemed to me he was approaching. He would certainly be wanting to know in which room it was. What struck me as odd was his really exaggerated considerations. He could have noticed just now that quiet was of no account in that house. Why in all the world did he smother his steps? For a moment I thought he was at my door; and then I heard him, there was no doubt about it, entering the next room. He walked straight in next door.

And now (how shall I describe it?), now all was still. Still, as when some pain ceases. A peculiarly palpable, prickling stillness, as if a wound were healing. I could have gone to sleep at once; could have taken a deep breath and gone off. My amazement alone kept me awake. Someone was speaking in the next room, but that, too, belonged in with the stillness. One must have experienced that stillness to know what it was like, it cannot be rendered. Outside, too, everything seemed to have been smoothed out. I sat up, I listened, it was like being in the country. My God, I thought, his mother is there. She was sitting beside the lamp, talking to him, perhaps he had leaned his head a little against his shoulder. In a minute she would be putting him to bed. Now I understood the faint steps outside in the passage. Ah, that this could be. A being such as this, before whom doors yield quite otherwise than they do for us. Yes, now we could sleep.

I have nearly forgotten my neighbor already. I fully realize that it was no real sympathy I had for him. Occasionally, indeed, I ask downstairs as I pass whether there is news of him, and what news. And I am glad when it is good. But I exaggerate. In reality I do not need to know. It no longer has any connection with him if I sometimes sense a sudden impulse to enter the next room. It is but a step from my door to the other, and the room is not locked. It would interest me to know what that room is really like. It is easy to form an idea of any particular room, and often the idea just about corresponds to the reality. Only the room one has next door to one is always entirely different from what one imagines it.

I tell myself that it is this circumstance that attracts me. But I know perfectly well that it is a certain tin object awaiting me. I have assumed that some tin lid is really in question, though of course I may be mistaken. That does not trouble me. It simply accords with my predisposition to lay the whole affair to a tin lid. He was not likely, one thinks, to take it away with him. Probably the room has been cleaned and the lid put back on the tin as is proper. And now the two together form the concept tin, a round tin, to express it exactly, a simple, very familiar concept. I seem to recall them standing on the mantel, these two parts that constitute the tin. Yes, they even stand before the mirror, so that another tin appears behind it, a deceptively similar, imaginary tin. A tin on which we place no value, but which a monkey, for example, would try to seize. In fact, there would even be two monkeys grabbing for it, for the monkey too would be duplicated as soon as it got to the edge of the mantelpiece. Now then, it is the lid of this tin that had designs on me.

Let us agree on this: the lid of a tin, of a sound tin, whose edge curves no differently than its own—such a lid should have no other desire than to find itself upon the tin; this would be the utmost it could imagine for itself; an insurpassable satisfaction, the fulfillment of all its desires. Indeed, there is something almost ideal in evenly reposing, patiently and gently turned to fit against the small projecting rim and feeling its dovetailing edge within you, elastic and just as sharp as one is at one's own edge when one lies there alone. But, alas, how few lids there are that still appreciate this. Here it is very evident what confusion their association with people has worked on things. For human beings, if it is feasible to compare them just in passing with such tin lids, sit most unwillingly and badly on their occupations. Partly because in their haste they have not come upon the right ones, partly because they have been put on crooked and in anger, partly because the rims that belong upon each other have been bent, each in a different way. Let us say it honestly: their chief thought is, as soon as they get a chance, to jump down and roll around and sound tinny. Else where do all these so-called distractions come from and the noise they cause?

Things have been looking on at this for centuries now. It is no wonder if they are spoiled, if they lose their taste for their natural, silent functions and want to make the most of existence, as they see it being made the most of all around them. They make attempts to evade their uses, they grow listless and negligent, and people are not at all surprised when they catch them at some dissipation. They know that so well from themselves. They are annoyed because they are the stronger, because they think they have more right to change, because they feel they are being aped; but they let the matter go, as they let themselves go. Where however there is one who pulls himself together, some solitary, for example, who wants to rest all roundly upon himself day and night, he at once provokes the contradiction, the contempt, the hatred of those degenerate objects which, in their own bad consciences, can no longer endure that anything should contain itself and strive according to its own nature. Then they combine to trouble, to frighten, to mislead him, and know they can do it. Winking to one another, they begin their seduction, which then grows on into the unlimited and sweeps along all creatures, and God himself, against the solitary one, who will perhaps hold out: the saint.

How I understand now those strange pictures in which things meant for restricted and regular uses relax and wantonly touch and tempt one another in their curiosity, quivering with the random lechery of dissipation. These cauldrons that go about boiling, these pistons that hit upon ideas, and the useless funnels that squeeze themselves into holes for their pleasure. And behold among them, too, thrown up by the jealous void, limbs and parts of limbs, and faces that warmly vomit into them, and windy buttocks offering them satisfaction.

And the saint writhes and shrinks into himself; yet in his eyes there was still a look that held this possible: he had glimpsed it. And already his senses are precipitating out of the bright solution of his spirit. Already his prayer is losing its leaves and stands up out of his mouth like a wilted bush. His heart has fallen over and flowed out into the murk. His scourge falls weakly upon him as a tail that flicks off flies. His sex is once again in one place only, and when a woman comes upright through the huddle toward him, her open bosom full of breasts, it points at her like a finger.

There was a time when I thought these pictures obsolete. Not as though I doubted their reality. I could imagine that this happened to the saints, in those days, those overhasty zealots, who wanted to begin with God immediately at any price. We no longer expect this of ourselves. We sense that God is too difficult for us, that we must defer him, in order slowly to do the long work that separates us from him. But now I know that this work is just as much contested as sainthood; that these things spring up around everyone who for its sake is solitary, as they formed around God's solitaries in their caves and bare retreats, long ago.

When one speaks of solitaries, one always takes too much for granted. One supposes that people know what one is talking about. No, they do not. They have never seen a solitary, they have simply hated him without knowing him. They have been his neighbors who used him up, and the voices in the next room that tempted him. They have incited things against him, so that they made a great noise and drowned him out. Children were in league against him, when he was tender and a child, and with every growth he grew up against the grown-ups. They tracked him to his hiding place, like a beast to be hunted, and his long youth had no closed season. And when he refused to be worn out and got away, they cried out upon that which emanated from him, and called it ugly and cast suspicion upon it. And when he would not listen, they became more distinct and ate away his food and breathed out his air and spat into his poverty so that it became repugnant to him. They brought down disrepute upon him as upon an infectious person and cast stones at him to make him go away more quickly. And they were right in their ancient instinct: for he was indeed their foe.

But then, when he did not raise his eyes, they began to reflect. They suspected that with all this they had done what he wanted; that they had fortified him in his solitude and helped him to separate himself from them for ever. And now they changed about and, resorting to the final, the extreme, used that other resistance: fame. And at this clamor almost every one has looked up and been distracted.

L ast night I thought again of the little green book which I must once have possessed as a boy; and I don't know why I imagine it came down from Manthilde Brahe. It did not interest me when I got it, and I did not read it until several years later, I believe during my holidays at Ulsgaard. But important it was to me from the very first moment. It was meaningful through and through, even considered from the outside. The green of its binding meant something, and one understood at once that inside it had to be as it was. As if by pre-arrangement, there came first that smooth fly-leaf, watered white on white, and then the title-page which one held to be mysterious. There might well have been illustrations in it, the way it looked; but there were none, and one had to admit, almost grudgingly, that this too belonged in the arrangement. It compensated one somehow to find at a particular place the narrow book-mark, which, friable and a little awry, pathetic in its confidence that it was still rose-colored, had lain since God knows when between the same pages. Perhaps it had never been used, and the bookbinder had hastily and busily folded it in without looking properly. But possibly it was no accident. It may be that someone had ceased reading at that point, who never read again; that fate had at the moment knocked at his door to occupy him so that he went off far away from all books, which after all are not life. It was impossible to tell whether the book had been read further. One could also imagine that it was simply a question of this passage having been turned to again and again, and that this had been done, even though sometimes not until late at night. In any case I felt a certain shyness before those two pages, such as one feels before a mirror in front of which someone is standing. I never read them. I do not even know whether I read the whole book. It was not very thick, but there were a lot of stories in it, especially of an afternoon; then there was always one that one did not yet know.

I remember only two. I will tell which they were: The End of Grishka Otrepioff and The Downfall of Charles the Bold.

God knows whether it impressed me at the time. But now, after so many years, I recall the description of how the corpse of the false czar had been thrown among the crowd and lay there three days, mangled and stabbed, with a mask before its face. There is, of course, not the least prospect that the little book will ever come into my hands again. But this passage must have been remarkable. I should also like to read over again how the encounter with his mother went off. He must have felt very secure, since he had her come to Moscow; I am even convinced that he believed in himself so strongly at that period, that he really thought he was summoning his mother. And this Maria Nagoi, who arrived from her mean convent by rapid day-journeys, had, after all, everything to gain by assenting. But did not his uncertainty begin with the very fact that she acknowledged him? I am not disinclined to believe that the strength of his transformation lay in his no longer being anybody's son.

* (This, in the end, is the strength of all young people who have gone away.)

The people, which desired him without picturing anyone in par-

---

* Written on the margin of the MS.

ticular, made him only more free and more unbounded in his possibilities. But his mother's declaration, even though a conscious deception, still had the power to belittle him; it lifted him out of the fulness of his inventions; it limited him to a weary imitation; it reduced him to the individual he was not; it made him an impostor. And now there also came, more gently dissolvent, that Marina Mniczek, who in her own fashion denied him, since, as it afterward appeared, she believed not in him but in anyone. Naturally, I cannot vouch for the extent to which all this was considered in that story. It seems to me it should have been told.

But even aside from that, this incident is not at all out of date. One might now conceive of a writer who would devote much care to these last moments; he would not be wrong. A lot happens in them: how, waking from the deepest sleep, he leaps to the window and out over the window into the courtyard between the sentinels. He cannot get up alone; they have to help him. Probably he has broken his foot. Leaning on the two men, he feels that they believe in him. He looks round: the others too believe in him. He is almost sorry for them, these gigantic Strelitzers; things must have come to a pretty pass with them: they have known Ivan Grosny in all his reality, and they believe in *him*. He is almost tempted to enlighten them; but to open his lips would simply mean to scream. The pain in his foot is maddening, and he thinks so little of himself at this moment that he knows nothing but the pain. And then there is no time. They are crowding in: he sees Shuisky and behind him all the others. Soon it will be over. But now his guards close round him. They do not give him up. And a miracle happens. The faith of these old men spreads, suddenly not one of them will advance. Shuisky, close before him, calls up in desperation to a window above. The false czar does not look round. He knows who is standing there; he realizes that there is silence, with no transition whatever. Now the voice will come that he knows of old, the shrill, false voice that overstrains itself. And then he hears the czarina-mother disowning him.

Up to this point the incident moves of itself; but now, please, a narrator, a narrator: for from the few lines that still remain to be written a force must emerge transcending all contradiction. Whether it is stated or not, one must swear that between voice and pistol-shot, infinitely compressed, there was once more within him the will and the power to be everything. Otherwise one fails to understand how brilliantly logical it is that they should have pierced through his night-shirt and stabbed all around in him, to see whether they would strike the hard core of a personality. And that in death he should still have worn, for three days, the mask which already he had almost renounced.

When I consider it now, it seems strange to me that in the same book the end of a man should have been told who was all his life long one and the same, hard and unalterable as granite and weighing always more heavily upon those who endured him. There is a portrait of him in Dijon. But even so one knows that he was squat, square, defiant, and desperate. Only his hands, perhaps, one would not have thought of. They are excessively warm hands, that continually want to cool themselves and involuntarily lay themselves on any cold object, outspread, with air between the fingers. Into those hands the blood could shoot, as it mounts to a person's head, and when clenched, they were indeed like the heads of madmen, raging with fancies.

It required incredible caution to live with this blood. The duke was locked in with it inside himself, and at times he was afraid of it, when it moved round him, cringing and dark. Even to him it could be terrifyingly foreign, this nimble, half-Portuguese blood he scarcely knew. He was often frightened lest it attack him as he slept and rend him in pieces. He made as if to master it, but he stood always in fear of it. He never dared love a woman lest it turn jealous, and so ravening was it that wine never passed his lips; instead of drinking, he gentled it with a marmalade of roses. Yet once he drank, in the camp at Lausanne, when Granson was lost. He was ill then and in seclusion and he took much straight wine. But at that time his blood slept. During his irrational last years it sometimes fell into this heavy, bestial sleep. Then it appeared how completely he was in its power; for when it slept, he was nothing. On these occasions none of his entourage was allowed to enter; he did not understand what they said. To the foreign envoys he could not show himself, desolate as he was. Then he sat and waited until his blood should awake. And most often it would leap up suddenly and break out of his heart and roar.

For the sake of this blood he dragged about with him all those things for which he cared nothing. The three great diamonds and all the precious stones; the Flemish laces and the Arras tapestries, in piles. His silken pavilion with its cords of twisted gold, and the four hundred tents for his suite. And pictures painted on wood, and the twelve Apostles of solid silver. And the Prince of Taranto and the Duke of Cleves and Philip of Baden and the seigneur of Château-Guyon. For he wanted to persuade his blood that he was emperor and nothing above him: so that it might fear him. But his blood did not believe him, despite such proofs; it was a distrustful blood. Perhaps he kept it for a little while in doubt. But the horns of Uri betrayed him. After that his blood knew it inhabited a lost man: and wanted to get out.

That is how I see it now, but at that time what impressed me above all was to read of that Epiphany when they were searching for him.

The young Lothringian prince, who the day before, right after that oddly hasty battle, had ridden into his miserable town of Nancy, had wakened his entourage very early and asked for the duke. Messenger after messenger was dispatched, and he himself appeared at the window from time to time, restless and anxious. He did not always recognize those whom they carried in on their carts and litters, he only saw that it was not the duke. Nor was he among the wounded, and none of the prisoners, whom they were still continually bringing in, had seen him. But the fugitives carried different accounts in every direction and were confused and scared, as though they were afraid of running into him. Night had already begun to fall and nothing had been heard of him. The news that he had disappeared had time to get about during the long winter evening. And, wherever it came, it engendered in everybody a brusque, exaggerated certainty that he was alive. Never perhaps had the duke been so real to the imagination of all as on that night. There was no house where people did not keep watch and expect him and imagine his knocking. And if he did not come, it was because he had already gone by.

It froze that night, and it was as though the idea that he still existed had frozen as well; so hard did it become. And years and years passed before it dissolved. All these people, without really knowing it, insisted on his being alive. The fate he had brought upon them was tolerable only through his person. They had learned with such difficulty that he existed; but now that they knew him, they found that he was easy to remember and not to be forgotten.

But next morning, the seventh of January, a Tuesday, the search was nevertheless resumed. And this time there was a guide. He was a page of the duke's, and it was said that from a distance he had seen his master fall; now he was to show the spot. He himself had told nothing; Count Campobasso had brought him and had spoken for him. Now he walked in front, the others keeping close behind him. Whoever saw him so, muffled up and strangely uncertain, would have found it difficult to believe this really was Gian-Battista Colonna, who was beautiful as a young girl and slender-jointed. He shivered with cold; the air was stiff with the night-frost, under foot the sound was like gnashing of teeth. They were all cold, for that matter. The duke's fool, nicknamed Louis-Onze, kept himself in motion. He played dog, ran ahead, came back and trotted a while on all fours beside the boy; but whenever he saw a corpse in the distance he leaped toward it and bowed and exhorted it to pull itself together and be him they were seeking. He would leave it a little time for reflection, but then he came back grumbling to the others and threatened and swore, and complained of the obstinacy and the sloth of the dead. And they went on and on, and there was no end. The town could scarcely be seen now; for the weather had meantime closed down, despite the cold, and had become grey and impenetrable. The country lay there flat and indifferent, and the little compact group looked more and more lost, the further it moved on. No one spoke; only an old woman, who had been running along with them, mumbled something and shook her head; perhaps she was praying.

Suddenly the leader stood still and looked about him. Then he turned brusquely to Lupi, the duke's Portuguese doctor, and pointed ahead. A few steps further on there was a stretch of ice, a kind of pond or marsh, and in it there lay, half broken through the ice, ten or twelve dead bodies. They were almost completely stripped and despoiled. Lupi went, bowed and attentive, from one to the other. And now as they went about thus separately, they recognized Olivier de la Marche and the chaplain. But the old woman was already kneeling in the snow, whimpering as she bent over a large hand whose outspread fingers pointed stiffly toward her. They all ran up. Lupi with some of the attendants tried to turn over the body, for it was lying face down. But the face was frozen into the ice, and as they pulled it out, one of the cheeks peeled off, thin and brittle, and it appeared that the other cheek had been torn out by dogs or wolves; and the whole was cleft by a great wound beginning at the ear, so that one could not speak of a face at all.

One after the other looked round; each expected to find the Roman behind him. But they saw only the fool, who came running toward them angry and bloody. He held a cloak away from him and shook it as if something should fall out; but the cloak was empty. Then they began to look for identifying marks and found a few. A fire had been kindled and the body was washed with warm water and wine. The scar on the throat appeared, and the traces of the two large abscesses. The doctor no longer had any doubt. But they made other comparisons. Louis-Onze had discovered a few steps further on, the cadaver of the big black charger Moreau, whom the duke had ridden the day of Nancy. He was sitting astride it, letting his short legs hang down. The blood was still running from his nose into his mouth, and one could see him tasting it. One of the attendants on the other side remembered that the duke had had an ingrown nail on his left foot; now they all began to search for this nail. But the fool wriggled, as if he were being tickled, and cried: "Ah! Monseigneur, forgive them for uncovering your gross defects, the dolts, not recognizing you by my long face, in which your virtues are written!"

*(The duke's fool was also the first to enter when the corpse was laid out. It was in the house of a certain Georges Marquis, no one could say for what reason. The bier-cloth had not yet been spread, so the fool received the full impression. The white of the doublet and the crimson of the cloak parted harsh and unfriendly from each other between the two blacks of baldachin and couch. Scarlet long-boots stood in front, pointing toward him with great, gilded spurs. And that that up there was a head there could be no disputing, as soon as one saw the crown. It was a large, ducal crown with jewels of some sort. Louis-Onze moved about, inspecting everything carefully. He handled even the satin, though he knew little about it. It would be good satin, perhaps a trifle cheap for

---

* Written on the margin of the MS.

the house of Burgundy. He stepped back once more to survey the whole. The colors were singularly unrelated in the light from the snow. He stamped each one separately on his memory. "Well-dressed," he acknowledged finally, "perhaps a trace too conspicuously." Death seemed to him like a puppet-master in instant need of a duke.)

It is well simply to recognize certain things that will never change, without deploring the facts or even judging them. Thus it became clear to me that I never was a real reader. In childhood I considered reading a profession one would take upon oneself, later some time, when all the professions came along, one after the other. I had, to tell the truth, no clear idea when that might be. I trusted that one would notice when life somehow turned and came only from without, as hitherto from within. I imagined that it would then become intelligible and unambiguous and not at all liable to misunderstanding. Not simple by any means; on the contrary, quite exacting, complicated and difficult, if you like, but nevertheless visible. All that in childhood was singularly unlimited, disproportionate, never altogether within sight, would then have been got through. Though indeed one did not at all know how. In reality it still continued to grow, closing together on all sides; and the more one looked outside, the more did one stir up inside oneself; God knows whence it came. But probably it grew to an extreme and then suddenly broke off. It was easy to observe that grown people were very little troubled by it: they went about judging and doing, and if ever they got into difficulties, that lay with external circumstances.

Until the beginning of such changes I postponed reading too. One would then treat books as one treated friends, there would be time for them, a definite time that would pass regularly, complaisantly, just so much of it as happened to suit one. Naturally some of them would be closer to one, and this is not to say that one would be secure from losing half-an-hour over them now and again, missing a walk, an appointment, the opening of a play, or a pressing letter. But that one's hair should become untidy and dishevelled, as if one had been lying on it, that one should get burning ears and hands as cold as metal, that a long candle beside one should burn right down into its holder, that, thank God, would then be entirely excluded. I mention these symptoms because I experienced them rather strikingly in myself, during those holidays at Ulsgaard when I so suddenly took to reading. It became clear at once that I did not know how to do it. I had indeed begun before the period I had assigned to it ahead of time. But that year I spent at Sorö among so many others of about my own age had made me mistrustful of such reckonings. There sudden and unexpected experiences had come up with me; and it was plain to see that they dealt with me as a grown-up. They were life-sized experiences that made themselves as heavy as they were. In the same degree, however, as I apprehended their actuality, my eyes opened also to the infinite reality of my childhood. I knew that it would not cease, any more than the other was only now beginning. I said to myself that everyone was naturally at liberty to make divisions, but they were artificial. And it appeared that I was too unskilled to think out any for myself. Every time I tried, life gave me to understand that it knew nothing of them. If, however, I persisted in thinking that my childhood was past, then in that same moment my whole future was also gone and there was left me only just so much as a lead soldier has beneath his feet to stand on.

This discovery naturally set me still more apart. It preoccupied me within myself and filled me with a kind of ultimate joy, which I mistook for sadness because it was far beyond my age. I was disquieted also, as I recollect, lest, since nothing had been provided for any fixed time one might miss many things altogether. And so when I returned to Ulsgaard and saw all the books, I set to; in great haste, almost with a bad conscience. Of what I so often felt later, I now somehow had a premonition: that one had no right to open a book at all, unless one pledged oneself to read them all. With every line one broke off a bit of the world. Before books it was intact and perhaps it would be again after them. But how could I, who was unable to read, cope with them all? There they stood, even in that modest library, in such hopeless abundance and solidarity. I flung myself stubborn and despairing from book to book and battled through their pages, like one who has to perform a disproportionate task. At that time I read Schiller and Baggesen, Öhlenschläger and Schack-Staffeldt, all that was there of Walter

Scott and Calderon. Many things came into my hands which ought in a way to have been read before, for others it was much too soon; to my present of that day almost nothing was due. And nevertheless I read.

In later years it occasionally happened that I awoke at night, and the stars stood out so real and proceeded so meaningfully that I could not understand how one brought oneself to miss so much world. I had a similar feeling, I believe, whenever I lifted my eyes from my books and looked outside, where summer was, where Abelone called. It was quite unexpected for us, that she had to call and that I did not even answer. It happened in the midst of our happiest time. But since this had now taken hold of me, I clung convulsively to reading, and hid, important and obstinate, from our daily holidays. Awkward as I was in making use of the numerous, often not too obvious opportunities of enjoying a natural happiness, I not unwillingly accepted the promise our growing dissension afforded of future reconciliations, which became the more delightful the longer one postponed them.

Furthermore, my reading trance ended one day as suddenly as it had begun; and then we thoroughly angered one another. For Abelone now spared me no teasing or superiority, and when I met her in the arbor she would declare she was reading. On a certain Sunday morning the book was indeed lying unopened beside her, but she seemed rather too busily employed over the currants, which with the aid of a fork she was carefully stripping out of their little clusters.

It must have been one of those early mornings such as there are in July, new, rested hours, in which joyful spontaneous things are happening everywhere. From a million tiny insuppressible movements a mosaic of most convincing life is assembled; objects vibrate one into another and out into the air, and their cool freshness makes the shadows clear and the sun into a light and spiritual clarity. Then there is no main object in the garden; everything is everywhere diffused, and one would have to be in everything in order to miss nothing.

And in Abelone's little action it was all there once again. It was such a happy thought, to be doing just that, and exactly as she did it. Her hands, bright in the shade, worked so lightly and harmoniously toward each other, and before the fork the round berries leaped gaily into the dish lined with dew-dimmed vineleaves, to join the others heaping up there, red and blond ones, lustrous, with sound grains inside the tart pulp. In these circumstances I desired nothing save to look on; but, as I should probably be reproved for that, also to appear at ease, I took the book, sat down on the other side of the table and, without long turning of pages, started in at random.

"If you would at least read aloud, bookworm," said Abelone after a little. That did not sound nearly so quarrelsome, and since I thought it high time for a reconciliation, I promptly read aloud, going right on to the end of a section, and on again to the next heading: To Bettina.

"No, not the answers," Abelone interrupted, and suddenly, as if she were exhausted, laid down the little fork. Then she laughed at the way I was looking at her.

"My goodness, Malte, how badly you've been reading."

Then I had to admit that not for one moment had my mind been on what I was doing. "I read simply to get you to interrupt me," I confessed, and grew hot and turned back the pages till I came to the title of the book. Only then did I know what it was. "And why not the answers?" I asked with curiosity.

Abelone seemed not to have heard me. She sat there in her bright dress, as though she were growing dark all over inside, as her eyes were now.

"Give it to me," she said suddenly, as if in anger, taking the book out of my hand and opening it right at the page she wanted. And then she read one of Bettina's letters.

I do not know how much of it I took in, but it was as though a solemn promise were being given me that one day I should understand it all. And while her voice rose and at last almost resembled the voice I knew from her singing, I was ashamed that I had had so trivial a conception of our reconciliation. For I well knew that this was it. But it was now taking place somewhere on a grand scale, far above me, where I did not reach.

The promise is still being fulfilled; at some time that same volume got in among my books, among the few books from which I never part. It opens now, for me too, at the passages I happen to have in mind, and when I read them it remains undecided whether I am thinking of Bettina or of Abelone. No, Bettina has become more real in me; Abelone, whom I knew, was like a preparation for her and has now become merged for me in Bettina, as if in her own unconscious being. For this strange Bettina gave space with all her letters, most spacious stature. From the beginning she spread out in everything, as though she were after her death. Everywhere she settled deep into existence, belonging to it, and whatever happened to her has eternally been in nature: there she recognized herself and thence she almost painfully freed herself; laboriously divined herself back again, as though out of traditions, conjured herself and was able to sustain herself.

Just now, Bettina, you still were; I understand you. Is not the earth still warm with you, and do not the birds still leave room for your voice? The dew is different, but the stars are still the stars of your nights. Or is not the whole world of your making? For how often you have set it afire with your love, and seen it flare and blaze and replaced it secretly with another world, when all were asleep. You felt yourself so well in harmony with God, when every morning you sought a new earth from him, so that all those he had created might have their turn. You thought it petty to spare them or to mend them and you used them up and stretched out your hands for always more world. For your love was equal to everything.

How is it possible that everyone does not still speak of your love? What has since happened that was more remarkable? What is it that occupied them? You yourself knew the worth of your love; you recited it aloud to your greatest poet, so that he should make it human; for it was still element. But he, in writing to you, dissuaded people from it. They have all read his answers and believe them rather, because the poet is clearer to them than nature. But perhaps it will someday appear that here lay the limit of his greatness. This lover was imposed upon him, and he was not equal to her. What does it signify that he could not respond? Such love needs no response, itself containing both the mating-call and the reply; it answers its own prayers. But he should have humbled himself before her in all his splendor and written what she dictated, with both hands, like John on Patmos, kneeling. There was no choice for him before this voice which "fulfilled the angels' function," which had come to wrap him round and carry him off into eternity. Here was the chariot of his fiery ascension. Here was prepared against his death the dark myth he left empty.

Fate loves to invent patterns and designs. Its difficulty lies in complexity. But life itself is difficult because of its simplicity. It has only a few things of a grandeur not fit for us. The saint, rejecting fate, chooses these, face to face with God. But the fact that woman, following her nature, must make the same choice relative to man, conjures up the doom of all love-relationships: resolute and without fate, like an eternal being, she stands beside him who changes. The woman who loves always transcends the man she loves, because life is greater than fate. Her devotion wants to be immeasurable; that is her happiness. But the nameless suffering of her love has always been this: that she is required to restrict this devotion.

No other plaint have women ever raised. The two first letters of Heloïse contain only this, and five hundred years later it rises from the letters of the Portuguese nun; one recognizes it as one does a bird-call. And suddenly through the clear field of this insight passes the very distant figure of Sappho, whom the centuries did not find, since they sought her in destiny.

I have never dared buy a newspaper from him. I am not sure that he really always has any copies with him, as he shuffles slowly back and forth outside the Luxembourg Gardens all evening long. He turns his back to the railings, and his hand rubs along the stone coping in which the bars are set. He presses himself so flat that every day many pass by who have never seen him. True, he still has a remnant of voice in him and gives warning; but that is no different from a noise in a lamp or in the stove, or when water drips at peculiar intervals in a grotto. And the world is so arranged that there are people who all their lives long pass by during the pauses, when he, more soundless than anything that stirs, moves on like a pointer, like the shadow of that pointer, like time.

How wrong I was to look at him reluctantly. I am ashamed to write down that often when I came near I adopted the tread of the others, as though I did not know about him. Then I heard "La Presse" pronounced inside him and immediately repeated and a third time, at hurried intervals. And the people beside me looked round and sought the voice. Only I acted as though I were in more haste than any of them, as though I had noticed nothing, as though I were inwardly altogether absorbed.

And in fact I was so. I was busy picturing him to myself; I undertook the task of imagining him, and I broke out in sweat at the exertion. For I had to make him as one does a dead man, of whom there remain no proofs, no components; who has to be achieved entirely inwardly. I know now that it helped me a little to think of those many demounted Christs of striated ivory that lie about in every antiquary's shop. The thought of some Pietà came and went—: all this no doubt simply to evoke a particular angle at which his long face was held, and the desolate aftergrowth of beard in the shadows of his cheeks, and the definitively painful blindness of his sealed expression, held obliquely upward. But there were so many other things besides that were part of him; for this I knew even then, that nothing about him was incidental: not the manner in which his coat or cloak, gaping at the back, let his collar be seen all the way round, that low collar, which curved in a wide arc round the stretched and pitted neck without touching it; not the greenish black cravat loosely buckled about the whole; and most particularly not the hat, an old, high-crowned, stiff felt hat which he wore as all blind men wear their hats; without regard to the lines of their faces, without the possibility of forming between this accession and themselves any new external unity; merely as some conceded foreign object. In my cowardly refusal to look I arrived at the point where finally the image of this man, often without provocation, firmly and painfully contracted in me to such sharp misery that, harried by it, I determined to intimidate and suppress the increasing skill of my imagination through the external reality. It was toward evening. I resolved to walk attentively past him at once.

Now one should know that spring was approaching. The wind of day had fallen; the side streets lay long and contented; where they debouched, the houses gleamed new as freshly broken fragments of some white metal. But it was a metal that surprised one by its lightness. In the broad thoroughfares many people mingled, passing, almost without fear of the carriages, which were few. It must have been a Sunday. The tower-caps of Saint Sulpice stood out serene and unexpectedly high in the still air, and through the narrow, almost Roman alleys one had an involuntary glimpse out into the season. In the garden and before it there was such an activity of people that I did not see him at once. Or did I not recognize him at first through the crowd?

I knew immediately that my conception was worthless. The utter abandonment of his misery, restricted by no precaution or disguise, exceeded my means. I had grasped neither the angle of inclination in his attitude, nor the terror with which the inner side of his eyelids seemed constantly to fill him. I had never thought of his mouth, which was contracted like the exit of a gutter. Possibly he had memories, but now nothing was ever added to his soul any more, save daily the amorphous feeling of the stone coping behind him, on which his hand was wearing itself away. I had stood still, and while I saw all this almost simultaneously, I felt that he was wearing another hat and a cravat that was undoubtedly a Sunday one; it had a pattern of oblique yellow and violet checks, and as for the hat—it was a cheap new straw with a green band. There is nothing to these colors, of course, and it is petty of me to have retained them. I only want to say that on him they were like the softest down on the underside of a bird. He himself got no pleasure from them, and who among all those people (I looked about me) could imagine that all this finery was for them?

My God, it struck me with vehemence, so indeed you *are*. There are proofs of your existence. I have forgotten them all and have never demanded any, for what an immense responsibility would lie in the certainty of you. And yet, I am now being shown. This, then, is to your liking, in this you take pleasure. That we should learn to endure before all and not to judge. What are the grievous things? What the gracious? You alone know.

When winter comes again and I need a new coat—grant that I may wear it like that, so long as it is new.

It is not that I want to distinguish myself from them, when I go about in better clothes that have belonged to me from the start, and set store on living somewhere. I have not got so far. I haven't the heart for their life. If my arm were to wither, I believe I should hide it. But she (beyond this I do not know who she was), she appeared every day in front of the café terraces, and although it was very difficult for her to take off her cloak and disentangle herself from her confused garments and undergarments, she did not shrink from the trouble and took so long putting off this and getting out of that, that one could scarcely wait any longer. And then she stood before us, modestly, with her stunted, withered stump, and one saw that it was something rare.

No, it is not that I want to distinguish myself from them; but I should be presumptuous if I sought to be like them. I am not. I possess neither their strength nor their standard. I take nourishment, and so I exist from meal to meal, quite unmysteriously; while they subsist almost as if they were eternal. They stand in their daily corners, even in November, and do not cry out because of winter. The fog comes and makes them indistinct and uncertain: they exist, notwithstanding. I went travelling, I fell ill, much is over for me: but they did not die.

* (I don't even know how it is possible for school-children to get up in bedrooms filled with grey-smelling cold; who encourages them, those little precocious skeletons, to run out into the grown-up city, into the gloomy dregs of the night, into the everlasting school-day, still always small, always full of foreboding, always late. I have no conception of the amount of succour that is constantly being used up.)

This city is full of people who are slowly gliding down to their level. Most of them resist at first; but then there are those faded girls who are growing older, who constantly let themselves slip over without a struggle, strong girls, still unused in their innermost depths, who have never been loved.

Perhaps you mean, O God, that I should leave everything and love them? Else why is it so difficult for me not to follow them when they overtake me? Why do I suddenly invent the sweetest, most nocturnal words, while my voice stays tenderly between my throat and my heart? Why do I imagine how I would hold them with infinite precaution to my breath, these dolls with whom life has played, spring-time after spring-time flinging their arms open

---

* Written on the margin of the MS.

for nothing and again for nothing, till they grew loose in their shoulders? They have never fallen very deep down from any hope, so they are not broken; but chipped they are and already too bad for life. Only stray cats come to them evenings in their rooms and secretly scratch them up, and lie sleeping on them. Sometimes I follow one of them the length of two streets. They walk along past the houses, people keep coming who screen them from view, they vanish away behind them like nothing.

And yet I know that if someone tried to love them, they would weigh upon him, like people who have gone too far and stop walking. I believe only Jesus could endure them, who still has resurrection in all his limbs; but they matter little to him. It is only those who love that seduce him, not those who wait with a small talent for being lovers, as with a cold lamp.

I know that if I am destined for the worst it will avail me nothing to disguise myself in my better clothes. Did he not in the midst of his kingship slip down among the last of men? He, who instead of rising sank to the very bottom? It is true that at times I have believed in the other kings, although the parks no longer prove anything. But it is night, it is winter, I am freezing, I believe in him. For glory is but an instant, and we have never seen anything more lasting than misery. But the king shall endure.

Is he not the only one who held up under his madness like wax flowers under a glass case? For the others they implored long life in their churches; but of him the Chancellor Jean Charlier Gerson demanded that he should be eternal, and this when he was already the neediest of all, wretched and in sheer poverty despite his crown.

It was in the days when men like strangers, with blackened faces, from time to time attacked him in his bed, to tear from him the shirt, putrefied into his ulcers, that for a long while now he had taken for part of himself. The room had been darkened, and they ripped away the flabby rags under his rigid arms as they seized them. One brought a light, and only then did they discover the purulent sore on his breast, into which the iron amulet had sunk because he pressed it to him every night with all the force of his ardor; now it lay deep in him, terribly precious, in a pearly border of pus, like some miraculous relic in the hollow of a reliquary.

Hardened men had been chosen for the task, but they were not proof against nausea when the worms, disturbed, stood out toward them from the Flemish fustian and, fallen out of the folds, pulled themselves up somewhere along their sleeves. His condition had undoubtedly grown worse since the days of the parva regina; for she had still been willing to lie beside him, young and radiant as she was. Then she had died. And now no one dared any more to bed a sleeping-companion beside that carrion. She had not left behind her the words and endearments with which the king was to be soothed. So no one penetrated the thicket of this spirit any more; none helped him out of the ravines of his soul; none understood, when he suddenly came out of them himself with the round-eyed gaze of an animal that goes to pasture. Then when he recognized the preoccupied countenance of Juvenal, he remembered the empire as it had been at the last. And he wanted to retrieve what he had neglected.

But it was characteristic of the events of these times that they could not be imparted with any mitigation. Where anything happened, it happened with all its weight, and seemed to be all of a piece when one told it. Or what could be subtracted from the fact that his brother had been murdered; that yesterday Valentina Visconti, whom he always called his dear sister, had kneeled before him, lifting away all her widow's black from the grieving and the grievance of her disfigured countenance? And today a tough, talkative advocate had stood there for hours demonstrating the right of the princely murderer, until the crime became transparent and as though it would ascend in clarity to heaven. And being just meant acknowledging that everybody was right; for Valentina of Orléans died brokenhearted, though vengeance had been promised her. And of what avail was it to pardon the Burgundian duke, and pardon him again; him the sinister ardor of despair had overcome, so that for weeks now he had been living in a tent deep in the forest of Argilly, declaring that for his solace he must hear the stags belling in the night.

When one had pondered all this, over and over to the end, brief as it was, the people demanded to see one, and they saw one: perplexed. But the people rejoiced at the sight; they realized that this was the king, this silent, this patient man, who was only there in order to let God, in his tardy impatience, act over his head. In these lucid moments on the balcony of his palace at Saint-Pol, the king perhaps divined his own secret progress: he remembered the day of Roosbecke, when his uncle de Berry had taken him by the hand to lead him to the place of his first ready-made victory; there in that remarkably longlit November day he had surveyed the masses of the men of Ghent, just as they had throttled themselves with their own density, when the cavalry had attacked them from every side. Intertwined with one another, like an immense brain, they lay there in the clusters into which they had bound themselves in order to stand solid. The air failed one at sight here and there of their suffocated faces; one could not cease imagining that it had been displaced far above these corpses, still standing by virtue of their own congestion, through the sudden exit of so many desperate souls.

This they had impressed upon him as the beginning of his glory. And he had retained the memory of it. But if that had been the triumph of death, this, his standing here with his weak knees; upright in all these eyes: this was the mystery of love. He had seen by the others that that field of battle could be comprehended, immense though it was. But this which was happening now would not be comprehended; it was just as marvelous as, long ago, the stag with the golden collar in the forest of Senlis. Only this time he himself was the apparition and others were lost in contemplation. And he did not doubt that they were breathless and of the same wide expectation that had once overtaken him on that adolescent's hunting day, when the quiet face, peering, came out from among the branches. The mystery of his visibility spread over all his gentle form; he did not stir, timid lest he fade away; the thin smile on his broad, simple face took on a natural permanence as with sculptured saints and cost him no effort. Thus he offered himself, and it was one of those moments that are eternity seen in foreshortening. The crowd was hardly able to endure it. Fortified, nourished by a consolation inexhaustibly multiplied, it broke through the silence with a cry of joy. But above on the balcony there was only Juvenal des Ursins left, and into the next calm he shouted that the king would come to the rue Saint-Denis, to the Brotherhood of the Passion, to witness the Mysteries.

On such days the king was filled with benign awareness. Had a painter of that time been seeking some indication for existence in

Paradise, he could have found no more perfect model than the assuaged figure of the king, as it stood at one of the high windows in the Louvre under the droop of its shoulders. He was turning the pages of the little book by Christine de Pisan which is called "The Way of Long Learning" and was dedicated to him. He was not reading the erudite polemics of that allegorical parliament which had undertaken to discover the prince who should be worthy to rule over the whole earth. The book always opened for him at the simplest passages: where it spoke of the heart which for thirteen long years, like a retort over the fire of suffering, had only served to distil the water of bitterness for the eyes; he understood that true consolation only began when happiness was long enough gone and over for ever. Nothing was more precious to him than this comfort. And while his gaze seemed to embrace the bridge beyond, he loved to see the world through this heart moved to great ways by the powerful Cumæan,—the world of those days: the adventurous seas, the strange-towered cities held shut by the pressure of distances, the ecstatic loneliness of the assembled mountains, and the heavens, explored in fearsome doubt, which were only now closing like an infant's skull.

But when anyone entered, the king took fright and slowly his spirit clouded. He allowed them to lead him away from the window and give him some occupation. They had accustomed him to spend hours over illustrations and he was content with that; only one thing annoyed him: that in turning the pages one could never keep several pictures in sight and that they were fixed in their folios so that one could not shift them about. Then someone remembered a game of cards that had been quite forgotten, and the king took into favor the person who brought it, so after his own heart were those variegated cardboards that could be separately handled and were full of figures. And while card-playing became the fashion among the courtiers, the king sat in his library and played alone. Just as he now turned up two kings side by side, so the Lord had recently placed him beside the Emperor Wenceslas; sometimes a queen died and then he would lay an ace of hearts upon her that was like a gravestone. It did not astonish him that at the edge of the table, and here, under his right hand, was Avignon. He had no interest in Rome; for some reason or other he pictured it to himself as round and dropped the matter there. But Avignon he knew.

And hardly had he thought it, when his memory repeated the high hermetic palace and overtaxed itself. He closed his eyes and had to take a deep breath. He feared bad dreams that night.

On the whole, however, it was really a soothing occupation, and they were right in bringing him back to it again and again. Such hours confirmed him in the opinion that he was the king, King Charles the Sixth. This is not to say that he exaggerated himself; he was far from considering himself anything more than one of these pasteboards; but the certitude grew strong in him that he too was a definite card, perhaps a bad one, played in anger, and always losing: but always the same card: but never any other. And yet when a week had passed thus in regular self-confirmation, he would begin to feel a certain tightness inside him. His skin bound him across the forehead and at the back of his neck, as if he suddenly felt his own too distinct contour. No one knew to what temptation he yielded then, when he asked about the Mysteries and could hardly wait for them to begin. And once it came time, he lived more in rue Saint-Denis than in his Hôtel of Saint-Pol.

The fatal thing about these acted poems was that they continually added to and extended themselves, growing to tens of thousands of verses, so that ultimately the time in them was the actual time; somewhat as if one were to make a globe on the scale of the earth. The hollow platform, beneath which was hell and above which, attached to a pillar, the unrailed scaffolding of a balcony represented the level of Paradise, only helped to weaken the illusion. For this century had indeed made heaven and hell terrestial: it lived on the forces of both in order to survive itself.

These were the days of that Avignonese Christianity which, a generation earlier, had drawn together round John the Twenty-second with so much involuntary recourse to shelter that at the place of his pontificate, immediately after him, the mass of that palace had arisen, closed and ponderous, like some last body of refuge for the homeless soul of all. But he himself, the little, ethereal, spiritual old man, still lived in the open. When, but just arrived, he began without delay to act swiftly and concisely in every direction, dishes spiced with poison stood on his table; the first goblet had always to be poured away, for the piece of unicorn was discolored when the cupbearer drew it out again. In his uncertainty, not knowing where to conceal them, this septuagenarian carried about the wax images that had been made of him so that he should be destroyed in them; and he scratched himself on the long needles with which they had been transpierced. One could melt them down. But these secret simulacra had filled him with such terror that, against his own strong will, he repeatedly conceived the idea that he might thereby deal himself a mortal blow and vanish like the wax at the fire. His diminished frame became only more dry with this horror and more enduring. And now they even dared attack the body of his empire; from Granada the Jews had been incited to exterminate all Christians, and this time they had hired more terrible executioners. No one, from the first rumors, doubted the conspiracy of the lepers; already several people had seen them throwing bundles of their horrible decomposition into the wells. It was no gullibility, promptly to hold this possible; faith, on the contrary, had become so heavy that it dropped from those trembling creatures and fell down to the bottom of the wells. And once more the zealous old man had to keep poison from his blood. During his superstitious spells he had prescribed the Angelus for himself and his entourage against the demons of the twilight; and now throughout the whole agitated world this calming prayer was sounded every evening. But with this exception all the bulls and epistles that emanated from him were like spiced wine rather than any tisane. The empire had not trusted itself to his treatment; but he never tired of overwhelming it with evidences of its sickness, and from the farthest Orient already they were turning to consult this imperious physician.

But then the incredible happened. On All Saints' Day he had preached, longer, more fervently than usual; in some sudden need, as though to see it again himself, he had exhibited his faith; had lifted it slowly and with all his strength out of its eighty-five-year-old tabernacle and displayed it on the pulpit: and immediately they cried out at him. All Europe cried out: this was an evil faith.

Then the pope disappeared. For days no action issued from him; he remained on his knees in his oratory, and explored the secret of those who act and do harm to their souls. Finally he reappeared, exhausted by this difficult self-communion, and recanted. He recanted again and again. It became the senile passion of his spirit to recant. He would even have the cardinals wakened at night in order to converse with them about his repentance. And perhaps what extended his life beyond all bounds was in the end simply the hope of humbling himself before Napoleon Orsini, too, who hated him and who would not come.

Jacob of Cahors had recanted. And one might think God himself had wished to show him his error, since he so soon after let that son of the Count de Ligny come up, who seemed to await his coming-of-age on earth only that he might share heaven's sensuous delights of the soul in all his virility. Many were alive who remembered this radiant youth in the days of his cardinalate, and recalled how on the threshold of his young manhood he had become a bishop and had died when scarcely eighteen in an ecstasy of his consummation. One met people who had been dead; for around his tomb the air, in which sheer life lay freed, wrought long upon the corpses. But was there not something desperate even in that precocious sanctity? Was it not an injustice to all that the pure fabric of this soul should have been no more than drawn through life, as if only to dye it brightly in the boiling scarlet vat of that time? Did they not feel something like a counter-blow when this young prince sprang off from earth into his passionate ascension? Why did not these shining ones abide among the laborious candlemakers? Was it not this darkness that had led John the Twenty-second to affirm that *before* the last judgment there could be no complete beatitude, not anywhere, even among the blessed? And indeed, how much stubborn tenacity was required to imagine that, while here such dense confusion reigned, somewhere there were faces already basking in the light of God, reclining upon angels and assuaged by the inexhaustible sight of him.

Here I sit in the cold night, writing, and I know all this. I know it, perhaps, because I met that man once when I was little. He was very tall; indeed, I believe his height must have been striking.

Unlikely though it seems, I had somehow managed to escape from the house alone, toward evening; I was running, I turned the corner of a street, and at the same instant I collided with him. I do not see how what now happened could take place within some five seconds. However compactly one tells it, it lasts much longer. I had hurt myself in running against him; I was small, it seemed a good deal to me that I was not crying. Also I was involuntarily expecting to be comforted. As he did nothing, I took it that he was embarrassed; I supposed that he could not find the right pleasantry to unravel the situation. I was happy enough by then to help him at it, but for that it was necessary to look him in the face. I have said that he was tall. Now he had not bent over me, as would have been natural, with the result that he stood at a height for which I was not prepared. Before me there was still nothing but the smell and the peculiar roughness of his suit, which I had felt. Suddenly his face appeared. What was it like? I do not know, I don't want to know. It was the face of a foe. And beside that face, close beside it, on the level of his terrible eyes, like a second head, was his fist. Ere I had time to lower my own face, I was already running; I dodged past him on the left and ran straight down an empty, horrible alley, an alley of a foreign town, of a town in which nothing is ever forgiven.

That time I experienced what I now comprehend: that heavy, massive, desperate age. The age in which the kiss of reconciliation between two men was only a signal for the murderers who were standing round. They drank from the same cup, they mounted the same saddle-horse before the eyes of all, and it was spread abroad that they would sleep in the same bed at night: and at all these contacts their aversion to one another became so strong that whenever one of them saw the pulsing veins of the other, a sickly disgust made him pull back as at sight of a toad. The age in which brother attacked brother and held him prisoner, for the sake of his larger share of their inheritance; the king, indeed, intervened on behalf of the ill-used brother and secured him his freeedom and possessions; taken up with other more distant adventures, the elder brother granted him peace and in letters repented of his injustice. But all this prevented the released brother from regaining his composure. The century shows him in pilgrim's habit going from church to church, inventing ever more curious vows. Hung with amulets, he whispers his apprehensions to the monks of Saint Denis, and for long there stood inscribed in their registers the hundred-pound wax candle he thought good to dedicate to Saint Louis. He never came to a life of his own; until the end he felt his brother's envy and anger as a grimacing constellation over his heart. And that Count de Foix, Gaston Phoebus, admired of all, had he not openly killed his cousin Ernault, the English king's captain at Lourdes? But what was that manifest murder compared to the terrible incident of his not having put aside the sharp little nail-knife, when in quivering reproach he touched with his famously beautiful hand against the naked throat of his son lying on the bed? The room was dark, light had to be brought to see this blood that had come from so far and was now leaving a noble race for ever, as it secretly issued from the tiny wound of this exhausted boy.

Who could be strong and refrain from murder? Who in that age did not know that the worst was inevitable? Here and there a man, whose eyes had during the day encountered the relishing glance of his murderer, would be overtaken by a strange presentiment. He would withdraw and shut himself up, finish writing out his will, and finally order the litter of osier twigs, the cowl of the Celestines, and the strewing of ashes. Foreign minstrels would appear before his castle, and he would give them princely rewards for their voice that was at one with his vague forebodings. There was doubt in the eyes of his dogs as they looked up at him, and they became less sure in their begging. From the device that had counted a whole life long, there quietly emerged a secondary meaning, new and clear. Many long-established customs appeared antiquated, but no substitutes for them seemed to be forming any more. If projects came up, one dealt with them on the whole without really believing in them; on the other hand, certain memories took on an unexpected finality. Evenings, by the fire, one meant to abandon oneself to them, but the night outside, which one no longer knew, became suddenly very loud in one's hearing. One's ear, accustomed to so many free or dangerous nights, distinguished separate pieces of the silence. And yet it was different this time. Not the night between yesterday and today: a night. Night. Beau Sire Dieu, and then the resurrection. Scarcely could the glorifying of some loved woman penetrate into such hours: they were all masked under aubes and saluts d'amour; had become incomprehensible under long, trailing, pompous names. At most, in the dark, like the full, womanly upward glance of a bastard son.

And then, before late supper this pensive consideration of the hands in the silver washbasin. One's own hands. Could any coherence be brought into what was theirs? any sequence, any continuity in grasping and refraining? No. All men attempted part and counterpart. They all neutralized one another, action there was none.

There was no action except at the mission brothers'. The king, when he had seen how they bore themselves in their acting, himself devised the charter for them. He addressed them as "his dear brothers"; never had anyone so affected him. They were accorded literal permission to go about among the laity as the characters they represented; for the king desired nothing more than that they should contaminate many and sweep them into their own vigorous action, in which there was order. For himself, he longed to learn from them. Did he not wear, just as they did, symbols and garments that had significance? When he watched them, he could believe it must be possible to learn this: how to come and go, how to speak out and turn away, in a manner that left no doubt. Vast hopes flooded his heart. In this hall in the Hospital of the Trinity, so restlessly lighted and so strangely indefinite, he sat every day in his best seat, standing up in his excitement, intent and wary as a school-boy. Others wept; but he was full inside with shining tears and only pressed his cold hands together in order to endure it. Occasionally at critical moments, when an actor who had done speaking stepped suddenly out of the range of his wide glance, he lifted his face and was afraid: how long now had He been present, Monseigneur Saint Michael, up there, advanced to the edge of the scaffolding in his mirroring armor of silver?

At such moments he sat up. He looked about him as though meditating a decision. He was very near to understanding the counterpart of this acting here: the great, fearful, profane passion, in which he was playing. But suddenly it was over. Everybody moved in meaningless fashion. Open torches advanced upon him, and formless shadows flung themselves into the vaulting above. Men whom he did not know were pulling at him. He wanted to take part in the play; but from his lips nothing came, his movements yielded no gestures. They pressed so strangely round him, the idea came to him that he ought to be carrying the cross. And he wanted to wait for them to bring it. But they were stronger than he, and they shoved him slowly out.

Outside much has changed. I don't know how. But inside and before you, O my God, inside before you, spectator, are we not without action? We discover, indeed, that we do not know our part, we look for a mirror, we want to rub off the make-up and remove the counterfeit and be real. But somewhere a bit of mummery still sticks to us that we forget. A trace of exaggeration remains in our eyebrows, we do not notice that the corners of our lips are twisted. And thus we go about, a laughing-stock, a mere half-thing: neither existing, nor actors.

It was in the theatre at Orange. Without really looking up, merely conscious of the rustic fracture that now forms its façade, I had entered by the attendant's little glass door. I found myself among prone column-bodies and small mallow shrubs; but they hid from me only for a moment the open shell of the sloping auditorium, which lay there, divided by the afternoon shadows, like a gigantic concave sundial. I advanced quickly toward it. I felt, as I mounted between the rows of seats, how I diminished in these surroundings. A little higher up a few visitors, unequally distributed, were standing about in idle curiosity; their clothes were unpleasantly evident, but their size made them scarcely worth mentioning. For a while they looked at me, wondering at my littleness. That made me turn round.

Oh, I was completely unprepared. A play was on. An immense, a superhuman drama was in progress, the drama of that powerful backdrop, the vertical articulation of which appeared, tripartite, resonant with grandeur, annihilating almost, and suddenly measured in its sheer immensity.

I sat down with a shock of amazed pleasure. This which towered before me, with its shadows ordered in the semblance of a face, with the darkness gathered in the mouth of its centre, bounded, up there, by the symmetrically curling hairdress of the cornice: this was the strong, all-covering antique mask, behind which the world condensed into a face. Here, in this great incurved amphitheatre of seats, there reigned a life of expectancy, void, absorbent: all happening was yonder: gods and destiny; and thence (when one looked, up high) came lightly, over the wall's rim: the eternal entry of the heavens.

That hour, I realize now, shut me for ever out of our theatres. What should I do there? What should I do before a stage on which this wall (the icon-screen of the Russian churches) has been pulled down, because one no longer has the strength to press the action, gas-like, through its hardness, to issue forth in full, heavy oil-drops? Now plays fall in lumps through the holes torn in the coarse sieve of our stages, and collect in heaps and are swept away when we have had enough. It is the same underdone reality that litters our streets and our houses, save that more of it collects there than can be put into one evening.

* (Let us be honest about it, then; we have no theatre, any more than we have a God: for this, community is needed. Everyone has his own special inspirations and misgivings, and he allows his fellow-man to see as much of them as serves him and suits him. We continually dilute our understanding, so that it may reach, instead of crying out for the wall of a common need, behind which the inscrutable would have time to gather and to brace itself.)

Had we a theatre, would you, tragic one, stand there again and again—so slight, so bare, so without pretext of a role—before those who rejoice their hurried curiosity at your exhibited grief? You, so unutterably touching, foresaw the reality of your own suffering, that time in Verona, when, almost a child still, you just held many roses before your face, as a masklike front-view that should the more intensely conceal you.

It is true you were an actor's child, and when your people played they wanted to be seen; but you did not run true. This profession was to become for you what, without her suspecting it, nunhood was for Marianna Alcoforado: a disguise, thick and durable enough to let one be unrestrainedly miserable behind it, with the ardor with which the invisible blessed are blissful. In all the cities you came to they described that gesture of yours; but they did not understand how, from day to day more hopeless, again and again you lifted up a poem before you, hoping it would hide you. You held your hair, your hands, or any other opaque object, before the translucent passages. You dimmed with your breath those that were transparent; you made yourself small; you hid as children hide, and then you raised that brief, happy cry—and only an angel should

---

* Written on the margin of the MS.

have been allowed to look for you. But if then you cautiously glanced up, there was no doubt that they had seen you all the time, everybody in that hateful, hollow, peering hall: you, you, you, and nothing but you.

And it came to you to hold your arm foreshortened toward them with the finger-sign that wards off the evil eye. It came to you to snatch your face from them, on which they preyed. It came to you to be yourself. Your fellow-actors' courage failed; as if they had been caged with a pantheress, they crept along the wings and spoke what they had to, only not to irritate you. But you drew them forward, and you posed them and dealt with them as if they were real. Those limp doors, those simulated curtains, those objects that had no reverse side, drove you to protest. You felt how your heart intensified unceasingly toward an immense reality and, frightened, you tried once more to take people's gaze off you like long gossamer threads—: but now, in their fear of the worst, they were already breaking into applause: as though at the last moment to ward off something that would compel them to change their life.

Those who are loved live poorly and in danger. Ah, that they might surmount themselves and become lovers. Around those who love is sheer security. No one casts suspicion on them any more, and they themselves are not in a position to betray themselves. In them the secret has grown inviolate, they cry it out whole, like nightingales, it is undivided. They make lament for one alone, but the whole of nature unites with them: it is the lament for one who is eternal. They hurl themselves after him they have lost, but even with their first steps they overtake him, and before them is only God. Theirs is the legend of Byblis, who pursued Caunus as far as Lycia. The urge of her heart drove her through many lands upon his track, and at last she came to the end of her strength; but so strong was the mobility of her nature that, sinking to earth, she reappeared beyond her death as a spring, hurrying on, as a hurrying spring.

What else happened to the Portuguese nun, save that inwardly she became a spring? Or to you, Heloïse? To you all, lovers, whose laments have come down to us: Gaspara Stampa; Countess of Die and Clara d'Anduze; Louise Labbé, Marceline Desbordes, Elisa

Mercoeur? But you, poor fleeing Aïssé, you began to hesitate and you gave in. Weary Julie Lespinasse! Disconsolate story of the happy park: Marie-Anne de Clermont!

I still remember exactly, one day long ago, at home, I found a jewel-casket. It was two handsbreadths large, fan-shaped with a border of flowers stamped into the dark-green morocco. I opened it: it was empty. I can say this now after so many years. But at the time, when I had opened it, I saw only in what its emptiness consisted: in velvet, in a little mound of light-colored, no longer fresh velvet; in the jewel-groove, which, empty, and lighter by a trace of melancholy, disappeared into it. For an instant this was endurable. But to those who, being beloved, remain behind, it is perhaps always like this.

Leaf back in your diaries. Was there not always a time around spring when the bursting year struck you as a reproach? A desire to be glad was in you, and yet, when you stepped out into the spacious open, an astonishment arose outside in the air, and you became uncertain in your progress, as on a ship. The garden was beginning; but you (that was it), you dragged into it winter and the year that had passed; for you it was at best but a continuation. While you waited for your soul to take part, you suddenly felt the weight of your limbs, and something like the possibility of becoming ill invaded your open presentiment. You blamed your too light dress, you threw your shawl round your shoulders, you ran up to the end of the drive: and then you stood, with beating heart, in the wide turnaround, determined to be at one with all this. But a bird sang and was alone and denied you. Alas, should you have been dead?

Perhaps. Perhaps it is new, our surviving these: the year and love. Blossoms and fruit are ripe when they fall; animals are self-aware and find each other and are content with this. But we, who have undertaken God, can never finish. We keep putting off our nature, we need more time. What is a year to us? What all the years? Before we have even begun God, we are already praying to him: let us survive this night. And then the being ill. And then love.

That Clémence de Bourges should have had to die in her dawn. She who had not her peer; among the instruments she knew how to play as no one else could, the loveliest, unforgettably played even in the least tone of her voice. So loftily resolute was her maiden-hood that a girl-lover in her flooding love could dedicate to this upsurging heart the book of sonnets in which every verse was in-satiate. Louise Labbé was not afraid of frightening this child with the long-suffering of love. She revealed to her the nightly mount-ing of desire; she promised her pain like a more spacious universe; and she guessed that she herself, with her experienced woe, fell short of that, so darkly expected, because of which this adolescent girl was beautiful.

Girls in my native land. May the loveliest of you on an after-noon in summer in the darkened library find herself the little book that Jan des Tournes printed in 1556. May she take the cooling, glossy volume out with her into the murmurous orchard, or yonder to the phlox, in whose oversweet fragrance there lies a sediment of sheer sweetness. May she find it early. In the days when her eyes begin to be watchful, while her mouth, being younger, is still able to bite off much too big pieces of an apple and be full.

And then, when the time for more mobile friendships comes, may it be your secret, girls, to call one another Dika and Anactoria, Gyrinno and Atthis. May someone, a neighbor perhaps, an older man who has travelled in his youth and has long been counted an eccentric, reveal these names to you. May he invite you to his house sometimes, to taste his famous peaches or to inspect, up in the white corridor, his Ridinger engravings illustrating equitation, which are so much talked about that one ought to have seen them.

Perhaps you will persuade him to tell you things. Perhaps among you is the one who can induce him to bring out his old travel-diaries; who knows? The same who will someday manage to make him tell about fragmentary passages of Sappho's poems having come down to us, and who will not rest until she knows what is almost a secret: that this secluded man loved now and again to employ his leisure in translating these bits of verse. He has to admit that, for a long time now, he has not given it a thought, and what there is on hand, he declares, is not worth mentioning. Yet he is glad now to say a stanza for these ingenuous friends, if they press him hard. He even discovers the Greek text in his memory, and recites it, because the translation, to his mind, does not give it, and in order to show the young people this fracture, beautiful and authentic, of the massive ornamental language that was wrought in so intense a flame.

All this warms him again to his work. Lovely, almost youthful evenings come for him, autumn evenings, for example, that have much silent night before them. Then the light burns late in his study. He does not always remain bent over his pages; he often leans back and closes his eyes over a line he has been reading again, and its meaning spreads through his blood. Never before has he been so certain of antiquity. He could almost smile at the generations that have mourned it as a lost play in which they would have liked to act. Now he instantaneously grasps the dynamic significance of that early world-unity, which was something like a new and simultaneous assumption of all human work. It does not trouble him that that consistent civilization, with its almost total visualization, seemed to many later eyes to form a whole, and that whole wholly past. There, it is true, the celestial half of life was really fitted against the halfround bowl of terrestial existence, as two full hemispheres connect to form a perfect orb of gold. Yet scarcely had this occurred, when the spirits confined within it felt this utter realization to be no more than allegory; the massive star lost weight and rose into space, and in its golden sphere the sadness was reflected, hesitant, of that which could not yet be mastered.

As he thinks this, the recluse in his night, thinks it and understands, he notices a plate with fruit on the window-seat. Involuntarily he takes an apple from it and lays it before him on the table. How my life stands round about this fruit, he thinks. Around all that is finished that which has still to be done rises and takes increase.

And then, beyond the not yet done, there comes up before him, almost too quickly, that slight figure straining out into the infinite, which (according to Galen's testimony) they all meant when they said: the poetess. For as after the labors of Heracles destruction and changing of the world stood up, demanding, so from the stocks of existence all the ecstasies and despairs with which the ages have to manage pressed, in order to be lived, toward the deeds of her heart.

Suddenly he knows this resolute heart that was ready to achieve to the end the whole of love. It does not surprise him that people misconstrued this heart; that in this lover, so altogether of the future, they saw only excess, not the new unit of measure for love and heart's distress. That they interpreted her life's epigraph as it happened to be credible at that time; that finally they ascribed to her the death of those whom the god incites singly, to love out of their own selves, without return. Perhaps even among the girl-lovers whom she molded there were some who did not understand: how at the height of her action she mourned not for any man who had left her embrace empty, but for the one, no longer possible, who had grown equal to her love.

Here he rises from his meditations and goes to his window; his high room is too close to him, he would like to see stars, if that is possible. He has no delusions about himself. He knows that this emotion fills him because among the young girls of his neighborhood there is the one who matters to him. He has wishes (not for himelf, no, but for her); on her account he understands, in a nocturnal hour that is passing, the exigence of love. He promises himself to tell her nothing of it. It seems to him the utmost he can do is to be alone and wakeful and on her account to think how right that lover had been: when she knew that nothing can be meant by union save increased loneliness; when she broke through the temporal aim of sex with its infinite purpose; when in the darkness of embracing she delved not for satisfaction but for longing. When she disdained one of two being the lover and one beloved, and at her own self kindled to lovers that left her those feeble beloved ones whom she bore to her couch. By such lofty farewells her heart became part of nature. Above fate she sang her last year's favorites their epithalamia; exalted their nuptials for them; magnified the coming bridegroom, so that they should prepare themselves for him as for a god and survive *his* splendor, too.

O nce more, Abelone, in these last years I sensed you and understood you, unexpectedly, after I had long ceased to think of you.

It was at Venice, in autumn, in one of those salons where foreigners, passing, gather round the lady of the house, who is foreign as they are. These people stand about with their cups of tea and are delighted whenever a well-informed fellow-guest turns them swiftly and surreptitiously toward the door, to whisper a name that sounds Venetian. They are prepared for the most extravagant names, nothing can surprise them; for thrifty as they may otherwise be in experience, in this city they abandon themselves nonchalantly to the most exaggerated possibilities. In their customary existence they constantly confound the extraordinary with the forbidden, so that the expectation of something wonderful, which they now permit themselves, appears in their faces as an expression of coarse licentiousness. What at home happens to them just momentarily in concerts or when they are alone with a novel, they openly exhibit as a legitimate condition in these flattering surroundings. Just as they let themselves, quite unprepared and unaware of danger, be stimulated by the almost fatal avowals of music as by physical indiscretions, so without in the least mastering the existence of Venice they abandon themselves to the rewarding swoon of gondolas. No longer newly married couples, who during their whole trip have had only ill-natured rejoinders for one another, sink into silent accord; the husband is overcome with the agreeable weariness of his ideals, while she feels young again and nods encouragingly to the lazy natives, smiling as if she had teeth of sugar that were continually melting. And if one listens, it appears that they are leaving tomorrow or the day after or at the end of the week.

So I stood there among them and rejoiced that I was not going away. Soon it would be cold. The soft and opiate Venice of their prejudices and demands disappears with these somnolent foreigners, and one morning the other Venice is there, the real one, awake, brittle to the breaking point, and not in the least imaginary: this Venice, willed in the midst of the void on sunken forests, enforced and in the end so extant, through and through. This hardened body, stripped to necessities, through which the sleepless arsenal drove the blood of its toil, and this body's penetrating spirit, continually expanding, stronger than the fragrance of aromatic lands. This resourceful state, that bartered the salt and glass of its poverty for the treasures of the nations. This beautiful counterpoise of the world, which even in its ornaments stands full of latent energies ever more finely ramified—: this Venice.

The awareness that I knew this city overcame me among all these self-deluding people with such a sense of opposition, that I looked up, wondering how I could unburden myself. Was it thinkable that in these great rooms there was not one person who unconsciously waited for enlightenment upon the nature of these surroundings? Some young person, who would at once understand that here no mere enjoyment was being opened up, but an example of will more exacting and severe than could be found elsewhere? I moved about; this truth of mine made me restless. Since it had seized me here among so many people, it brought with it the desire to be expressed, defended, demonstrated. The grotesque notion arose in me to clap my hands next moment in hate against all their gabbled misunderstanding.

In this ridiculous mood I noticed her. She was standing alone before a bright window, observing me; not precisely with her eyes, which were serious and thoughtful, but, one would have said, with her mouth, which ironically imitated the obviously angry expression of my face. I felt at once the impatient tension of my features and assumed an indifferent look, whereupon her mouth became natural and haughty. Then, after an instant's reflection, we smiled to each other simultaneously.

She reminded me, if you will, of a certain youthful portrait of the beautiful Benedicte von Qualen, who plays a part in Baggesen's life. One could not see the dark calm of her eyes without guessing the clear darkness of her voice. Furthermore, the plaiting of her hair and the way her light dress was cut out at the neck were so Copenhaguesque, that I made up my mind to address her in Danish.

But I was not yet near enough to do so, when a stream of people pressed toward her from the other side; our guest-happy countess, warm, enthusiastic and scatter-brained, with a number of supporters, flung herself upon the young girl, intending to carry her off on the spot to sing. I was sure she would excuse herself on the ground that nobody there could possibly be interested in hearing someone sing in Danish. And this she did, when they allowed her to reply at all. The throng around the light figure became more urgent; someone knew that she also sang German. "And Italian, too," a laughing voice added with malicious conviction. I knew of no excuse I might have wished for her, but I did not doubt that she would hold out. Already an expression of dry mortification was overspreading the importuners' faces, tired with too prolonged smiling; already the good countess, to preserve her importance, had stepped back a pace with an air of pity and dignity—and then, when it was altogether unnecessary, she consented. I felt myself paling with disappointment; my gaze filled with reproach, but I turned away; there was no use letting her see that. She freed herself from the others, however, and was suddenly beside me. Her dress shone upon me, the flowery perfume of her warmth was about me.

"I am really going to sing," she said in Danish, along my cheek, "not because they demand it, nor for appearance' sake, but because at this moment I must sing."

Through her words broke the same irritated impatience from which she had just delivered me.

I slowly followed the group with whom she moved away. But near a high door I remained behind, allowing people to move about and arrange themselves. I leaned against the black-mirroring doorway and waited. Someone asked what was going on, whether there was to be singing. I pretended I did not know. As I told the lie, she had already begun to sing.

I could not see her. Space gradually formed around one of those Italian songs foreigners consider so very genuine because they are of such manifest conventionality. She, singing it, did not believe in it. She lifted it up with effort; she took it much too heavily. By the applause in front, one could note when it was over. I was sad and ashamed. People began to move about, and I decided that when anybody left, I would join them.

But then suddenly all was still. A silence fell which a moment ago no one would have thought possible; it lasted, it grew more tense, and now arose in it that voice. (Abelone, I thought. Abelone.) This time it was strong, full and yet not heavy; of one piece, without rent, without seam. She sang an unknown German song. She sang it with singular simplicity, like something necessary. She sang:

> "You, whom I do not tell that in the night
> I lie weeping,
> whose being makes me weary
> like a cradle,
> you, who do not tell me when you lie wakeful
> for my sake:

how if we should endure
this glory in us
without assuaging?"

(short pause, then hesitating:)

"Look at those who are lovers,
when avowal has once begun
how soon they lie."

Again the silence. God knows who made it. Then the people
stirred, jostled one another, apologized, coughed. They were about
to pass over into a general obliterating hubbub, when suddenly the
voice broke out, resolute, broad and intense:

"You make me alone. Only you can I interchange.
A while it is you, then again it is a murmuring,
or it is a fragrance with no trace.
Alas, in my arms I have lost them all,
only you, you are born always again:
because I never held you close, I hold you forever."

No one had expected it. They all stood as if bowed beneath
that voice. And in the end there was an assurance in her so great
that it seemed she had known for years that at that moment she
would have to start singing.

I had sometimes wondered why Abelone did not use the calories
of her magnificent feeling on God. I know she yearned to re-
move from her love all that was transitive, but could her truthful
heart be deceived about God's being only a direction of love, not
an object of love? Didn't she know that she need fear no return
from him? Didn't she know the restraint of this superior beloved,
who quietly defers delight in order to let us, slow as we are, ac-
complish our whole heart? Or did she want to avoid Christ? Did
she fear to be delayed by him halfway, and by this to become a
beloved? Was that why she did not like to think of Julie Reven-
tlow?

I almost believe so, when I recall how a lover as simple as Mechthild, as passionate as Theresa of Avila, as wounded as Blessed Rose of Lima, could sink back, yielding, yet beloved, upon this alleviation of God. Alas, he who was a succour for the weak is to these strong souls a wrong: when they were expecting nothing more but the endless road, once again, in the suspense of heaven's gate, a palpable figure comes to meet them, pampering them with shelter and bewildering them with virility. The lens of his vigorously refracting heart once again assembles their already parallel heart-rays, and they, whom the angels were now hoping to keep intact for God, flame up in the aridity of their longing.

*(To be loved means to be consumed. To love is to give light with inexhaustible oil. To be loved is to pass away, to love is to endure.)

It is nevertheless possible that Abelone attempted in later years to think with her heart, in order to come inconspicuously and directly into relation with God. I can imagine that there are letters of hers which recall the attentive inward contemplation of Princess Amalie Galitzin; but if these letters were addressed to someone to whom for years she had been close, how must he have suffered from the transformation in her. And she herself: I suspect she feared nothing but that spectral changing which one does not notice because one constantly lets slip all evidences for it as entirely unconnected with oneself.

It will be difficult to persuade me that the story of the Prodigal Son is not the legend of him who did not want to be loved. When he was a child, everybody in the house loved him. He grew up knowing nothing else and came to feel at home in their softness of heart, when he was a child.

But as a boy he sought to lay aside such habits. He could not have put it into words, but when he wandered about outside all day and did not even want to have the dogs along, it was because they too loved him; because in their glances there was observation and sympathy, expectancy and solicitude; because even in their presence one could do nothing without gladdening or giving pain. But what he meant in those days was that profound indifference

---

* Written on the margin of the MS.

of his heart, which sometimes, of an early morning in the fields, seized him with such purity that he began to run, in order to have neither time nor breath to be more than an airy moment in which the morning comes to consciousness.

The secret of that life of his which never yet had been, spread out before him. Involuntarily he forsook the footpath and ran on into the fields, with arms outstretched, as if in this wide reach he could master several directions at once. And then he would throw himself down behind some hedge, and mattered to no one. He peeled himself a willow flute, flung a stone at some little wild animal, bent over and compelled a beetle to turn round: all this became no destiny, and the skies passed on as over nature. At last came afternoon with all its inspirations; one was a buccaneer on the island of Tortuga, and there was no obligation in being that; one besieged Campêche, one took Vera Cruz by storm; it was possible to be the whole army or a commander on horseback or a ship on the ocean, according to the way one felt. But if it entered one's head to kneel, then swiftly one became Deodatus of Gozon and had slain the dragon and, learned, all hot, that this heroism was arrogant, without obedience. For one spared oneself nothing that belonged to the business. But however numerous the imaginings that came to one, in between there was always time to be nothing but a bird, uncertain what kind. Only then came the return home.

Heavens, how much there was then to cast off and forget; for it was necessary to forget thoroughly; otherwise one betrayed oneself when they pressed one. However one lingered and looked about, the gable always did loom up at last. The first window up there kept its eye on one; somebody might very well be standing there. The dogs, in whom expectation had been growing all day, scurried through the bushes and drove one together into the person they believed one to be. And the house did the rest. Once one entered into the full smell of it, most things were already decided. Details might still be changed; in the main one was the person for whom they took one here; the person for whom, out of his little past and their own wishes, they had long fashioned a life; the creature belonging to them all, who stood day and night under the suggestion of their love, between their hope and their suspicion, before their blame or praise.

Useless for such a person to go upstairs with indescribable caution. They will all be in the sittingroom, and if the door merely opens they will look his way. He remains in the dark, he wants to wait for their questioning. But then comes the worst. They take him by the hands, they draw him toward the table, and all of them, as many as are present, stretch inquisitively into the lamplight. They have the best of it; they keep in the shadow, while on him alone falls, with the light, all the shame of having a face.

Shall he stay, imitating with a lie the vague life they ascribe to him, and grow to resemble them all in his every feature? Shall he divide himself between the delicate truthfulness of his will and the clumsy deceit that spoils it for himself? Shall he give up trying to become the thing that might hurt those of his family who have nothing left but a weak heart?

No, he will go away. For example, while they are all busy setting out on his birthday table those badly conceived gifts meant, once again, to compensate for everything. Go away for ever. Not until long afterward was it to become clear to him how much he had then intended never to love, in order not to put anyone in the terrible position of being loved. It occurred to him years later and, like other projects, this too had been impossible. For he had loved and loved again in his solitude; each time with waste of his whole nature and with unspeakable fear for the liberty of the other. Slowly he learned to penetrate the beloved object with the rays of his feeling, instead of consuming it in them. And he was spoiled by the fascination of recognizing through the ever more transparent form of his beloved, the expanses it opened to his desire infinitely to possess.

How he could weep for nights then with yearning to be himself penetrated by such rays. But a woman loved, who yields, is still far from being a woman who loves. O disconsolate nights, when he received back again his flooding gifts, in pieces, heavy with transience. How he thought then of the troubadours who feared nothing more than being answered. All his money, acquired and increased, he gave in order not to experience this too. He hurt them with his gross paying, anxious from day to day lest they try to enter into his love. For he no longer had hope of experiencing the lover who should pierce him.

Even at the time when poverty terrified him daily with new hardnesses, when his head was the favorite toy of misery and utterly worn bare, when ulcers opened all over his body like auxiliary eyes against the blackness of tribulation, when he shuddered at the rubbish upon which he had been abandoned because he himself was like it: even then still, when he reflected, his greatest terror was lest anyone should respond to him. What were all obscurities since, compared to the opaque sadness of those embraces in which everything lost itself? Did one not wake feeling one had no future? Did one not go about, meaningless, without right to any danger whatever? Had not one had a hundred times to promise not to die? Perhaps it was the stubbornness of this bitter memory, which wanted to keep itself a place to return to again and again, that made his life endure amid the refuse. Finally he was found again. And not till then, not till his shepherd years, did all his past find calm.

Who shall describe what befell him then? What poet has the persuasiveness to reconcile the length of the days he now lived with the brevity of life? What art is vast enough to evoke simultaneously his slight, cloaked figure and the whole high spaciousness of his gigantic nights?

That was the time which began with his feeling of being general, anonymous, like a slowly recovering convalescent. He did not love, unless it were that he loved to be. The lowly affection of his sheep lay not too close to him; like light falling through clouds it dispersed about him and shimmered softly on the meadows. In the innocent track of their hunger he strode silently over the pastures of the world. Strangers saw him on the Acropolis, and perhaps he was for a long time one of the shepherds in Les Baux, and saw petrified time outlast that lofty race which, with all the conquests of seven and three, could not get the better of the sixteen rays of its own star. Or should I imagine him at Orange, resting against the rustic triumphal arch? Should I see him in the soul-accustomed shade of Aliscamps as, among graves that stand open like the graves of the resurrected, his eyes pursue a dragon-fly?

It is all the same. I see more than himself: I see his life, which at that time began its long love to God, that silent, aimless labor. For over him, who had wanted to withhold himself for always, there came once more the growing and undeviating urge of his heart. And this time he hoped to be answered. His whole nature, grown prescient and poised while he had been so long alone, promised

him that he whom he now meant, knew how to love with pene-
trating, radiant love. But while he longed to be loved at last in so
masterly a way, his senses, accustomed to far distances, grasped
the extreme remoteness of God. Nights came when he thought to
fling himself toward him into space; hours full of discovery, when
he felt strong enough to dive for the earth and pull it upward on
the storm tide of his heart. He was like one who hears a glorious
language and feverishly conceives plans to write, to create in it. He
had still to experience the dismay of learning how difficult this
language was; he was unwilling to believe at first that a long life
could pass away in forming the first short fictitious phrases that
have no sense. He flung himself into this study like a runner into
a race; but the density of what had to be mastered slowed him up.
Nothing more humiliating could be thought out than this appren-
ticeship. He had found the philosopher's stone, and now he was
being forced ceaselessly to transmute the swiftly made gold of his
happiness into the lumpy lead of patience. He, who had adapted
himself to space, like a worm traced crooked passages without outlet
or direction. Now that with so much labor and sorrow he was
learning to love, it was shown him how trivial and careless up to
now all the love had been which he thought to have achieved. How
none of it could have come to anything, because he had not begun
to work at it and make it real.

During those years the great changes were going on in him. He
almost forgot God over the hard work of drawing near him, and
all that he hoped perhaps to attain with him in time was "sa pa-
tience de supporter une âme." The accidents of fate, which men
hold important, had long ago deserted him, but now even what-
ever of pleasure and pain were necessary lost their spicy by-taste
and became pure and nourishing for him. From the roots of his
being developed the sturdy, evergreen plant of a fertile joy. He be-
came wholly engrossed in learning to master what constituted his
inner life; he wanted to omit nothing, for he did not doubt that
his love was in all this and growing. Indeed, his inward composure
went so far that he resolved to retrieve the most important of the
things he had hitherto been unable to accomplish, those that had
simply been waited through. He thought above all of his child-
hood, and, the more calmly he reflected, the more unachieved did
it seem to him; all its memories had about them the vagueness of

premonitions, and their counting as past made them almost future. To take all this once more, and this time really, upon himself—this was the reason he, the estranged, turned home. We do not know whether he remained; we only know that he came back.

Those who have told the story try at this point to remind us of the house as it then was; for there only a short time has passed, a little counted time, everyone in the house can say how much. The dogs have grown old, but they are still alive. It is reported that one of them let out a howl. An interruption cuts through the whole day's work. Faces appear at the windows, faces that have aged and faces that have grown up, touching in their resemblance. And in one quite old face recognition suddenly breaks through, pale. Recognition? Really only recognition?—Forgiveness. Forgiveness of what?—Love. My God: love.

He, the recognized, had not even been thinking, preoccupied as he was, that love could still exist. It is easy to understand how, of all that now happened, only this should have been transmitted to us: his gesture, the incredible gesture that had never before been seen—the gesture of supplication with which he threw himself at their feet, imploring them not to love. Scared and wavering, they lifted him to themselves. They interpreted his outburst in their own fashion, forgiving. It must have been an indescribable release for him that, despite the desperate evidence of his attitude, they all misunderstood him. Probably he was able to remain. For he recognized more clearly from day to day that the love of which they were so vain and to which they secretly encouraged one another, had nothing to do with him. He almost had to smile at their exertions, and it became clear how little they could have him in mind.

What did they know of him? He was now terribly difficult to love, and he felt that One alone was able for the task. But He was not yet willing.

END OF THE NOTEBOOKS

Translated by M. D. Herter Norton

Das Stunden-Buch

Das Buch vom mönchischen Leben

1

Da neigt sich die Stunde und rührt mich an
mit klarem, metallenem Schlag:
mir zittern die Sinne. Ich fühle: ich kann—
und ich fasse den plastischen Tag.

Nichts war noch vollendet, eh ich es erschaut,
ein jedes Werden stand still
Meine Blicke sind reif, und wie eine Braut
kommt jedem das Ding, das er will.

Nichts ist mir zu klein, und ich lieb es trotzdem
und mal' es auf Goldgrund und groß
und halte es hoch, und weiß nicht wem
löst es die Seele los . . .

2

Ich lebe mein Leben in wachsenden Ringen,
die sich über die Dinge ziehn.
Ich werde den letzten vielleicht nicht vollbringen,
aber versuchen will ich ihn.

The Book of Hours

First Book: The Book of the Monastic Life

1

With strokes that ring clear and metallic, the hour
to touch me bends down on its way:
my senses are quivering. I feel I've the power—
and I seize on the pliable day.

Not a thing was complete till by me it was eyed,
every kind of becoming stood still.
Now my glances are ripe and there comes like a bride
to each of them just what it will.

There's nothing so small but I love it and choose
to paint it gold-groundly and great
and hold it most precious and know not whose
soul it may liberate . . .

2

I live in expanding rings that are weaving
over these things below.
The last, perhaps, is beyond my achieving,
I'll make an attempt at it though.

Ich kreise um Gott, um den uralten Turm,
und ich kreise jahrtausendelang;
und ich weiß noch nicht: bin ich ein Falke, ein Sturm
oder ein großer Gesang.

6

Du, Nachbar Gott, wenn ich dich manches Mal
in langer Nacht mit hartem Klopfen störe,—
so ists, weil ich dich selten atmen höre
und weiß: Du bist allein im Saal.
Und wenn du etwas brauchst, ist keiner da,
um deinem Tasten einen Trank zu reichen:
ich horche immer. Gib ein kleines Zeichen.
Ich bin ganz nah.

Nur eine schmale Wand ist zwischen uns,
durch Zufall; denn es könnte sein:
ein Rufen deines oder meines Munds—
und sie bricht ein
ganz ohne Lärm und Laut.

Aus deinen Bildern ist sie aufgebaut.

Und deine Bilder stehn vor dir wie Namen.
Und wenn einmal das Licht in mir entbrennt,
mit welchem meine Tiefe dich erkennt,
vergeudet sichs als Glanz auf ihren Rahmen.

Und meine Sinne, welche schnell erlahmen,
sind ohne Heimat und von dir getrennt.

26

Werkleute sind wir: Knappen, Jünger, Meister,
und bauen dich, du hohes Mittelschiff.
Und manchmal kommt ein ernster Hergereister,
geht wie ein Glanz durch unsre hundert Geister
und zeigt uns zitternd einen neuen Griff.

Round God, the old tower, my gyres I perform,
and I've gyred there centuries long;
and don't know whether I'm falcon or storm
or, maybe, a mighty song.

6

If sometimes, neighbour God, my knocking on
your wall at night disturbs you out of season,
that I've scarce heard you breathing is the reason,
and know you're in your room alone.
And no one's present there to understand
what you are groping for and bring it you:
I'm always listening. Just a rap will do.
I'm close at hand.

Nothing's between us but a slender wall,
fortuitously; for if there came perhaps
from your mouth or from mine a sudden call,
it might collapse
forthwith, quite noiselessly.

It's been constructed from your imagery.

Before you stand your images like names.
And if at times the light in me leaps high,
that light the depths of me discern you by,
it spends itself as radiance on their frames.

And senses which a sudden tiredness lames
homelessly separated from you lie.

26

We're workmen, all the millions of us, whether
craftsman or prentice, huge Nave, building you.
And sometimes some grave traveller comes hither,
goes like a gleam through all our minds together,
and shows us tremblingly a grip that's new.

Wir steigen in die wiegenden Gerüste,
in unsern Händen hängt der Hammer schwer,
bis eine Stunde uns die Stirnen küßte
die strahlend und als ob sie alles wüßte
von dir kommt wie der Wind vom Meer.

Dann ist ein Hallen von dem vielen Hämmern,
und durch die Berge geht es Stoß um Stoß.
Erst wenn es dunkelt, lassen wir dich los:
Und deine kommenden Konturen dämmern.

Gott, du bist groß.

36

Was wirst du tun, Gott wenn ich sterbe?
Ich bin dein Krug (wenn ich zerscherbe?)
Ich bin dein Trank (wenn ich verderbe?)
Bin dein Gewand und dein Gewerbe,
mit mir verlierst du deinen Sinn.

Nach mir hast du kein Haus, darin
dich Worte, nah und warm, begrüßen.
Es fällt von deinen müden Füßen
die Samtsandale, die ich bin.
Dein großer Mantel läßt dich los.
Dein Blick, den ich mit meiner Wange
warm, wie mit einem Pfühl, empfange,
wird kommen, wird mich suchen, lange—
und legt beim Sonnenuntergange
sich fremden Steinen in den Schoß.

Was wirst du tun, Gott? Ich bin bange.

Up to the rocking scaffold we are going,
the hammer in our hands hangs heavily,
until some hour upon our brows be blowing
that radiantly, as though it were all-knowing,
comes from you like the wind from sea.

Then hammer upon hammer rings out gaily,
and through the mountains blows reverberate.
We do not let you go till it's grown late:
and now your future contours glimmer greyly.

God, you are great.

36

What will you do, God, if Death takes me?
I am your jug (if someone breaks me?)
I am your drink (if curdling cakes me?)
I am your trim, your trade,—it makes me
think: with me goes your meaning too.

You'll have no house to turn into,
where words, so near and warm, will greet then.
They'll fall from off your weary feet then,
those velvet sandals I'm for you.

Your cloak will slip from off your shoulders.
Your glance, which on my cheek would rest,
warmly as by a pillow pressed,
will come, and, after much vain quest,
sink, as the sun goes down the west,
into some lap of alien boulders.

What will you do, God? I'm distressed.

Das Buch von der Pilgerschaft

24

Die Könige der Welt sind alt
und werden keine Erben haben.
Die Söhne sterben schon als Knaben,
und ihre bleichen Töchter gaben
die kranken Kronen der Gewalt.
Der Pöbel bricht sie klein zu Geld,
der zeitgemäße Herr der Welt
dehnt sie im Feuer zu Maschinen,
die seinem Wollen grollend dienen;
aber das Glück ist nicht mit ihnen.
Das Erz hat Heimweh. Und verlassen
will es die Münzen und die Räder,
die es ein kleines Leben lehren.
Und aus Fabriken und aus Kassen
wird es zurück in das Geäder
der aufgetanen Berge kehren,
die sich verschließen hinter ihm.

25

Alles wird wieder groß sein und gewaltig,
die Lande einfach und die Wasser faltig,
die Bäume riesig und sehr klein die Mauern;
und in den Tälern, stark und vielgestaltig,
ein Volk von Hirten und von Ackerbauern.

Und keine Kirchen, welche Gott umklammern
wie einen Flüchtling und ihn dann bejammern
wie ein gefangenes und wundes Tier,—
die Häuser gastlich allen Einlaßklopfern
und ein Gefühl von unbegrenztem Opfern
in allem Handeln und in dir und mir.

Second Book: The Book of Pilgrimage

24

The world's kings have grown old, and hence-
forth heirs to them will be denied.
Their sons in infancy have died,
and their pale daughters have supplied
their sickly crowns to Violence.

These crowns the mob breaks up and spends them,
the world's progressive lord extends them
with fire into machines, until
they grumblingly perform his will,
but little happiness attends them.

The ore is sick for home. And hankers to
quit the coins and wheels that train
it up in all their pettiness.
And out of factories and bankers'
tills it will yet return again
into the opened veiness
of mountains that will close behind it.

25

Grandeur in all things shall be reinstated,
the lands outsmoothed, the waters corrugated,
walls inconspicuous and trees tremendous;
and in the valleys, strong and variegated,
a race of shepherds and of crop-attenders.

No churches, which first capture God and gaol him
like some absconder, and which then bewail him
like some trapped creature panting woundedly,—
houses to every knocker hospitable
and sense of sacrifice immeasurable
in all transactions and in you and me.

Kein Jenseitswarten und kein Schaun nach drüben,
nur Sehnsucht, auch den Tod nicht zu entweihn
und dienend sich am Irdischen zu üben,
um seinen Händen nicht mehr neu zu sein.

Das Buch von der Armut und vom Tode

4

Denn, Herr, die großen Städte sind
Verlorene und Aufgelöste;
wie Flucht vor Flammen ist die größte,—
und ist kein Trost, daß er sie tröste,
und ihre kleine Zeit verrinnt.

Da leben Menschen, leben schlecht und schwer,
in tiefen Zimmern, bange von Gebärde,
geängsteter denn eine Erstlingsherde;
und draußen wacht und atmet deine Erde,
sie aber sind und wissen es nicht mehr.

Da wachsen Kinder auf an Fensterstufen,
die immer in demselben Schatten sind,
und wissen nicht, daß draußen Blumen rufen
zu einem Tag voll Weite, Glück und Wind,—
und müssen Kind sein und sind traurig Kind.

Da blühen Jungfraun auf zum Unbekannten
und sehnen sich nach ihrer Kindheit Ruh;
das aber ist nicht da, wofür sie brannten,
und zitternd schließen sie sich wieder zu.
Und haben in verhüllten Hinterzimmern
die Tage der enttäuschten Mutterschaft,
der langen Nächte willenloses Wimmern
und kalte Jahre ohne Kampf und Kraft.

No waiting for, no gaze at, things celestial,
just longing to give even Death his due
and humbly train ourselves on the terrestrial
so that his hands shan't find us wholly new.

Third Book: The Book of Poverty and of Death

4

For, Lord, the great towns, without doubt,
are lost and broken; and the chief's[1]
like flight from flames,—and no relief's
awaiting to relieve her griefs,
and her brief time is running out.

There men are living lives of cark and care
in deep rooms, shy in gesture and in word,
more terror-stricken than a yearling herd;
and outside wakes the Earth your breath has stirred
to life of which these now live unaware.

Children grow up at window-ledges where
at every hour the self-same shadow's falling,
and do not know that outside flowers are calling
to days all full of distance, joy and air,
and must be children, but sad children, there.

Girls are upgrowing there for something distant
and yearning for their childhood's lost repose;
there, though, the thing they've burned for 's non-existent,
and tremblingly their opened petals close.
They spend that motherhood they've so awaited
in endless days of back-roomed hiddenness;
to nights of will-less whimpering are fated
and years of uncontending powerlessness.

---

[1] Paris. It was after his first six months in that city that Rilke escaped to Viareggio and wrote this last part of *The Book of Hours*.

Und ganz im Dunkel stehn die Sterbebetten,
und langsam sehnen sie sich dazu hin;
und sterben lange, sterben wie in Ketten
und gehen aus wie eine Bettlerin.

8

Herr: wir sind ärmer denn die armen Tiere,
die ihres Todes enden, wenn auch blind,
weil wir noch alle ungestorben sind.
Den gib uns, der die Wissenschaft gewinnt,
das Leben aufzubinden in Spaliere,
um welche zeitiger der Mai beginnt.

Denn dieses macht das Sterben fremd und schwer,
daß es nicht unser Tod ist; einer, der
uns endlich nimmt, nur weil wir keinen reifen;
drum geht ein Sturm, uns alle abzustreifen.

Wir stehn in deinem Garten Jahr und Jahr
und sind die Bäume, süßen Tod zu tragen;
aber wir altern in den Erntetagen,
und so wie Frauen, welche du geschlagen,
sind wir verschlossen, schlecht und unfruchtbar.

Oder ist meine Hoffart ungerecht:
sind Bäume besser? Sind wir nur Geschlecht
und Schooß von Frauen, welche viel gewähren?—
Wir haben mit der Ewigkeit gehurt,
und wenn das Kreißbett da ist, so gebären
wir unsres Todes tote Fehlgeburt;
den krummen, kummervollen Embryo,
der sich (als ob ihn Schreckliches erschreckte)
die Augenkeime mit den Händen deckte
und dem schon auf der ausgebauten Stirne
die Angst von allem steht, was er nicht litt,—
und alle schließen so wie eine Dirne
in Kindbettkrämpfen und am Kaiserschnitt.

And somewhere in the dark death-beds are lying,
and thither all their yearnings slowly tend,
and long, as though in fetters, they're a-dying,
and like some beggar-woman's is their end.

8

Lord, we are poorer than poor beasts, for they
can die their deaths, if but instinctively,
while we are all going on undyingly.
Send us someone who'll learn devotedly
to train life on espaliers which May
will then begin around more seasonably.

For what in dying so alienly shakes us
is that it's not our death, but one that takes us
only because we've not matured our own;
therefore there comes a storm and down we're blown.

We stand within your garden year by year
as trees from which sweet death's desiderated;
by harvest, though, we're superannuated,
and, like those women you have castigated,
closed, useless and unfruitful we appear.

Or is this arrogance of mine unjust?
Are the trees better? Are we merely lust
and sex and womb of women without caution?

We with Eternity have played the whore,
and, when our time has come, the dead abortion
of our own death is all we labour for;
that twisted, miserable embryo
which (as in terror of some dread surprise)
has covered with its hands its budding eyes,
and on whose bulging brow even now protrude
its fears of all the suffering still to be,—
and all of us, like prostitutes, conclude
in child-bed spasms and hysterotomy.

9

Mach Einen herrlich, Herr, mach Einen groß,
bau seinem Leben einen schönen Schooß,
und seine Scham errichte wie ein Tor
in einem blonden Wald von jungen Haaren,
und ziehe durch das Glied des Unsagbaren
den Reisigen den weißen Heeresscharen,
den tausend Samen, die sich sammeln, vor.
Und eine Nacht gib, daß der Mensch empfinge,

was keines Menschen Tiefen noch betrat;
gib eine Nacht: da blühen alle Dinge,
und mach sie duftender als die Syringe
und wiegender denn deines Windes Schwinge
und jubelnder als Josaphat.

Und gib ihm eines langen Tragens Zeit
und mach ihn weit in wachsenden Gewändern,
und schenk ihm eines Sternes Einsamkeit,
daß keines Auges Staunen ihn beschreit,
wenn seine Züge schmelzend sich verändern.

Erneue ihn mit einer reinen Speise,
mit Tau, mit ungetötetem Gericht,
mit jenem Leben, das wie Andacht leise
und warm wie Atem aus den Feldern bricht.

Mach, daß er seine Kindheit wieder weiß;
das Unbewußte und das Wunderbare
und seiner ahnungsvollen Anfangsjahre
unendlich dunkelreichen Sagenkreis.

Und also heiß ihn seiner Stunde warten,
da er den Tod gebären wird, den Herrn:
allein und rauschend wie ein großer Garten
und ein Versammelter aus fern.

9

Make someone glorious, Lord, make someone great,
build a fine womb for him, and, like a gate
within a flaxen forest of young hair,
erect its entrance, and, yourself advancing
through the unmentioned member, lead those prancing
cavalry in, those hosts all whitely glancing,
those myriad seeds that are assembled there.

And grant a night that to mankind here brings
more than all human depths have quivered at;
make it a night all full of flowering things,
and sweeter than syringa's perfumings,
and more sleep-rocking than your wind's own wings,
and more rejoicing than Jehosaphat.

And grant him a long period of gestation,
set him, in growing garments, out of range,
bestow upon him a star's isolation,
lest any eye bewitch with admiration
when meltingly his features start to change.

Renew him with some purer sustenance,
with dew, with dishes for which nothing dies,
with that same life which, soft as suppliance
and warm as breathing, from the fields will rise.

Make him re-know his childhood, make him see
the mystery and the marvel, till he hears
the saga of those first divining years
in all its vastly rich obscurity.

And thus command him wait his hour and bear,
when it shall come upon him, Death the Lord:
lone-murmuring like some great garden there
and one convened from far abroad.

15

Dann sah ich auch Paläste, welche leben;
sie brüsten sich den schönen Vögeln gleich,
die eine schlechte Stimme von sich geben.
Viele sind reich und wollen sich erheben,—
aber die Reichen sind nicht reich.

Nicht wie die Herren deiner Hirtenvölker,
der klaren, grünen Ebenen Bewölker,
wenn sie mit schummerigem Schafgewimmel
darüber zogen wie ein Morgenhimmel.
Und wenn sie lagerten und die Befehle
verklungen waren in der neuen Nacht,
dann wars, als sei jetzt eine andre Seele
in ihrem flachen Wanderland erwacht—:
die dunklen Höhenzüge der Kamele
umgaben es mit der Gebirge Pracht.

Und der Geruch der Rinderherden lag
dem Zuge nach bis an den zehnten Tag,
war warm and schwer und wich dem Wind nicht aus.
Und wie in einem hellen Hochzeitshaus
die ganze Nacht die reichen Weine rinnen:
so kam die Milch aus ihren Eselinnen.

Und nicht wie jene Scheichs der Wüstenstämme,
die nächtens auf verwelktem Teppich ruhten,
aber Rubinen ihren Lieblingsstuten
einsetzen ließen in die Silberkämme.

Und nicht wie jene Fürsten, die des Golds
nicht achteten, das keinen Duft erfand,
und deren stolzes Leben sich verband
mit Ambra, Mandelöl und Sandelholz.

15

Live palaces would also meet my eye,
flaunting themselves like those fine birds from which
no sound emerges but a hideous cry.
Many are rich and want to sit on high,—
these rich, though, are not really rich.

Not like the rulers of your shepherd-trains,
those old beclouders of the clear, green plains,
who with their fleecy multitudes would ply
through those expanses like a morning sky.
And when they had encamped, and every pealing
order had died into night's youthfulness,
it seemed as though another soul were feeling
in their flat nomad-land for consciousness:—
the dusky ridges of humped camels kneeling
surrounded it with mountain splendidness.

And far behind their line of march would hang
for ten days long their herded cattle's tang,
heavy and warm and wind-resistingly.
And as at bright-lit bridals flowingly
rich vintages throughout the night regale,
milk came from their she-asses pail on pail.

Not like those desert sheikhs who spent the night in
sleep on a faded carpet and who yet
were always having silver combs inset
with rubies for the mares they took delight in.

Not like those princes whom such gold as could
invent no perfume never fascinated,
and whose proud lives were so consociated
with amber, almond-oil and sandalwood.

Nicht wie des Ostens weißer Gossudar,
dem Reiche eines Gottes Recht erwiesen;
er aber lag mit abgehärmtem Haar,
die alte Stirne auf des Fußes Fliesen,
und weinte,—weil aus allen Paradiesen
nicht eine Stunde seine war.

Nicht wie die Ersten alter Handelshäfen,
die sorgten, wie sie ihre Wirklichkeit
mit Bildern ohnegleichen überträfen
und ihre Bilder wieder mit der Zeit;
und die in ihres goldnen Mantels Stadt
zusammgefaltet waren wie ein Blatt,
nur leise atmend mit den weißen Schläfen . . .

Das waren Reiche, die das Leben zwangen,
unendlich weit zu sein und schwer und warm.
Aber der Reichen Tage sind vergangen,
und keiner wird sie dir zurückverlangen,
nur mach die Armen endlich wieder arm.

16

Sie sind es nicht. Sie sind nur die Nicht-Reichen,
die ohne Willen sind und ohne Welt;
gezeichnet mit der letzten Ängste Zeichen
und überall entblättert und entstellt.
Zu ihnen drängt sich aller Staub der Städte,
und aller Unrat hängt sich an sie an.
Sie sind verrufen wie ein Blatternbette,
wie Scherben fortgeworfen, wie Skelette,
wie ein Kalender, dessen Jahr verrann,—
und doch: wenn deine Erde Nöte hätte:
sie reihte sie an eine Rosenkette
und trüge sie wie einen Talisman.

Not like that Eastern Gossudar,[1] with share
of godlike honour by whole kingdoms shown,
who none the less with desolated hair
beat his old brow against the flooring stone
and wept, because not one hour for his own
those regal paradises had to spare.

Not like old harbour-cities' signory,
trying to surpass their own reality
with portraits unsurpassably sublime,
and then those portraits too with their own time;
those figures that like parchment-sheets would fold
into their civic robes of silk and gold
and breathe with their white temples, silently . . .

Those were the rich who forced life to attain
such breadth and warmth and full maturity.
Gone, though, for ever is such rich men's reign,
and none will beg it back from you again:
let but the poor regain their poverty.

16

They are not poor. They're only not-rich, living
without a will, without a world achieved;
marked with the marks of ultimate misgiving
and utterly disfigured and disleaved.

On them the cities' dust has all collected,
they are the dump all refuse settles on.
They're shunned with loathing like a bed infected;
like broken pots, like skeletons, rejected,
like calendars whose year's already gone,—
and yet, were this your Earth enough dejected,
all these upon a rosary chain collected
it would be wearing for a talisman.

[1] Gossudar: the Russian word for 'ruler'.

Denn sie sind reiner als die reinen Steine
und wie das blinde Tier, das erst beginnt,
und voller Einfalt und unendlich deine
und wollen nichts und brauchen nur das eine:

so arm sein dürfen, wie sie wirklich sind.

17

Denn Armut ist ein großer Glanz aus Innen . . .

31

Die Städte aber wollen nur das Ihre
und reißen alles mit in ihren Lauf.
Wie hohles Holz zerbrechen sie die Tiere
und brauchen viele Völker brennend auf.

Und ihre Menschen dienen in Kulturen
und fallen tief aus Gleichgewicht und Maß,
und nennen Fortschritt ihre Schneckenspuren
und fahren rascher, wo sie langsam fuhren,
und fühlen sich und funkeln wie die Huren
und lärmen lauter mit Metall und Glas.

Es ist, als ob ein Trug sie täglich äffte,
sie können gar nicht mehr sie selber sein;
das Geld wächst an, hat alle ihre Kräfte
und ist wie Ostwind groß, und sie sind klein
und ausgeholt und warten, daß der Wein
und alles Gift der Tier- und Menschensäfte
sie reize zu vergänglichem Geschäfte.

For they are purer than the purest stone
and like blind beasts in earliest infancy
and simple and so endlessly your own
and wish for nothing and need this alone:

leave to be poor as they have come to be.

17

For poverty's a great shine from within . . .

31

The cities, though, want only what will speed them,
and drag all with them on their headlong course.
They smash the beasts like rotten wood to feed them
and use whole nations up without remorse.

Their people serve some culture's domination
and fall afar from measure and from poise,
and give the name of progress to gyration,
and travel with a growing acceleration,
and have a harlot's soul and scintillation,
and louder rings their glass and metal noise.

Some phantom seems to lure them every hour,
they can no longer be themselves at all;
their money grows, engrosses all their power,
and swells to east wind size, and they are small
and vacuous and wait there for the call
of wine and every poisonous distillation
to rouse them to some transient occupation.

Translated by J. B. Leishman

Neue Gedichte

Der Ölbaum-Garten

Er ging hinauf unter dem grauen Laub
ganz grau und aufgelöst im Ölgelände
und legte seine Stirne voller Staub
tief in das Staubigsein der heißen Hände.

Nach allem dies. Und dieses war der Schluß.
Jetzt soll ich gehen, während ich erblinde,
und warum willst Du, daß ich sagen muß
Du seist, wenn ich Dich selber nicht mehr finde.

Ich finde Dich nicht mehr. Nicht in mir, nein.
Nicht in den andern. Nicht in diesem Stein.
Ich finde Dich nicht mehr. Ich bin allein.

Ich bin allein mit aller Menschen Gram,
den ich durch Dich zu lindern unternahm,
der Du nicht bist. O namenlose Scham . . .

Später erzählte man: ein Engel kam—.

Warum ein Engel? Ach es kam die Nacht
und blätterte gleichgültig in den Bäumen.
Die Jünger rührten sich in ihren Träumen.
Warum ein Engel? Ach es kam die Nacht.

New Poems

The Olive Garden

And still he climbed, and through the grey leaves thrust,
quite grey and lost in the grey olive lands,
and laid his burning forehead full of dust
deep in the dustiness of burning hands.

After all, this. And, this, then, was the end.
Now I'm to go, while I am going blind;
and, oh, why wilt Thou have me still contend
Thou art, whom I myself no longer find.

No more I find Thee. In myself no tone
of Thee; nor in the rest; nor in this stone.
I can find Thee no more. I am alone.

I am alone with all that human fate
I undertook through Thee to mitigate,
Thou who art not. Oh, shame too consummate . . .

An angel came, those afterwards relate.

Wherefore an angel? Oh, there came the night,
and turned the leaves of trees indifferently,
and the disciples stirred uneasily.
Wherefore an angel? Oh, there came the night.

Die Nacht, die kam, war keine ungemeine;
so gehen hunderte vorbei.
Da schlafen Hunde und da liegen Steine.
Ach eine traurige, ach irgendeine,
die wartet, bis es wieder Morgen sei.

Denn Engel kommen nicht zu solchen Betern,
und Nächte werden nicht um solche groß.
Die Sich-Verlierenden läßt alles los,
und sie sind preisgegeben von den Vätern
und ausgeschlossen aus der Mütter Schooß.

Gott im Mittelalter

Und sie hatten Ihn in sich erspart
und sie wollten, daß er sei und richte,
und sie hängten schließlich wie Gewichte
(zu verhindern seine Himmelfahrt)

an ihn ihrer großen Kathedralen
Last und Masse. Und er sollte nur
über seine grenzenlosen Zahlen
zeigend kreisen und wie eine Uhr

Zeichen geben ihrem Tun und Tagwerk.
Aber plötzlich kam er ganz in Gang,
und die Leute der entsetzten Stadt

ließen ihn, vor seiner Stimme bang,
weitergehn mit ausgehängtem Schlagwerk
und entflohn vor seinem Zifferblatt.

The night that came requires no specifying;
just so a hundred nights go by,
while dogs are sleeping and while stones are lying—
just any melancholy night that, sighing,
lingers till morning mount the sky.

For angels never come to such men's prayers,
nor nights for them mix glory with their gloom.
Forsakenness is the self-loser's doom,
and such are absent from their father's cares
and disincluded from their mother's womb.

Paris, May–June 1906
Luke, xxii, 39–46

God in the Middle Ages

And they'd got him in themselves upstored,
and they wanted him to reign forever,
and they hung on him (a last endeavour
to withhold his journey heavenward

and to have him near them in their slumbers)
their cathedrals' massive weights. He must
merely wheel across his boundless numbers
pointingly and, like a clock, adjust

what they daily toiled at or transacted.
But he suddenly got into gear,
and the people of the stricken town

left him—for his voice inspired such fear—
running with his striking-works extracted,
and absconded from his dial's frown.

Paris, 19–23 July 1907

Der Panther

Im Jardin des Plantes, Paris

Sein Blick ist vom Vorübergehn der Stäbe
so müd geworden, daß er nichts mehr hält.
Ihm ist, als ob es tausend Stäbe gäbe
und hinter tausend Stäben keine Welt.

Der weiche Gang geschmeidig starker Schritte,
der sich im allerkleinsten Kreise dreht,
ist wie ein Tanz von Kraft um eine Mitte,
in der betäubt ein großer Wille steht.

Nur manchmal schiebt der Vorhang der Pupille
sich lautlos auf—. Dann geht ein Bild hinein,
geht durch der Glieder angespannte Stille—
und hört im Herzen auf zu sein.

Römische Sarkophage

Was aber hindert uns zu glauben, daß
(so wie wir hingestellt sind und verteilt)
nicht eine kleine Zeit nur Drang und Haß
und dies Verwirrende in uns verweilt,

wie einst in dem verzierten Sarkophag
bei Ringen, Götterbildern, Gläsern, Bändern,
in langsam sich verzehrenden Gewändern
ein langsam Aufgelöstes lag—

bis es die unbekannten Munde schluckten,
die niemals reden. (Wo besteht und denkt
ein Hirn, um ihrer einst sich zu bedienen?)

The Panther

Jardin des Plantes, Paris

His gaze those bars keep passing is so misted
with tiredness, it can take in nothing more.
He feels as though a thousand bars existed,
and no more world beyond them than before.

Those supply-powerful paddings, turning there
in tiniest of circles, well might be
the dance of forces round a centre where
some mighty will stands paralyticly.

Just now and then the pupil's noiseless shutter
is lifted.—Then an image will indart,
down through the limbs' intensive stillness flutter,
and end its being in the heart.

Paris, 1903 or (possibly) end of 1902

Roman Sarcophagi

Why should we too, though, not anticipate
(set down here and assigned our places thus)
that only for a short time rage and hate
and this bewildering will remain in us,

as in the ornate sarcophagus, enclosed
with images of gods, rings, glasses, trappings,
there lay in slowly self-consuming wrappings
something being slowly decomposed—

till swallowed by those unknown mouths at last,
that never speak. (Where bides a brain that may
yet trust the utterance of its thinking to them?)

Da wurde von den alten Aquädukten
ewiges Wasser in sie eingelenkt—:
das spiegelt jetzt und geht und glänzt in ihnen.

Der Schwan

Diese Mühsal, durch noch Ungetanes
schwer und wie gebunden hinzugehn,
gleicht dem ungeschaffnen Gang des Schwanes.

Und das Sterben, dieses Nichtmehrfassen
jenes Grunds, auf dem wir täglich stehn,
seinem ängstlichen Sich-Niederlassen—:

in die Wasser, die ihn sanft empfangen
und die sich, wie glücklich und vergangen,
unter ihm zurückziehn, Flut um Flut;
während er unendlich still und sicher
immer mündiger und königlicher
und gelassener zu ziehn geruht.

Die Spitze

I

Menschlichkeit: Namen schwankender Besitze,
noch unbestätigter Bestand von Glück:
ist das unmenschlich, daß zu dieser Spitze,
zu diesem kleinen dichten Spitzenstück
zwei Augen wurden?—Willst du sie zurück?

Then from the ancient aqueducts there passed
eternal water into them one day:—
that mirrors now and moves and sparkles through them.

Paris, May–June 1906

The Swan

This laborious going on and on,
bound and heavy, through the still-to-do is
like the unshaped walking of the swan.

Dying too, that no more hold-providing
by the ground we daily trusted to, is
like his so unconfident subsiding

into waters that receive him gently
and, as though departed and contently,
wave on wave retire from under him;
while he, infinitely still and surely,
ever kinglier and more maturely,
more composedly, condescends to swim.

Meudon, winter 1905–6

The Lace

I

Humanness: name for wavering possession,
still undetermined term of happiness:
is it inhuman that there went to fashion
this piece of lace-work's fine enwovenness
two eyes?—Do you regret their absentness?

Du Langvergangene und schließlich Blinde,
ist deine Seligkeit in diesem Ding,
zu welcher hin, wie zwischen Stamm und Rinde,
dein großes Fühlen, kleinverwandelt, ging?

Durch einen Riß im Schicksal, eine Lücke
entzogst du deine Seele deiner Zeit;
und sie ist so in diesem lichten Stücke,
daß es mich lächeln macht vor Nützlichkeit.

II

Und wenn uns eines Tages dieses Tun
und was an uns geschieht gering erschiene
und uns so fremd, als ob es nicht verdiene,
daß wir so mühsam aus den Kinderschuhn
um seinetwillen wachsen—: Ob die Bahn
vergilbter Spitze, diese dichtgefügte
blumige Spitzenbahn, dann nicht genügte,
uns hier zu halten? Sieh: Sie ward *getan*.

Ein Leben ward vielleicht verschmäht, wer weiß?
Ein Glück war da und wurde hingegeben,
und endlich wurde doch, um jeden Preis,
dies Ding daraus, nicht leichter als das Leben
und doch vollendet und so schön als sei's
nicht mehr zu früh, zu lächeln und zu schweben.

You long-departed and at last benighted,
is all your heaven in this thing, where went,
as between trunk and bark, your lofty-flighted
feeling in magical diminishment?

Through some small chink in destiny, some gaping,
you drew your soul from temporality;
and it's so present in this airy shaping,
I have to smile at the expediency.

Paris, early summer 1906

II

And if one day our doing and our ado's
and all that happens to us should appear
trivial and strange, and it were far from clear
why we should struggle out of children's shoes
merely for that—would not, perhaps, this run
of yellowed lace, this finely woven length
of flowery lace, then have sufficient strength
to keep us here? For look, it all got done.

A life perhaps was slighted, who can know?
A chance of happiness let slip—yet, spite
of all, there still emerged, however slow,
this thing, not easier than life, but quite
perfect, and, oh, so beautiful—as though
now were no more too soon for smiles and flight.

Capri, c. 10 February 1907

Die Kurtisane

Venedigs Sonne wird in meinem Haar
ein Gold bereiten: aller Alchemie
erlauchten Ausgang. Meine Brauen, die
den Brücken gleichen, siehst du sie

hinführen ob der lautlosen Gefahr
der Augen, die ein heimlicher Verkehr
an die Kanäle schließt, so daß das Meer
in ihnen steigt und fällt und wechselt. Wer

mich einmal sah, beneidet meinen Hund,
weil sich auf ihm oft in zerstreuter Pause
die Hand, die nie an keiner Glut verkohlt,

die unverwundbare, geschmückt, erholt—.
Und Knaben, Hoffnungen aus altem Hause,
gehn wie an Gift an meinem Mund zugrund.

Das Karussell

Jardin du Luxembourg

Mit einem Dach und seinem Schatten dreht
sich eine kleine Weile der Bestand
von bunten Pferden, alle aus dem Land,
das lange zögert, eh es untergeht.
Zwar manche sind an Wagen angespannt,
doch alle haben Mut in ihren Mienen;
ein böser roter Löwe geht mit ihnen
und dann und wann ein weißer Elefant.

The Courtesan

The sun of Venice in my hair's prepairing
a gold where lustrously shall culminate
all alchemy. My brows, which emulate
her bridges, you can contemplate

over the silent perilousness repairing
of eyes which some communion secretly
unites with her canals, so that the sea
rises and ebbs and changes in them. He

who once has seen me falls to envying
my dog, because, in moments of distraction,
this hand no fieriness incinerates,

scathless, bejewelled, there recuperates.—
And many a hopeful youth of high extraction
will not survive my mouth's envenoming.

Capri, mid-March 1907

The Merry-go-round

Jardin du Luxembourg

With roof and shadow for a while careers
the stud of horses, variously bright,
all from that land that long remains in sight
before it ultimately disappears.
Several indeed pull carriages, with tight-
held rein, but all have boldness in their bearing;
with them a wicked scarlet lion's faring
and now and then an elephant all white.

Sogar ein Hirsch ist da, ganz wie im Wald,
nur daß er einen Sattel trägt und drüber
ein kleines blaues Mädchen aufgeschnallt.

Und auf dem Löwen reitet weiß ein Junge
und hält sich mit der kleinen heißen Hand,
dieweil der Löwe Zähne zeigt und Zunge.

Und dann und wann ein weißer Elefant.

Und auf den Pferden kommen sie vorüber,
auch Mädchen, helle, diesem Pferdesprunge
fast schon entwachsen; mitten in dem Schwunge
schauen sie auf, irgendwohin, herüber—

Und dann und wann ein weißer Elefant.

Und das geht hin und eilt sich, daß es endet,
und kreist und dreht sich nur und hat kein Ziel.
Ein Rot, ein Grün, ein Grau vorbeigesendet,
ein kleines kaum begonnenes Profil—.
Und manchesmal ein Lächeln, hergewendet,
ein seliges, das blendet und verschwendet
an dieses atemlose blinde Spiel . . .

Spanische Tänzerin

Wie in der Hand ein Schwefelzündholz, weiß
eh es zur Flamme kommt, nach allen Seiten
zuckende Zungen streckt—: beginnt im Kreis
naher Beschauer hastig, hell und heiß
ihr runder Tanz sich zuckend auszubreiten.

Und plötzlich ist er Flamme, ganz und gar.

Just as in woods, a stag comes into view,
save that it has a saddle and tied fast
thereon a little maiden all in blue.

And on the lion a little boy is going,
whose small hot hands hold on with all his might,
while raging lion's tongue and teeth are showing.

And now and then an elephant all white.

And on the horses they come riding past,
girls too, bright-skirted, whom the horse-jumps here
scarce now preoccupy: in full career
elsewhither, hitherwards, a glance they cast—

And now and then an elephant all white.

And on it goes and hastens to be ended,
and aimlessly rotates until it's done.
A red, a green, a grey is apprehended,
a little profile, scarcely yet begun.—
And now and then a smile, for us intended,
blissfully happy, dazzlingly expended
upon this breathless, blindly followed fun . . .

Paris, June 1906

Spanish Dancer

As in the hand a sulphur match, sheer white
before it flames, will stretch out scintillating
tongues on all sides, her round dance, in the tight
ring of spectators, hasty, hot, alight,
has started scintillatingly dilating.

And suddenly it's only flame that's there.

Mit einem Blick entzündet sie ihr Haar
und dreht auf einmal mit gewagter Kunst
ihr ganzes Kleid in diese Feuersbrunst,
aus welcher sich, wie Schlangen die erschrecken,
die nackten Arme wach und klappernd strecken.

Und dann: als würde ihr das Feuer knapp,
nimmt sie es ganz zusamm und wirft es ab
sehr herrisch, mit hochmütiger Gebärde
und schaut: da liegt es rasend auf der Erde
und flammt noch immer und ergiebt sich nicht—.
Doch sieghaft, sicher und mit einem süßen
grüßenden Lächeln hebt sie ihr Gesicht
und stampft es aus mit kleinen festen Füßen.

Archaïscher Torso Apollos

Wir kannten nicht sein unerhörtes Haupt,
darin die Augenäpfel reiften. Aber
sein Torso glüht noch wie ein Kandelaber,
in dem sein Schauen, nur zurückgeschraubt,

sich hält und glänzt. Sonst könnte nicht der Bug
der Brust dich blenden, und im leisen Drehen
der Lenden könnte nicht ein Lächeln gehen
zu jener Mitte, die die Zeugung trug.

Sonst stünde dieser Stein entstellt und kurz
unter der Schultern durchsichtigem Sturz
und flimmerte nicht so wie Raubtierfelle;

und bräche nicht aus allen seinen Rändern
aus wie ein Stern: denn da ist keine Stelle,
die dich nicht sieht. Du mußt dein Leben ändern.

With one glance she has set alight her hair,
and all at once with daring artfulness
spins her whole dress into this fieriness,
from which, like serpents terribly abashing,
her naked arms stretch out aroused and gnashing.

And then, as though her fire would not suffice,
she gathers it all up, and in a trice
flings it away with proud gesticulation
and gazes: still in raging conflagration
it's writhing on the ground unyieldingly.—
She, though, inflexible and with a sweet
saluting smile, looks up victoriously
and stamps it out with little steadfast feet.

Paris, June 1906

Archaic Torso of Apollo

Though we've not known his unimagined head
and what divinity his eyes were showing,
his torso like a branching street-lamp's glowing,
wherein his gaze, only turned down, can shed

light still. Or else the breast's insurgency
could not be dazzling you, or you discerning
in that slight twist of loins a smile returning
to where was centred his virility.

Or else this stone would not stand so intact
beneath the shoulders' through-seen cataract
and would not glisten like a wild beast's skin;

and would not keep from all its contours giving
light like a star: for there's no place therein
that does not see you. You must change your living.

Paris, early summer 1908

Leichen-Wäsche

Sie hatten sich an ihn gewöhnt. Doch als
die Küchenlampe kam und unruhig brannte
im dunkeln Luftzug, war der Unbekannte
ganz unbekannt. Sie wuschen seinen Hals,

und da sie nichts von seinem Schicksal wußten,
so logen sie ein anderes zusamm,
fortwährend waschend. Eine mußte husten
und ließ solang den schweren Essigschwamm

auf dem Gesicht. Da gab es eine Pause
auch für die zweite. Aus der harten Bürste
klopften die Tropfen; während seine grause
gekrampfte Hand dem ganzen Hause
beweisen wollte, daß ihn nicht mehr dürste.

Und er bewies. Sie nahmen wie betreten
eiliger jetzt mit einem kurzen Huster
die Arbeit auf, so daß an den Tapeten
ihr krummer Schatten in dem stummen Muster

sich wand und wälzte wie in einem Netze,
bis daß die Waschenden zu Ende kamen.
Die Nacht im vorhanglosen Fensterrahmen
war rücksichtslos. Und einer ohne Namen
lag bar und reinlich da und gab Gesetze.

Corpse-washing

They'd got quite used to him by now. But when
the kitchen-lamp came and its flame was blowing
in the dark draughtiness, beyond all knowing
was the unknown. They washed his neck, and then,

knowing nothing of his history, bit by bit
they fabricated one without demur,
washing away. One had a coughing fit,
and let the heavy sponge of vinegar

lie on his face. And then a little rest
was taken by the second. Drops descended
with thuds from the hard brush, while his compressed
horrific hand was trying to manifest
to the whole house that now his thirst was ended.

And he succeeded. As though guiltily
surprised, they now with some acceleration
resumed their task, and on the tapestry
their bending shadows in the figuration

as in a net contorted and gyrated,
till with their washing to an end they came.
The night in each uncurtained window-frame
was pitiless. And one without a name
lay bare and cleanly there and legislated.

Paris, summer 1908

Spätherbst in Venedig

Nun treibt die Stadt schon nicht mehr wie ein Köder,
der alle aufgetauchten Tage fängt.
Die gläsernen Paläste klingen spröder
an deinen Blick. Und aus den Gärten hängt

der Sommer wie ein Haufen Marionetten
kopfüber, müde, umgebracht.
Aber vom Grund aus alten Waldskeletten
steigt Willen auf: als sollte über Nacht

der General des Meeres die Galeeren
verdoppeln in dem wachen Arsenal,
um schon die nächste Morgenluft zu teeren

mit einer Flotte, welche ruderschlagend
sich drängt und jäh, mit allen Flaggen tagend,
den großen Wind hat, strahlend und fatal.

Corrida

In Memoriam Montez, 1830

Seit er, klein beinah, aus dem Toril
ausbrach, aufgescheuchten Augs und Ohrs,
und den Eigensinn des Picadors
und die Bänderhaken wie im Spiel

hinnahm, ist die stürmische Gestalt
angewachsen—sieh: zu welcher Masse,
aufgehäuft aus altem schwarzen Hasse,
und das Haupt zu einer Faust geballt,

Late Autumn in Venice

The city drifts no longer like a bait now,
upcatching all the days as they emerge.
Brittlier the glassy palaces vibrate now
beneath your gaze. And from each garden verge

the summer like a bunch of puppets dangles,
headforemost, weary, made away.
Out of the ground, though, from dead forest tangles
volition mounts: as though before next day

the sea-commander must have rigged and ready
the galleys in the sleepless Arsenal,
and earliest morning air be tarred already

by an armada, oaringly outpressing,
and suddenly, with flare of flags, possessing
the great wind, radiant and invincible.

Paris, early summer 1908

Corrida

In Memoriam Montez, 1830

Since, small almost, through the opened door
with upstartled eyes and ears he came
and supposed the baiting picador
and beribboned barbs to be a game,

that wild figure seems now to consist
of an ever-concentrating weight
of accumulated old black hate,
and his head is clenched into a fist,

nicht mehr spielend gegen irgendwen,
nein: die blutigen Nackenhaken hissend
hinter den gefällten Hörnern, wissend
und von Ewigkeit her gegen Den,

der in Gold und mauver Rosaseide
plötzlich umkehrt und, wie einen Schwarm
Bienen und als ob ers eben leide,
· den Bestürzten unter seinem Arm

durchläßt,—während seine Blicke heiß
sich noch einmal heben, leichtgelenkt,
und als schlüge draußen jener Kreis
sich aus ihrem Glanz und Dunkel nieder
und aus jedem Schlagen seiner Lider,

ehe er gleichmütig, ungehässig,
an sich selbst gelehnt, gelassen, lässig
in die wiederhergerollte große
Woge über dem verlornen Stoße
seinen Degen beinah sanft versenkt.

no more meeting any playfully:
no, but rearing bloody barbs behind
those presented horns, and in his mind
his opponent from eternity,

who, in gold and mauve-pink silk arrayed,
suddenly turns round and, like a swarm
of bees, and as if vexed but undismayed,
lets the baffled beast beneath his arm

rush by,—while his burning looks are lifting
up once more in tremulous accord,
as if all that circling throng were drifting
down from their own shine and sombering
and his eyelids' every fluttering,

till, so unexcitedly, unhating,
leaning on himself, deliberating,
into that great wave's refluctuance
over its dispersed precipitance
almost softly he insheathes his sword.

Paris, 3 August 1907

Translated by J. B. Leishman

Duineser Elegien

Die erste Elegie

Wer, wenn ich schriee, hörte mich denn aus der *Engel*
Ordnungen? und gesetzt selbst, es nähme
einer mich plötzlich ans Herz: ich verginge von seinem
stärkeren Dasein. Denn das Schöne ist nichts
als des Schrecklichen Anfang, den wir noch grade ertragen,
und wir bewundern es so, weil es gelassen verschmäht,
uns zu zerstören. Ein jeder Engel ist schrecklich.
Und so verhalt ich mich denn und verschlucke den Lockruf
dunkelen Schluchzens. Ach, wen vermögen
wir denn zu brauchen? Engel nicht, Menschen nicht,
und die findigen Tiere merken es schon,
daß wir nicht sehr verläßlich zu Haus sind
in der gedeuteten Welt. Es bleibt uns vielleicht
irgend ein Baum an dem Abhang, daß wir ihn täglich
wiedersähen; es bleibt uns die Straße von gestern
und das verzogene Treusein einer Gewohnheit,
der es bei uns gefiel, und so blieb sie und ging nicht.
O und die Nacht, die Nacht, wenn der Wind voller Weltraum
uns am Angesicht zehrt—, wem bliebe sie nicht, die ersehnte,
sanft enttäuschende, welche dem einzelnen Herzen
mühsam bevorsteht. Ist sie den Liebenden leichter?
Ach, sie verdecken sich nur mit einander ihr Los.
Weißt du's *noch* nicht? Wirf aus den Armen die Leere
zu den Räumen hinzu, die wir atmen; vielleicht daß die Vögel
die erweiterte Luft fühlen mit innigerm Flug.

Duino Elegies

The First Elegy

Who, if I cried, would hear me among the angelic
orders? And even if one of them suddenly
pressed me against his heart, I should fade in the strength of his
stronger existence. For Beauty's nothing
but beginning of Terror we're still just able to bear,
and why we adore it so is because it serenely
disdains to destroy us. Every angel is terrible.
And so I repress myself, and swallow the call-note
of depth-dark sobbing. Alas, who is there
we can make use of? Not angels, not men;
and even the noticing beasts are aware
that we don't feel very securely at home
in this interpreted world. There remains, perhaps,
some tree on a slope, to be looked at day after day,
there remains for us yesterday's walk and the long-drawn loyalty
of a habit that liked us and stayed and never gave notice.
Oh, and there's Night, there's Night, when wind full of cosmic space
feeds on our faces: for whom would she not remain,
longed for, mild disenchantress, painfully there
for the lonely heart to achieve? Is she lighter for lovers?
Alas, with each other they only conceal their lot!
Don't you know yet?—Fling the emptiness out of your arms
to broaden the spaces we breathe—maybe that the birds
will feel the extended air in more fervent flight.

Ja, die Frühlinge brauchten dich wohl. Es muteten manche
Sterne dir zu, daß du sie spürtest. Es hob
sich eine Woge heran im Vergangenen, oder
da du vorüberkamst am geöffneten Fenster,
gab eine Geige sich hin. Das alles war Auftrag.
Aber bewältigtest du's? Warst du nicht immer
noch von Erwartung zerstreut, als kündigte alles
eine Geliebte dir an? (Wo willst du sie bergen,
da doch die großen fremden Gedanken bei dir
aus und ein gehn und öfters bleiben bei Nacht.)
Sehnt es dich aber, so singe die Liebenden; lange
noch nicht unsterblich genug ist ihr berühmtes Gefühl.
Jene, du neidest sie fast, Verlassenen, die du
so viel liebender fandst als die Gestillten. Beginn
immer von neuem die nie zu erreichende Preisung;
denk: es erhält sich der Held, selbst der Untergang war ihm
nur ein Vorwand, zu sein: seine letzte Geburt.
Aber die Liebenden nimmt die erschöpfte Natur
in sich zurück, als wären nicht zweimal die Kräfte,
dieses zu leisten. Hast du der Gaspara Stampa
denn genügend gedacht, daß irgend ein Mädchen,
dem der Geliebte entging, am gesteigerten Beispiel
dieser Liebenden fühlt: daß ich würde wie sie?
Sollen nicht endlich uns diese ältesten Schmerzen
fruchtbarer werden? Ist es nicht Zeit, daß wir liebend
uns vom Geliebten befrein und es bebend bestehn:
wie der Pfeil die Sehne besteht, um gesammelt im Absprung
mehr zu sein als er selbst. Denn Bleiben ist nirgends.
Stimmen, Stimmen. Höre, mein Herz, wie sonst nur
Heilige hörten: daß sie der riesige Ruf
aufhob vom Boden; sie aber knieten
Unmögliche, weiter und achtetens nicht:
So waren sie hörend. Nicht, daß du *Gottes* ertrügest
die Stimme, bei weitem. Aber das Wehende höre,
die ununterbrochene Nachricht, die aus Stille sich bildet.

Yes, the Springs had need of you. Many a star
was waiting for you to perceive it. Many a wave
would rise in the past towards you; or else, perhaps,
as you went by an open window, a violin
would be utterly giving itself. All this was commission.
But were you equal to it? Were you not still
distraught by expectancy, as though all were announcing
some beloved's approach? (As if you could hope
to house her, with all those great strange thoughts
going in and out and often staying overnight!)
Should you be longing, though, sing the great lovers: the fame
of all they can feel is far from immortal enough.
Those—you envied them almost, those forsaken, you found
so far beyond the requited in loving. Begin
ever anew their never-attainable praise.
Consider: the Hero continues, even his setting
was a pretext for further existence, an ultimate birth.
But lovers are taken back by exhausted Nature
into herself, as though such creative force
could not be exerted twice. Does Gaspara Stampa [1]
mean enough to you yet, and that any girl, whose beloved
has slipped away, might feel, from that far intenser
example of loving: 'Could I but become like her!'?
Should not these oldest sufferings be finally growing
fruitfuller for us? Is it not time that, in loving,
we freed ourselves from the loved one, and, quivering, endured:
as the arrow endures the string, to become, in the gathering
    out-leap,
something more than itself? For staying is nowhere.
Voices, voices. Hearken, my heart, as only
saints once hearkened: so, that the giant call
lifted them off the ground; they, though, impossibles,
went on kneeling and paid no heed:
such was their hearkening. Not that you could bear God's
voice, by a long way. But hark to the suspiration,
the uninterrupted news that grows out of silence.

---

[1] Gaspara Stampa (1523–1554), an Italian poetess of noble family who recorded
her at first happy and then unrequited love in some two hundred sonnets.

Es rauscht jetzt von jenen jungen Toten zu dir.
Wo immer du eintratst, redete nicht in Kirchen
zu Rom und Neapel ruhig ihr Schicksal dich an?
Oder es trug eine Inschrift sich erhaben dir auf,
wie neulich die Tafel in Santa Maria Formosa.
Was sie mir wollen? leise soll ich des Unrechts
Anschein abtun, der ihrer Geister
reine Bewegung manchmal ein wenig behindert.

Freilich ist es seltsam, die Erde nicht mehr zu bewohnen,
kaum erlernte Gebräuche nicht mehr zu üben,
Rosen, und andern eigens versprechenden Dingen
nicht die Bedeutung menschlicher Zukunft zu geben;
das, was man war in unendlich ängstlichen Händen,
nicht mehr zu sein, und selbst den eigenen Namen
wegzulassen wie ein zerbrochenes Spielzeug.
Seltsam, die Wünsche nicht weiterzuwünschen. Seltsam,
alles, was sich bezog, so lose im Raume
flattern zu sehen. Und das Totsein ist mühsam
und voller Nachholn, daß man allmählich ein wenig
Ewigkeit spürt.—Aber Lebendige machen
alle den Fehler, daß sie zu stark unterscheiden.
Engel (sagt man) wüßten oft nicht, ob sie unter
Lebenden gehn oder Toten. Die ewige Strömung
reißt durch beide Bereiche alle Alter
immer mit sich und übertönt sie in beiden.

Schließlich brauchen sie uns nicht mehr, die Früheentrückten,
man entwöhnt sich des Irdischen sanft, wie man den Brüsten
milde der Mutter entwächst. Aber wir, die so große
Geheimnisse brauchen, denen aus Trauer so oft
seliger Fortschritt entspringt—: *könnten* wir sein ohne sie?
Ist die Sage umsonst, daß einst in der Klage um Linos
wagende erste Musik dürre Erstarrung durchdrang;
daß erst im erschrockenen Raum, dem ein beinah göttlicher Jüngling
plötzlich für immer enttrat, das Leere in jene
Schwingung geriet, die uns jetzt hinreißt und tröstet und hilft.

Rustling towards you now from those youthfully-dead.
Whenever you entered a church in Rome or in Naples
were you not always being quietly addressed by their fate?
Or else an inscripion sublimely imposed itself on you,
as, lately, the tablet in Santa Maria Formosa.
What they require of me? that I should gently remove
the appearance of suffered injustice, that hinders
a little, at times, their purely-proceeding spirits.

True, it is strange to inhabit the earth no longer,
to use no longer customs scarcely acquired,
not to interpret roses, and other things
that promise so much, in terms of a human future;
to be no longer all that one used to be
in endlessly anxious hands, and to lay aside
even one's proper name like a broken toy.
Strange, not to go on wishing one's wishes. Strange,
to see all that was once relation so loosely fluttering
hither and thither in space. And it's hard, being dead,
and full of retrieving before one begins to perceive
a little eternity.—All of the living, though,
make the mistake of drawing too sharp distinctions.
Angels (it's said) would be often unable to tell
whether they moved among living or dead. The eternal
torrent whirls all the ages through either realm
for ever, and sounds above their voices in both.

They've finally no more need of us, the early-departed,
one's gently weaned from terrestrial things as one mildly
outgrows the breasts of a mother. But we, that have need of
such mighty secrets, we, for whom sorrow's so often
source of blessedest progress, could we exist without them?
Is the story in vain, how once, in the mourning for Linos,
venturing earliest music pierced barren numbness, and how,
in the startled space an almost deified youth
suddenly quitted for ever, emptiness first
felt the vibration that now lifts us and comforts and helps?

Die dritte Elegie

Eines ist, die Geliebte zu singen. Ein anderes, wehe,
jenen verborgenen schuldigen Fluß-Gott des Bluts.
Den sie von weitem erkennt, ihren Jüngling, was weiß er
selbst von dem Herren der Lust, der aus dem Einsamen oft,
ehe das Mädchen noch linderte, oft auch als wäre sie nicht,
ach, von welchem Unkenntlichen triefend, das Gotthaupt
aufhob, aufrufend die Nacht zu unendlichem Aufruhr.
O des Blutes Neptun, o sein furchtbarer Dreizack.
O der dunkele Wind seiner Brust aus gewundener Muschel.
Horch, wie die Nacht sich muldet und höhlt. Ihr Sterne,
stammt nicht von euch des Liebenden Lust zu dem Antlitz
seiner Geliebten? Hat er die innige Einsicht
in ihr reines Gesicht nicht aus dem reinen Gestirn?

Du nicht hast ihm, wehe, nicht seine Mutter
hat ihm die Bogen der Braun so zur Erwartung gespannt.
Nicht an dir, ihn fühlendes Mädchen, an dir nicht
bog seine Lippe sich zum fruchtbarern Ausdruck.
Meinst du wirklich, ihn hätte dein leichter Auftritt
also erschüttert, du, die wandelt wie Frühwind?
Zwar du erschrakst ihm das Herz; doch ältere Schrecken
stürzten in ihn bei dem berührenden Anstoß.
Ruf ihn . . . du rufst ihn nicht ganz aus dunkelem Umgang.
Freilich, er *will*, er entspringt; erleichtert gewöhnt er
sich in dein heimliches Herz und nimmt und beginnt sich.
Aber begann er sich je?
Mutter, *du* machtest ihn klein, du warst, die ihn anfing;
dir war er neu, du beugtest über die neuen
Augen die freundliche Welt und wehrtest der fremden.
Wo, ach, hin sind die Jahre, da du ihm einfach
mit der schlanken Gestalt wallendes Chaos vertratst?
Vieles verbargst du ihm so; das nächtlich-verdächtige Zimmer
machtest du harmlos, aus deinem Herzen voll Zuflucht
mischtest du menschlichern Raum seinem Nacht-Raum hinzu.
Nicht in die Finsternis, nein, in dein näheres Dasein

The Third Elegy

One thing to sing the beloved, another, alas!
that hidden guilty river-god of the blood.
Him she discerns from afar, her lover, what does he know
of that Lord of Pleasure, who often, out of his lonely heart,
before she'd soothed him, often as though she didn't exist,
streaming from, oh, what unknowable depths, would uplift
his god-head, uprousing the night to infinite uproar?
Oh, the neptune within our blood, oh, his terrible trident!
Oh, the gloomy blast of his breast from the twisted shell!
Hark, how the night grows fluted and hollowed. You stars,
is it not from you that the lover's delight in the loved one's
face arises? Does not his intimate insight
into her purest face come from the purest star?

It wasn't you, alas! it wasn't his mother
that bent his brows into such an expectant arch.
Not to meet yours, girl feeling him, not to meet yours
did his lips begin to assume that more fruitful curve.
Do you really suppose your gentle approach could have so
convulsed him, you, that wander like wind at dawn?
You terrified his heart, indeed; but more ancient terrors
rushed into him in that instant of shattering touch.
Call him . . . you can't quite call him away from sombre
    consorting.
He certainly wants to, he does escape; disburdenedly settles
into your intimate heart, takes up and begins himself there.
Did he ever begin himself, though?
Mother, you made him small, it was you that began him;
for you he was new, you arched over those new eyes
the friendly world, averting the one that was strange.
Where, oh, where, are the years when you barred the way
for him, with your slender form, to the surging abyss?
You hid so much from him then; made the nightly-suspected room
harmless, and out of your heart full of refuge
mingled more human space with that night-space of his.
Not in the darkness, no, but within your far nearer presence

hast du das Nachtlicht gestellt, und es schien wie aus Freundschaft.
Nirgends ein Knistern, das du nicht lächelnd erklärtest,
so als wüßtest du längst, *wann* sich die Diele benimmt . . .
Und er horchte und linderte sich. So vieles vermochte
zärtlich dein Aufstehn; hinter den Schrank trat
hoch im Mantel sein Schicksal, und in die Falten des Vorhangs
paßte, die leicht sich verschob, seine unruhige Zukunft.

Und er selbst, wie er lag, der Erleichterte, unter
schläfernden Lidern deiner leichten Gestaltung
Süße lösend in den gekosteten Vorschlaf—:
schien ein Gehüteter . . . Aber *innen:* wer wehrte,
hinderte innen in ihm die Fluten der Herkunft?
Ach, da *war* keine Vorsicht im Schlafenden; schlafend,
aber träumend, aber in Fiebern: wie er sich ein-ließ.
Er, der Neue, Scheuende, wie er verstrickt war,
mit des innern Geschehns weiterschlagenden Ranken
schon zu Mustern verschlungen, zu würgendem Wachstum, zu
    tierhaft
jagenden Formen. Wie er sich hingab—. Liebte.
Liebte sein Inneres, seines Inneren Wildnis,
diesen Urwald in ihm, auf dessen stummem Gestürztsein
lichtgrün sein Herz stand. Liebte. Verließ es, ging die
eigenen Wurzeln hinaus in gewaltigen Ursprung,
wo seine kleine Geburt schon überlebt war. Liebend
stieg er hinab in das ältere Blut, in die Schluchten,
wo das Furchtbare lag, noch satt von den Vätern. Und jedes
Schreckliche kannte ihn, blinzelte, war wie verständigt.
Ja, das Entsetzliche lächelte . . . Selten
hast du so zärtlich gelächelt, Mutter. Wie sollte
er es nicht lieben, da es ihm lächelte. *Vor* dir
hat ers geliebt, denn, da du ihn trugst schon,
war es im Wasser gelöst, das den Keimenden leicht macht.

Siehe, wir lieben nicht, wie die Blumen, aus einem
einzigen Jahr; uns steigt, wo wir lieben,
unvordenklicher Saft in die Arme. O Mädchen,
dies: daß wir liebten *in* uns, nicht Eines, ein Künftiges, sondern

you placed the light, and it shone as though out of friendship.
Nowhere a creak you could not explain with a smile,
as though you had long known *when* the floor would behave itself
    thus . . .
And he listened to you and was soothed. So much it availed,
gently, your rising: his tall cloaked destiny stepped
behind the wardrobe then, and his restless future,
that easily got out of place, conformed to the folds of the curtain.

And he himself as he lay there in such relief,
dissolving, under his drowsy eyelids, the sweetness
of your light shaping into the sleep he had tasted,
seemed to be under protection . . . *Within*, though: who could
    avert,
divert, the floods of origin flowing within him?
Alas! there *was* no caution within that sleeper; sleeping,
yes, but dreaming, yes, but feverish: what he embarked on!
He, so new, so timorous, how he got tangled
in ever-encroaching creepers of inner event,
twisted to primitive patterns, to throttling growths, to bestial
preying forms! How he gave himself up to it! Loved.
Loved his interior world, his interior jungle,
that primal forest within, on whose mute overthrownness,
green-lit, his heart stood. Loved. Left it, continued
out through his own roots into violent beginning
where his tiny birth was already outlived. Descended,
lovingly, into the older blood, the ravines
where Frightfulness lurked, still gorged with his fathers. And every
terror knew him, winked, was as though it were waiting.
Yes, Horror smiled at him . . . Seldom
did you, Mother, smile so tenderly. How could he help
loving what smiled at him? Long before you
he loved it, for even while you bore him
it was there, dissolved in the water that lightens the seed.

Look, we don't love like flowers, with only a single
season behind us; immemorial sap
mounts in our arms when we love. Oh, maid,
this: that we've loved, *within* us, not one, still to come, but all

das zahllos Brauende; nicht ein einzelnes Kind,
sondern die Väter, die wie Trümmer Gebirgs
uns im Grunde beruhn; sondern das trockene Flußbett
einstiger Mütter—; sondern die ganze
lautlose Landschaft unter dem wolkigen oder
reinen Verhängnis—: *dies* kam dir, Mädchen, zuvor.

Und du selber, was weißt du—, du locktest
Vorzeit empor in dem Liebenden. Welche Gefühle
wühlten herauf aus entwandelten Wesen. Welche
Frauen haßten dich da. Wasfür finstere Männer
regtest du auf im Geäder des Jünglings? Tote
Kinder wollten zu dir . . . O leise, leise,
tu ein liebes vor ihm, ein verläßliches Tagwerk,—führ ihn
nah an den Garten heran, gieb ihm der Nächte
Übergewicht . . .
                    Verhalt ihn . . .

Die vierte Elegie

O Bäume Lebens, o wann winterlich?
Wir sind nicht einig. Sind nicht wie die Zug-
vögel verständigt. Überholt und spät,
so drängen wir uns plötzlich Winden auf
und fallen ein auf teilnahmslosen Teich.
Blühn und verdorrn ist uns zugleich bewußt.
Und irgendwo gehn Löwen noch und wissen,
solang sie herrlich sind, von keiner Ohnmacht.

Uns aber, wo wir Eines meinen, ganz,
ist schon des andern Aufwand fühlbar. Feindschaft
ist uns das Nächste. Treten Liebende
nicht immerfort an Ränder, eins im andern,
die sich versprachen Weite, Jagd und Heimat.
    Da wird für eines Augenblickes Zeichnung
ein Grund von Gegenteil bereitet, mühsam,
daß wir sie sähen; denn man ist sehr deutlich
mit uns. Wir kennen den Kontur

the innumerable fermentation; not just a single child,
but the fathers, resting like mountain-ruins
within our depths;—but the dry river-bed
of former mothers;—yes, and the whole of that
soundless landscape under its cloudy or
cloudless destiny:—*this* got the start of you, maid.

And you yourself, how can you tell,—you have conjured up
prehistoric time in your lover. What feelings
whelmed up from beings gone by! What women
hated you in him! What sinister men
you roused in his youthful veins! Dead children
were trying to reach you . . . Oh, gently, gently
show him daily an honest, confident task done,—guide him
close to the garden, give him preponderance
over his nights . . . . . .
                        Withhold him . . . . . .

The Fourth Elegy

O trees of life, what are your signs of winter?
We're not at one. We've no instinctive knowledge,
like migratory birds. Outstript and late,
we force ourselves on winds and find no welcome
from ponds where we alight. We comprehend
flowering and fading simultaneously.
And somewhere lions still roam, all unaware,
while yet their splendour lasts, of any weakness.

We, though, while we're intent upon one thing,
can feel the cost and conquest of another.
The Next's our enemy. Aren't lovers always
coming to precipices in each other,—
lovers, that looked for spaces, hunting, home?
Then, for the sudden sketchwork of a moment,
a ground of contrast's painfully prepared,
to make us see it. For they're very clear
with us, we that don't know our feeling's shape,

des Fühlens nicht: nur, was ihn formt von außen.
Wer saß nicht bang vor seines Herzens Vorhang?
Der schlug sich auf: die Szenerie war Abschied.
Leicht zu verstehen. Der bekannte Garten,
und schwankte leise: dann erst kam der Tänzer.
Nicht *der*. Genug! Und wenn er auch so leicht tut,
er ist verkleidet und er wird ein Bürger
und geht durch seine Küche in die Wohnung.
Ich will nicht diese halbgefüllten Masken,
lieber die Puppe. Die ist voll. Ich will
den Balg aushalten und den Draht und ihr
Gesicht aus Aussehn. Hier. Ich bin davor.
Wenn auch die Lampen ausgehn, wenn mir auch
gesagt wird: Nichts mehr—, wenn auch von der Bühne
das Leere herkommt mit dem grauen Luftzug,
wenn auch von meinen stillen Vorfahrn keiner
mehr mit mir dasitzt, keine Frau, sogar
der Knabe nicht mehr mit dem braunen Schielaug:
Ich bleibe dennoch. Es giebt immer Zuschaun.

Hab ich nicht recht? Du, der um mich so bitter
das Leben schmeckte, meines kostend, Vater,
den ersten trüben Aufguß meines Müssens,
da ich heranwuchs, immer wieder kostend
und, mit dem Nachgeschmack so fremder Zukunft
beschäftigt, prüftest mein beschlagnes Aufschaun,—
der du, mein Vater, seit du tot bist, oft
in meiner Hoffnung, innen in mir, Angst hast,
und Gleichmut, wie ihn Tote haben, Reiche
von Gleichmut, aufgiebst für mein bißchen Schicksal,
hab ich nicht recht? Und ihr, hab ich nicht recht,
die ihr mich liebtet für den kleinen Anfang
Liebe zu euch, von dem ich immer abkam,
weil mir der Raum in eurem Angesicht,
da ich ihn liebte, überging in Weltraum,
in dem ihr nicht mehr wart . . . wenn mir zumut ist,
zu warten vor der Puppenbühne, nein,
so völlig hinzuschaun, daß, um mein Schauen
am Ende aufzuwiegen, dort als Spieler

but only that which forms it from outside.
Who's not sat tense before his own heart's curtain?
Up it would go: the scenery was Parting.
Easy to understand. The well-known garden,
swaying a little. Then appeared the dancer.
Not *him*! Enough! However light he foots it,
he's just disguised, and turns into a bourgeois,
and passes through the kitchen to his dwelling.
I will not have these half-filled masks! No, no,
rather the doll. That's full. I'll force myself
to bear the husk, the wire, and even that face
of sheer appearance. Here! I'm in my seat.
Even if the lights go out, even if I'm told
'There's nothing more',—even if greyish draughts
of emptiness come drifting from the stage,—
even if of all my silent forbears none
sits by me any longer, not a woman,
not even the boy with the brown squinting eyes:
I'll still remain. For one can always watch.

Am I not right? You, to whom life would taste
so bitter, Father, when you tasted mine,
that turbid first infusion of my Must,
you kept on tasting as I kept on growing,
and, still arrested by the after-taste
of such queer future, tried my clouded gaze,—
you, who so often, since you died, my Father,
have been afraid within my inmost hope,
surrendering realms of that serenity
the dead are lords of for my bit of fate,—
am I not right? And you, am I not right,—
you that would love me for that small beginning
of love for you I always turned away from,
because the space within your faces changed,
even while I loved it, into cosmic space
where you no longer were . . . , when I feel like it,
to wait before the puppet stage,—no, rather
gaze so intensely on it that at last
a counterpoising angel has to come

ein Engel hinmuß, der die Bälge hochreißt.
Engel und Puppe: dann ist endlich Schauspiel.
Dann kommt zusammen, was wir immerfort
entzwein, indem wir da sind. Dann entsteht
aus unsern Jahreszeiten erst der Umkreis
des ganzen Wandelns. Über uns hinüber
spielt dann der Engel. Sieh, die Sterbenden,
sollten sie nicht vermuten, wie voll Vorwand
das alles ist, was wir hier leisten. Alles
ist nicht es selbst. O Stunden in der Kindheit,
da hinter den Figuren mehr als nur
Vergangnes war und vor uns nicht die Zukunft.
Wir wuchsen freilich und wir drängten manchmal,
bald groß zu werden, denen halb zulieb,
die andres nicht mehr hatten, als das Großsein.
Und waren doch, in unserem Alleingehn,
mit Dauerndem vergnügt und standen da
im Zwischenraume zwischen Welt und Spielzeug,
an einer Stelle, die seit Anbeginn
gegründet war für einen reinen Vorgang.

Wer zeigt ein Kind, so wie es steht? Wer stellt
es ins Gestirn und giebt das Maß des Abstands
ihm in die Hand? Wer macht den Kindertod
aus grauem Brot, das hart wird,—oder läßt
ihn drin im runden Mund, so wie den Gröps
von einem schönen Apfel? . . . Mörder sind
leicht einzusehen. Aber dies: den Tod,
den ganzen Tod, noch *vor* dem Leben so
sanft zu enthalten und nicht bös zu sein,
ist unbeschreiblich.

and play a part there, snatching up the husks?
Angel and doll! Then there's at last a play.
Then there unites what we continually
part by our mere existence. Then at last
emerges from our seasons here the cycle
of the whole process. Over and above us,
then, there's the angel playing. Look, the dying,—
surely they must suspect how full of pretext
is all that we accomplish here, where nothing
is what it really is. O hours of childhood,
hours when behind the figures there was more
than the mere past, and when what lay before us
was not the future! True, we were growing, and sometimes
made haste to be grown up, half for the sake
of those who'd nothing left but their grown-upness.
Yet, when alone, we entertained ourselves
with everlastingness: there we would stand,
within the gap left between world and toy,
upon a spot which, from the first beginning,
had been established for a pure event.

Who'll show a child just as it is? Who'll place it
within its constellation, with the measure
of distance in its hand? Who'll make its death
from grey bread, that grows hard,—or leave it there,
within the round mouth, like the seeded core
of a nice apple? . . . . . . Minds of murderers
can easily be fathomed. This, though: death,
the whole of death, before life's start, to hold it
so gently and so free from all resentment,
transcends description.

Die fünfte Elegie

Frau Hertha Koenig zugeeignet

Wer aber *sind* sie, sag mir, die Fahrenden, diese ein wenig
Flüchtigern noch als wir selbst, die dringend von früh an
wringt ein *wem, wem* zu Liebe
niemals zufriedener Wille? Sondern er wringt sie,
biegt sie, schlingt sie und schwingt sie,
wirft sie und fängt sie zurück; wie aus geölter,
glatterer Luft kommen sie nieder
auf dem verzehrten, von ihrem ewigen
Aufsprung dünneren Teppich, diesem verlorenen
Teppich im Weltall.
Aufgelegt wie ein Pflaster, als hätte der Vorstadt-
Himmel der Erde dort wehe getan.
                              Und kaum dort,
aufrecht, da und gezeigt: des Dastehns
großer Anfangsbuchstab . . . , schon auch, die stärksten
Männer, rollt sie wieder, zum Scherz, der immer
kommende Griff, wie August der Starke bei Tisch
einen zinnenen Teller.

Ach und um diese
Mitte, die Rose des Zuschauns:
blüht und entblättert. Um diesen
Stampfer, den Stempel, den von dem eignen
blühenden Staub getroffnen, zur Scheinfrucht
wieder der Unlust befruchteten, ihrer
niemals bewußten,—glänzend mit dünnster
Oberfläche leicht scheinlächelnden Unlust.
Da: der welke, faltige Stemmer,
der alte, der nur noch trommelt,
eingegangen in seiner gewaltigen Haut, als hätte sie früher
zwei Männer enthalten, und einer
läge nun schon auf dem Kirchhof, und er überlebte den andern,
taub und manchmal ein wenig
wirr, in der verwitweten Haut.

The Fifth Elegy

Dedicated to Frau Hertha Koenig

But tell me, who *are* they, these travellers, even a little
more fleeting than we ourselves,—so urgently, ever since childhood,
wrung by an (oh, for the sake of whom?)
never-contented will? That keeps on wringing them,
bending them, slinging them, swinging them,
throwing them and catching them back: as though from an oily,
smoother air, they come down on the threadbare
carpet, thinned by their everlasting
upspringing, this carpet forlornly
lost in the cosmos.
Laid on like a plaster, as though the suburban sky
had injured the earth there.
                              And hardly there,
upright, shown us: the great initial
letter of Thereness,—than even the strongest
men are rolled once more, in sport, by the ever-
returning grasp, as once by Augustus the Strong
a tin platter at table.

Alas, and round this
centre the rose of onlooking
blooms and unblossoms. Round this
pestle, this pistil, caught by its own
dust-pollen, and fertilised over again
to a sham-fruit of boredom, their own
never-realised, so thin-surfacedly gleaming,
lightly sham-smiling boredom.
There, the withered wrinkled lifter,
old now and only drumming,
shrivelled up in his massive hide as though it had once contained
two men, and one were already
lying in the churchyard, and this one here had survived him,
deaf and sometimes a little
lost in his widowed skin.

Aber der junge, der Mann, als wär er der Sohn eines Nackens
und einer Nonne: prall und strammig erfüllt
mit Muskeln und Einfalt.

Oh ihr,
die ein Leid, das noch klein war,
einst als Spielzeug bekam, in einer seiner
langen Genesungen . . .

Du, der mit dem Aufschlag,
wie nur Früchte ihn kennen, unreif,
täglich hundertmal abfällt vom Baum der gemeinsam
erbauten Bewegung (der, rascher als Wasser, in wenig
Minuten Lenz, Sommer und Herbst hat)—
abfällt und anprallt ans Grab:
manchmal, in halber Pause, will dir ein liebes
Antlitz entstehn hinüber zu deiner selten
zärtlichen Mutter; doch an deinen Körper verliert sich,
der es flächig verbraucht, das schüchtern
kaum versuchte Gesicht . . . Und wieder
klatscht der Mann in die Hand zu dem Ansprung, und eh dir
jemals ein Schmerz deutlicher wird in der Nähe des immer
trabenden Herzens, kommt das Brennen der Fußsohln
ihm, seinem Ursprung, zuvor mit ein paar dir
rasch in die Augen gejagten leiblichen Tränen.
Und dennoch, blindlings,
das Lächeln . . .

Engel! o nimms, pflücks, das kleinblütige Heilkraut.
Schaff eine Vase, verwahrs! Stells unter jene, uns *noch* nicht
offenen Freuden; in lieblicher Urne
rühms mit blumiger schwungiger Aufschrift:

»Subrisio Saltat.«.

    Du dann, Liebliche,
du, von den reizendsten Freuden
stumm Übersprungne. Vielleicht sind
deine Fransen glücklich für dich—,
oder über den jungen
prallen Brüsten die grüne metallene Seide

And the youngster, the man, like the son of a neck
and a nun: so tautly and smartly filled
with muscle and simpleness.

O you,
a pain that was still quite small
received as a plaything once in one of its
long convalescences. . . .

You, that fall with the thud
only fruits know, unripe,
daily a hundred times from the tree
of mutually built up motion (the tree that, swifter than water,
has spring and summer and autumn in so many minutes),
fall and rebound on the grave:
sometimes, in half-pauses, a tenderness tries
to steal out over your face to your seldomly
tender mother, but scatters over your body,
whose surface quickly absorbs the timidly rippling,
hardly attempted look . . . And again
that man is clapping his hands for the downward spring, and before
a single pain has got within range of your ever-
galloping heart, comes the tingling
in the soles of your feet, ahead of the spring that it springs from,
chasing into your eyes a few physical tears.
And still, all instinctive,
that smile. . . .

Angel! oh, take it, pluck it, that small-flowered herb of healing!
Get a vase to preserve it. Set it among those joys
not yet open to us: in a graceful urn
praise it, with florally soaring inscription:
                                    'Subrisio Saltat.'
Then you, my darling,
mutely elided
by all the most exquisite joys. Perhaps
your frills are happy on your behalf,—
or over your tight young breasts
the green metallic silk

fühlt sich unendlich verwöhnt und entbehrt nichts.
Du,
immerfort anders auf alle des Gleichgewichts schwankende Waagen
hingelegte Marktfrucht des Gleichmuts,
öffentlich unter den Schultern.

Wo, o *wo* ist der Ort—ich trag ihn im Herzen—,
wo sie noch lange nicht *konnten*, noch von einander
abfieln, wie sich bespringende, nicht recht
paarige Tiere;—
wo die Gewichte noch schwer sind;
wo noch von ihren vergeblich
wirbelnden Stäben die Teller
torkeln . . .

Und plötzlich in diesem mühsamen Nirgends, plötzlich
die unsägliche Stelle, wo sich das reine Zuwenig
unbegreiflich verwandelt—, umspringt
in jenes leere Zuviel.
Wo die vielstellige Rechnung
zahlenlos aufgeht.

Plätze, o Platz in Paris, unendlicher Schauplatz,
wo die Modistin, *Madame Lamort,*
die ruhlosen Wege der Erde, endlose Bänder,
schlingt und windet und neue aus ihnen
Schleifen erfindet, Rüschen, Blumen, Kokarden, künstliche Früchte—,
    alle
unwahr gefärbt,—für die billigen
Winterhüte des Schicksals.

                    . . . .

Engel!: Es wäre ein Platz, den wir nicht wissen, und dorten,
auf unsäglichem Teppich, zeigten die Liebenden, die's hier
bis zum Können nie bringen, ihre kühnen
hohen Figuren des Herzschwungs,
ihre Türme aus Lust, ihre
längst, wo Boden nie war, nur an einander
lehnenden Leitern, bebend,—und *könntens,*
vor den Zuschauern rings, unzähligen lautlosen Toten:

feels itself endlessly spoilt and in need of nothing.
You,
time after time, upon all of the quivering scale-pans of balance
freshly laid fruit of serenity,
publicly shown among shoulders.

Where, oh, where in the world is that place in my heart
where they still were far from being *able*, still fell away
from each other like mounting animals, not yet
ready for pairing;—
where weights are still heavy,
and hoops still stagger
away from their vainly
twirling sticks? . . . . .

And then, in this wearisome nowhere, all of a sudden,
the ineffable spot where the pure too-little
incomprehensibly changes, veering
into that empty too-much?
Where the many-digited sum
solves into zero?

Squares, O square in Paris, infinite show-place,
where the modiste Madame Lamort
winds and binds the restless ways of the world,
those endless ribbons, to ever-new
creations of bow, frill, flower, cockade and fruit,
all falsely coloured, to deck
the cheap winter-hats of Fate.

. . . .

Angel: suppose there's a place we know nothing about, and there,
on some indescribable carpet, lovers showed all that here
they're for ever unable to manage—their daring
lofty figures of heart-flight,
their towers of pleasure, their ladders,
long since, where ground never was, just quiveringly
propped by each other,—were able to manage it there,
before the ringed onlookers there, countless unmurmuring dead:

Würfen die dann ihre letzten, immer ersparten,
immer verborgenen, die wir nicht kennen, ewig
gültigen Münzen des Glücks vor das endlich
wahrhaft lächelnde Paar auf gestilltem
Teppich?

Die Siebente Elegie

Werbung nicht mehr, nicht Werbung, entwachsene Stimme,
sei deines Schreies Natur; zwar schrieest du rein wie der Vogel,
wenn ihn die Jahreszeit aufhebt, die steigende, beinah vergessend,
daß er ein kümmerndes Tier und nicht nur ein einzelnes Herz sei,
das sie ins Heitere wirft, in die innigen Himmel. Wie er, so
würbest du wohl, nicht minder—, daß, noch unsichtbar,
dich die Freundin erführ, die stille, in der eine Antwort
langsam erwacht und über dem Hören sich anwärmt,—
deinem erkühnten Gefühl die erglühte Gefühlin.

O und der Frühling begriffe—, da ist keine Stelle,
die nicht trüge den Ton der Verkündigung. Erst jenen kleinen
fragenden Auflaut, den, mit steigernder Stille,
weithin umschweigt ein reiner bejahender Tag.
Dann die Stufen hinan, Ruf-Stufen hinan, zum geträumten
Tempel der Zukunft—; dann den Triller, Fontäne,
die zu dem drängenden Strahl schon das Fallen zuvornimmt
im versprechlichen Spiel . . . Und vor sich, den Sommer.
  Nicht nur die Morgen alle des Sommers—, nicht nur
wie sie sich wandeln in Tag und strahlen vor Angang.
Nicht nur die Tage, die zart sind um Blumen, und oben,
um die gestalteten Bäume, stark und gewaltig.
Nicht nur die Andacht dieser entfalteten Kräfte,
nicht nur die Wege, nicht nur die Wiesen im Abend,
nicht nur, nach spätem Gewitter, das atmende Klarsein,
nicht nur der nahende Schlaf und ein Ahnen, abends . . .
sondern die Nächte! Sondern die hohen, des Sommers,
Nächte, sondern die Sterne, die Sterne der Erde.
O einst tot sein und sie wissen unendlich,
alle die Sterne: denn wie, wie, wie sie vergessen!

would not those then fling their last, their for ever reserved,
ever-concealed, unknown to us, ever-valid
coins of happiness down before the at last
truthfully smiling pair on the quietened
carpet?

The Seventh Elegy

Not wooing, no longer shall wooing, voice that's outgrown it,
be now the form of your cry; though you cried as pure as the bird
when the surging season uplifts him, almost forgetting
he's merely a fretful creature and not just a single heart
it's tossing to brightness, to intimate azure. No less
than he, you, too, would be wooing some silent companion
to feel you, as yet unseen, some mate in whom a reply
was slowly awaking and warming itself as she listened,—
your own emboldened feeling's glowing fellow-feeling.
Oh, and Spring would understand—not a nook would fail
to re-echo annunciation. Re-echoing first the tiny
questioning pipe a purely affirmative day
quietly invests all round with magnifying stillness.
Then the long flight of steps, the call-steps, up to the dreamt-of
temple of what's to come;—then the trill, that fountain
grasped, as it rises, by Falling, in promiseful play,
for another thrusting jet . . . And before it, the Summer!
Not only all those summer dawns, not only
the way they turn into day and stream with Beginning.
Not only the days, so gentle round flowers, and, above,
around the configured trees, so mighty and strong.
Not only the fervour of these unfolded forces,
not only the walks, not only the evening meadows,
not only, after late thunder, the breathing clearness,
not only, evenings, sleep coming and something surmised . . .
No, but the nights as well! the lofty, the summer
nights,—but the stars as well, the stars of the Earth!
Oh, to be dead at last and endlessly know them,
all the stars! For how, how, how to forget them!

Siehe, da rief ich die Liebende. Aber nicht *sie* nur
käme . . . Es kämen aus schwächlichen Gräbern
Mädchen und ständen . . . Denn, wie beschränk ich,
wie, den gerufenen Ruf? Die Versunkenen suchen
immer noch Erde.—Ihr Kinder, ein hiesig
einmal ergriffenes Ding gälte für viele.
Glaubt nicht, Schicksal sei mehr, als das Dichte der Kindheit;
wie überholtet ihr oft den Geliebten, atmend,
atmend nach seligem Lauf, auf nichts zu, ins Freie.

Hiersein ist herrlich. Ihr wußtet es, Mädchen, *ihr* auch,
die ihr scheinbar entbehrtet, versankt—, ihr, in den ärgsten
Gassen der Städte, Schwärende, oder dem Abfall
Offene. Denn eine Stunde war jeder, vielleicht nicht
ganz eine Stunde, ein mit den Maßen der Zeit kaum
Meßliches zwischen zwei Weilen—, da sie ein Dasein
hatte. Alles. Die Adern voll Dasein.
Nur, wir vergessen so leicht, was der lachende Nachbar
uns nicht bestätigt oder beneidet. Sichtbar
wollen wirs heben, wo doch das sichtbarste Glück uns
erst zu erkennen sich giebt, wenn wir es innen verwandeln.

Nirgends, Geliebte, wird Welt sein, als innen. Unser
Leben geht hin mit Verwandlung. Und immer geringer
schwindet das Außen. Wo einmal ein dauerndes Haus war,
schlägt sich erdachtes Gebild vor, quer, zu Erdenklichem
völlig gehörig, als ständ es noch ganz im Gehirne.
Weite Speicher der Kraft schafft sich der Zeitgeist, gestaltlos
wie der spannende Drang, den er aus allem gewinnt.
Tempel kennt er nicht mehr. Diese, des Herzens, Verschwendung
sparen wir heimlicher ein. Ja, wo noch eins übersteht,
ein einst gebetetes Ding, ein gedientes, geknietes—,
hält es sich, so wie es ist, schon ins Unsichtbare hin.
Viele gewahrens nicht mehr, doch ohne den Vorteil,
daß sie's nun *innerlich* baun, mit Pfeilern und Statuen, größer!

   Jede dumpfe Umkehr der Welt hat solche Enterbte,
denen das Frühere nicht und noch nicht das Nächste gehört.
Denn auch das Nächste ist weit für die Menschen. *Uns* soll

Look, I've been calling the lover. But not only she
would come . . . Out of unwithholding graves
girls would come and gather . . . For how could I limit
the call I had called? The sunken are always seeking
Earth again.—You children, I'd say, a single
thing comprehended here's as good as a thousand.
Don't think Destiny's more than what's packed into childhood.
How often you'd overtake the beloved, panting,
panting from blissful pursuit of nothing but distance!
Being here's glorious! Even you knew it, you girls,
who went without, as it seemed, sank under,—you, in the vilest
streets of cities, festering, or open for refuse.
For to each was granted an hour,—perhaps not quite
so much as an hour—some span that could scarcely be measured
by measures of time, in between two whiles, when she really
possessed an existence. All. Veins full of existence.
But we so lightly forget what our laughing neighbour
neither confirms nor envies. We want to be visibly
able to show it; whereas the most visible joy
can only reveal itself to us when we've transformed it, within.

Nowhere, beloved, can world exist but within.
Life passes in transformation. And, ever diminishing,
outwardness dwindles. Where once was a permanent house,
up starts some invented structure across our vision, as fully
at home among concepts as though it still stood in a brain.
Spacious garners of power are formed by the Time Spirit, formless
as that tense urge he's extracting from everything else.
Temples he knows no longer. We're now more secretly saving
such lavish expenses of heart. Nay, even where one survives,
one single thing once prayed or tended or knelt to,
it's reaching, just as it is, into the unseen world.
Many perceive it no more, but neglect the advantage
of building it grandlier now, with pillars and statues, *within*!

Each torpid turn of the world has such disinherited children,
those to whom former has ceased, next not yet come, to belong.
For even the next is far for mankind. Though this

dies nicht verwirren; es stärke in uns die Bewahrung
der noch erkannten Gestalt.—Dies *stand* einmal unter Menschen,
mitten im Schicksal stands, im vernichtenden, mitten
im Nichtwissen-Wohin stand es, wie seiend, und bog
Sterne zu sich aus gesicherten Himmeln. Engel,
dir noch zeig ich es, *da!* in deinem Anschaun
steh es gerettet zuletzt, nun endlich aufrecht.
Säulen, Pylone, der Sphinx, das strebende Stemmen,
grau aus vergehender Stadt oder aus fremder, des Doms.

War es nicht Wunder? O staune, Engel, denn *wir* sinds,
wir, o du Großer, erzähls, daß wir solches vermochten, mein Atem
reicht für die Rühmung nicht aus. So haben wir dennoch
nicht die Räume versäumt, diese gewährenden, diese
unseren Räume. (Was müssen sie fürchterlich groß sein,
da sie Jahrtausende nicht unseres Fühlns überfülln.)
Aber ein Turm war groß, nicht wahr? O Engel, er war es,—
groß, auch noch neben dir? Chartres war groß—, und Musik
reichte noch weiter hinan und überstieg uns. Doch selbst nur
eine Liebende—, oh, allein am nächtlichen Fenster . . .
reichte sie dir nicht ans Knie—?
                                        Glaub *nicht,* daß ich werbe.
Engel, und würb ich dich auch! Du kommst nicht. Denn mein
Anruf ist immer voll Hinweg; wider so starke
Strömung kannst du nicht schreiten. Wie ein gestreckter
Arm ist mein Rufen. Und seine zum Greifen
oben offene Hand bleibt vor dir
offen, wie Abwehr und Warnung,
Unfaßlicher, weitauf.

shall not confuse us, shall rather confirm us in keeping
still recognisable form. This *stood* once among mankind,
stood in the midst of Fate, the extinguisher, stood
in the midst of not-knowing-whither, as though it existed, and
     bowed
stars from established heavens towards it. Angel,
I'll show it to you as well—there! In your gaze
it shall stand redeemed at last, in a final uprightness.
Pillars, pylons, the Sphinx, all the striving thrust,
greyly from fading or foreign town, of the spire!
Was it not miracle? Angel, gaze, for it's *we*—
O mightiness, tell them that *we* were capable of it—my breath's
too short for this celebration. So, after all, we have *not*
failed to make use of the spaces, these generous spaces, these
our spaces. (How terribly big they must be,
when, with thousands of years of our feeling, they're not
     overcrowded.)
But a tower was great, was it not? Oh, Angel, it was, though,—
even compared with you? Chartres was great—and music
towered still higher and passed beyond us. Why, even
a girl in love, alone, at her window, at night . . .
did she not reach to your knee?—
                              Don't think that I'm wooing!
Angel, even if I were, you'd never come! For my call
is always full of outgoing; against such a powerful
current you cannot advance. Like an outstretched
arm is my call. And its hand, for some grasping,
skywardly opened, remains before you
as opened so wide but for warding
and warning, Inapprehensible.

Die achte Elegie

Rudolf Kassner zugeeignet

Mit allen Augen sieht die Kreatur
das Offene. Nur unsre Augen sind
wie umgekehrt und ganz um sie gestellt
als Fallen, rings um ihren freien Ausgang.
Was draußen *ist,* wir wissens aus des Tiers
Antlitz allein; denn schon das frühe Kind
wenden wir um und zwingens, daß es rückwärts
Gestaltung sehe, nicht das Offne, das
im Tiergesicht so tief ist. Frei von Tod.
Ihn sehen wir allein; das freie Tier
hat seinen Untergang stets hinter sich
und vor sich Gott, und wenn es geht, so gehts
in Ewigkeit, so wie die Brunnen gehen.
   Wir haben nie, nicht einen einzigen Tag,
den reinen Raum vor uns, in den die Blumen
unendlich aufgehn. Immer ist es Welt
und niemals Nirgends ohne Nicht: das Reine,
Unüberwachte, das man atmet und
unendlich *weiß* und nicht begehrt. Als Kind
verliert sich eins im Stilln an dies und wird
gerüttelt. Oder jener stirbt und *ists.*
Denn nah am Tod sieht man den Tod nicht mehr
und starrt *hinaus,* vielleicht mit großem Tierblick.
Liebende, wäre nicht der andre, der
die Sicht verstellt, sind nah daran und staunen . . .
Wie aus Versehn ist ihnen aufgetan
hinter dem andern . . . Aber über ihn
kommt keiner fort, und wieder wird ihm Welt.
Der Schöpfung immer zugewendet, sehn
wir nur auf ihr die Spiegelung des Frein,
von uns verdunkelt. Oder daß ein Tier,
ein stummes, aufschaut, ruhig durch uns durch.
Dieses heißt Schicksal: gegenüber sein
und nichts als das und immer gegenüber.

The Eighth Elegy

Dedicated to Rudolf Kassner

With all its eyes the creature-world beholds
the open. But our eyes, as though reversed,
encircle it on every side, like traps
set round its unobstructed path to freedom.
What *is* outside, we know from the brute's face
alone; for while a child's quite small we take it
and turn it round and force it to look backwards
at conformation, not that openness
so deep within the brute's face. Free from death.
We alone see *that*; the free animal
has its decease perpetually behind it
and God in front, and when it moves, it moves
within eternity, like running springs.
We've never, no, not for a single day,
pure space before us, such as that which flowers
endlessly open into: always world,
and never nowhere without no: that pure,
unsuperintended element one breathes,
endlessly knows, and never craves. A child
sometimes gets quietly lost there, to be always
jogged back again. Or someone dies and *is* it.
For, nearing death, one perceives death no longer,
and stares ahead—perhaps with large brute gaze.
Lovers—were not the other present, always
blocking the view!—draw near to it and wonder . . .
Behind the other, as though through oversight,
the thing's revealed . . . But no one gets beyond
the other, and so world returns once more.
Always facing Creation, we perceive there
only a mirroring of the free and open,
dimmed by our breath. Or that a dumb brute's calmly
raising its head to look us through and through.
For this is Destiny: being opposite,
and nothing else, and always opposite.

Wäre Bewußtheit unsrer Art in dem
sicheren Tier, das uns entgegenzieht
in anderer Richtung—, riß es uns herum
mit seinem Wandel. Doch sein Sein ist ihm
unendlich, ungefaßt und ohne Blick
auf seinen Zustand, rein, so wie sein Ausblick.
Und wo wir Zukunft sehn, dort sieht es Alles
und sich in Allem und geheilt für immer.

Und doch ist in dem wachsam warmen Tier
Gewicht und Sorge einer großen Schwermut.
Denn ihm auch haftet immer an, was uns
oft überwältigt,—die Erinnerung,
als sei schon einmal das, wonach man drängt,
näher gewesen, treuer und sein Anschluß
unendlich zärtlich. Hier ist alles Abstand,
und dort wars Atem. Nach der ersten Heimat
ist ihm die zweite zwitterig und windig.
    O Seligkeit der *kleinen* Kreatur,
die immer *bleibt* im Schooße, der sie austrug;
o Glück der Mücke, die noch *innen* hüpft,
selbst wenn sie Hochzeit hat: denn Schooß ist Alles.
Und sieh die halbe Sicherheit des Vogels,
der beinah beides weiß aus seinem Ursprung,
als wär er eine Seele der Etrusker,
aus einem Toten, den ein Raum empfing,
doch mit der ruhenden Figur als Deckel.
Und wie bestürzt eins, das fliegen muß
und stammt aus einem Schooß. Wie vor sich selbst
erschreckt, durchzuckts die Luft, wie wenn ein Sprung
durch eine Tasse geht. So reißt die Spur
der Fledermaus durchs Porzellan des Abends.

Und wir: Zuschauer, immer, überall,
dem allen zugewandt und nie hinaus!
Uns überfüllts. Wir ordnens. Es zerfällt.
Wir ordnens wieder und zerfallen selbst.

Did consciousness such as we have exist
in the sure animal that moves towards us
upon a different course, the brute would drag us
round in its wake. But its own being for it
is infinite, inapprehensible,
unintrospective, pure, like its outgazing.
Where we see Future, it sees Everything,
itself in Everything, for ever healed.

And yet, within the wakefully-warm beast
there lies the weight and care of a great sadness.
For that which often overwhelms us clings
to him as well,—a kind of memory
that what one's pressing after now was once
nearer and truer and attached to us
with infinite tenderness. Here all is distance,
there it was breath. Compared with that first home
the second seems ambiguous and fickle.

Oh, bliss of *tiny* creatures that *remain*
for ever in the womb that brought them forth!
Joy of the gnat, that can still leap *within,*
even on its wedding-day: for womb is all!
Look at the half-assurance of the bird,
through origin almost aware of both,
like one of those Etruscan souls, escaped
from a dead man enclosed within a space
on which his resting figure forms a lid.
And how dismayed is any womb-born thing
that has to fly! As though it were afraid
of its own self, it zigzags through the air
like crack through cup. The way a bat's track runs
rendingly through the evening's porcelain.

And we, spectators always, everywhere,
looking at, never out of, everything!
It fills us. We arrange it. It collapses.
We re-arrange it, and collapse ourselves.

Wer hat uns also umgedreht, daß wir,
was wir auch tun, in jener Haltung sind
von einem, welcher fortgeht? Wie er auf
dem letzten Hügel, der ihm ganz sein Tal
noch einmal zeigt, sich wendet, anhält, weilt—,
so leben wir und nehmen immer Abschied.

Die neunte Elegie

Warum, wenn es angeht, also die Frist des Daseins
hinzubringen, als Lorbeer, ein wenig dunkler als alles
andere Grün, mit kleinen Wellen an jedem
Blattrand (wie eines Windes Lächeln)—: warum dann
Menschliches müssen—und, Schicksal vermeidend,
sich sehnen nach Schicksal? . . .
                    Oh, *nicht,* weil Glück *ist,*
dieser voreilige Vorteil eines nahen Verlusts.
Nicht aus Neugier, oder zur Übung des Herzens,
das auch im Lorbeer *wäre* . . .

Aber weil Hiersein viel ist, und weil uns scheinbar
alles das Hiesige braucht, dieses Schwindende, das
seltsam uns angeht. Uns, die Schwindendsten. *Ein* Mal
jedes, nur *ein* Mal. *Ein* Mal und nichtmehr. Und wir auch
ein Mal. Nie wieder. Aber dieses
ein Mal gewesen zu sein, wenn auch nur *ein* Mal:
irdisch gewesen zu sein, scheint nicht widerrufbar.

Und so drängen wir uns und wollen es leisten,
wollens enthalten in unsern einfachen Händen,
im überfüllteren Blick und im sprachlosen Herzen.
Wollen es werden.—Wem es geben? Am liebsten
alles behalten für immer . . . Ach, in den andern Bezug,
wehe, was nimmt man hinüber? Nicht das Anschaun, das hier
langsam erlernte, und kein hier Ereignetes. Keins.
Also die Schmerzen. Also vor allem das Schwersein,
also der Liebe lange Erfahrung,—also
lauter Unsägliches. Aber später,

Who's turned us round like this, so that we always,
do what we may, retain the attitude
of someone who's departing? Just as he,
on the last hill, that shows him all his valley
for the last time, will turn and stop and linger,
we live our lives, for ever taking leave.

The Ninth Elegy

Why, when this span of life might be fleeted away
as laurel, a little darker than all
the surrounding green, with tiny waves on the border
of every leaf (like the smile of a wind):—oh, why
have to be human, and, shunning Destiny,
long for Destiny? . . .

                 Not because happiness really
exists, that precipitate profit of imminent loss.
Not out of curiosity, not just to practise the heart,
that could still be there in laurel. . . . .
But because being here is much, and because all this
that's here, so fleeting, seems to require us and strangely
concerns us. Us the most fleeting of all. Just once,
everything, only for once. Once and no more. And we, too,
once. And never again. But this
having been once, though only once,
having been once on earth—can it ever be cancelled?

And so we keep pressing on and trying to perform it,
trying to contain it within our simple hands,
in the more and more crowded gaze, in the speechless heart.
Trying to become it. To give it to whom? We'd rather
hold on to it all for ever . . . But into the other relation,
what, alas! do we carry across? Not the beholding we've here
slowly acquired, and no here occurrence. Not one.
Sufferings, then. Above all, the hardness of life,
the long experience of love; in fact,
purely untellable things. But later,

unter den Sternen, was solls: *die* sind *besser* unsäglich.
Bringt doch der Wanderer auch vom Hange des Bergrands
nicht eine Hand voll Erde ins Tal, die Allen unsägliche, sondern
ein erworbenes Wort, reines, den gelben und blaun
Enzian. Sind wir vielleicht *hier*, um zu sagen: Haus,
Brücke, Brunnen, Tor, Krug, Obstbaum, Fenster,—
höchstens: Säule, Turm . . . aber zu *sagen*, verstehs,
oh zu sagen *so*, wie selber die Dinge niemals
innig meinten zu sein. Ist nicht die heimliche List
dieser verschwiegenen Erde, wenn sie die Liebenden drängt,
daß sich in ihrem Gefühl jedes und jedes entzückt?
Schwelle: was ists für zwei
Liebende, daß sie die eigne ältere Schwelle der Tür
ein wenig verbrauchen, auch sie, nach den vielen vorher
und vor den künftigen . . . , leicht.

Hier ist des *Säglichen* Zeit, *hier* seine Heimat.
Sprich und bekenn. Mehr als je
fallen die Dinge dahin, die erlebbaren, denn,
was sie verdrängend ersetzt, ist ein Tun ohne Bild.
Tun unter Krusten, die willig zerspringen, sobald
innen das Handeln entwächst und sich anders begrenzt.
Zwischen den Hämmern besteht
unser Herz, wie die Zunge
zwischen den Zähnen, die doch,
dennoch, die preisende bleibt.

Preise dem Engel die Welt, nicht die unsägliche, *ihm*
kannst du nicht großtun mit herrlich Erfühltem; im Weltall,
wo er fühlender fühlt, bist du ein Neuling. Drum zeig
ihm das Einfache, das, von Geschlecht zu Geschlechtern gestaltet,
als ein Unsriges lebt, neben der Hand und im Blick.
Sag ihm die Dinge. Er wird staunender stehn; wie du standest
bei dem Seiler in Rom, oder beim Töpfer am Nil.
Zeig ihm, wie glücklich ein Ding sein kann, wie schuldlos und unser,
wie selbst das klagende Leid rein zur Gestalt sich entschließt,
dient als ein Ding, oder stirbt in ein Ding—, und jenseits
selig der Geige entgeht.—Und diese, von Hingang
lebenden Dinge verstehn, daß du sie rühmst; vergänglich,

under the stars, what use? the more deeply untellable stars?
Yet the wanderer too doesn't bring from mountain to valley
a handful of earth, of for all untellable earth, but only
a word he has won, pure, the yellow and blue
gentian. Are we, perhaps, *here* just for saying: House,
Bridge, Fountain, Gate, Jug, Fruit tree, Window,—
possibly: Pillar, Tower? . . . but for *saying*, remember,
oh, for such saying as never the things themselves
hoped so intensely to be. Is not the secret purpose
of this sly Earth, in urging a pair of lovers,
just to make everything leap with ecstasy in them?
Threshold: what does it mean
to a pair of lovers, that they should be wearing their own
worn threshold a little, they too, after the many before,
before the many to come, . . . as a matter of course!

Here is the time for the Tellable, *here* is its home.
Speak and proclaim. More than ever
things we can live with are falling away, for that
which is oustingly taking their place is an imageless act.
Act under crusts, that will readily split as soon
as the doing within outgrows them and takes a new outline.
Between the hammers lives on
our heart, as between the teeth
the tongue, which, in spite of all,
still continues to praise.

Praise this world to the Angel, not the untellable: you
can't impress him with the splendour you've felt; in the cosmos
where he more feelingly feels you're only a novice. So show him
some simple thing, refashioned by age after age,
till it lives in our hands and eyes as a part of ourselves.
Tell him *things*. He'll stand more astonished: as you did
beside the roper in Rome or the potter in Egypt.
Show him how happy a thing can be, how guileless and ours;
how even the moaning of grief purely determines on form,
serves as a thing, or dies into a thing,—to escape
to a bliss beyond the fiddle. These things that live on departure
understand when you praise them: fleeting, they look for

232 · *Rainer Maria Rilke*

traun sie ein Rettendes uns, den Vergänglichsten, zu.
Wollen, wir sollen sie ganz im unsichtbarn Herzen verwandeln
in—o unendlich—in uns! Wer wir am Ende auch seien.

Erde, ist es nicht dies, was du willst: *unsichtbar*
in uns erstehn?—Ist es dein Traum nicht,
einmal unsichtbar zu sein?—Erde! unsichtbar!
Was, wenn Verwandlung nicht, ist dein drängender Auftrag?
Erde, du liebe, ich will. Oh glaub, es bedürfte
nicht deiner Frühlinge mehr, mich dir zu gewinnen—, *einer,*
ach, ein einziger ist schon dem Blute zu viel.
Namenlos bin ich zu dir entschlossen, von weit her.
Immer warst du im Recht, und dein heiliger Einfall
ist der vertrauliche Tod.

Siehe, ich lebe. Woraus? Weder Kindheit noch Zukunft
werden weniger . . . Überzähliges Dasein
entspringt mir im Herzen.

Die zehnte Elegie

Dass ich dereinst, an dem Ausgang der grimmigen Einsicht,
Jubel und Ruhm aufsinge zustimmenden Engeln.
Daß von den klar geschlagenen Hämmern des Herzens
keiner versage an weichen, zweifelnden oder
reißenden Saiten. Daß mich mein strömendes Antlitz
glänzender mache; daß das unscheinbare Weinen
blühe. O wie werdet ihr dann, Nächte, mir lieb sein,
gehärmte. Daß ich euch knieender nicht, untröstliche Schwestern,
hinnahm, nicht in euer gelöstes
Haar mich gelöster ergab. Wir, Vergeuder der Schmerzen.
Wie wir sie absehn voraus, in die traurige Dauer,
ob sie nicht enden vielleicht. Sie aber sind ja
unser winterwähriges Laub, unser dunkeles Sinngrün,
eine der Zeiten des heimlichen Jahres—, nicht nur
Zeit—, sind Stelle, Siedelung, Lager, Boden, Wohnort.

rescue through something in us, the most fleeting of all.
Want us to change them entirely, within our invisible hearts,
into—oh, endlessly—into ourselves! Whosoever we are.

Earth, is it not just this that you want: to arise
invisibly in us? Is not your dream
to be one day invisible? Earth! invisible!
What is your urgent command, if not transformation?
Earth, you darling, I will! Oh, believe me, you need
no more of your spring-times to win me over: a single one,
ah, one, is already more than my blood can endure.
Beyond all names I am yours, and have been for ages.
You were always right, and your holiest inspiration
is Death, that friendly Death.
Look, I am living. On what? Neither childhood nor future
are growing less. . . . . Supernumerous existence
wells up in my heart.

The Tenth Elegy

Some day, emerging at last out of this fell insight,
may I lift up jubilant praise to assenting Angels!
May not one of the clear-struck keys of the heart
fail to respond through alighting on slack or doubtful
or rending strings! May a brighter radiance stream from
my streaming face! May inconspicuous Weeping
flower! How dear you will be to me then, you Nights
of Affliction! Why did I not, inconsolable sisters,
more kneelingly welcome you, more loosenedly render
myself to your loosened hair? We wasters of sorrows!
How we stare away into sad endurance beyond them,
trying to foresee their end! Whereas they are nothing else
than our winter foliage, our sombre evergreen, *one*
of the seasons of our interior year,—not only
season—they're also place, settlement, camp, soil, dwelling.

Freilich, wehe, wie fremd sind die Gassen der Leid-Stadt,
wo in der falschen, aus Übertönung gemachten
Stille, stark, aus der Gußform des Leeren der Ausguß
prahlt: der vergoldete Lärm, das platzende Denkmal.
O, wie spurlos zerträte ein Engel ihnen den Trostmarkt,
den die Kirche begrenzt, ihre fertig gekaufte:
reinlich und zu und enttäuscht wie ein Postamt am Sonntag.
Draußen aber kräuseln sich immer die Ränder von Jahrmarkt.
Schaukeln der Freiheit! Taucher und Gaukler des Eifers!
Und des behübschten Glücks figürliche Schießstatt,
wo es zappelt von Ziel und sich blechern benimmt,
wenn ein Geschickterer trifft. Von Beifall zu Zufall
taumelt er weiter; denn Buden jeglicher Neugier
werben, trommeln und plärrn. Für Erwachsene aber
ist noch besonders zu sehn, wie das Geld sich vermehrt, anatomisch,
nicht zur Belustigung nur: der Geschlechtsteil des Gelds,
alles, das Ganze, der Vorgang—, das unterrichtet und macht
fruchtbar . . .
      . . . Oh aber gleich darüber hinaus,
hinter der letzten Planke, beklebt mit Plakaten des »Todlos«,
jenes bitteren Biers, das den Trinkenden süß scheint,
wenn sie immer dazu frische Zerstreuungen kaun . . . ,
gleich im Rücken der Planke, gleich dahinter, ists *wirklich*.
Kinder spielen, und Liebende halten einander,—abseits,
ernst, im ärmlichen Gras, und Hunde haben Natur.
Weiter noch zieht es den Jüngling; vielleicht, daß er eine junge
Klage liebt . . . Hinter ihr her kommt er in Wiesen. Sie sagt:
—Weit. Wir wohnen dort draußen . . .
             Wo? Und der Jüngling
folgt. Ihn rührt ihre Haltung. Die Schulter, der Hals—, vielleicht
ist sie von herrlicher Herkunft. Aber er läßt sie, kehrt um,
wendet sich, winkt . . . Was solls? Sie ist eine Klage.

Nur die jungen Toten, im ersten Zustand
zeitlosen Gleichmuts, dem der Entwöhnung,
folgen ihr liebend. Mädchen
wartet sie ab und befreundet sie. Zeigt ihnen leise,

Strange, though, alas! are the streets of the City of Pain,
where, in the pseudo-silence of drowned commotion,
loudly swaggers the casting cast from vacuity's
mould: the begilded ado, the bursting memorial.
How an Angel would trample it down beyond trace, their market
        of comfort,
with the church alongside, bought ready for use: as clean
and disenchanted and shut as the Post on a Sunday!
Outside, though, there's always the billowing edge of the fair.
Swings of Freedom! Divers and Jugglers of Zeal!
And the figured shooting-range of bedizened Happiness: targets
tumbling in tinny contortions whenever some better shot
happens to hit one. Cheer-struck, on he goes reeling
after his luck. For booths that can please
the most curious tastes are drumming and bawling. Especially
worth seeing (for adults only): the breeding of Money!
Anatomy made amusing! Money's organs on view!
Nothing concealed! Instructive, and guaranteed
to increase fertility! . . . . . .
                        . . . Oh, but then just outside,
behind the last hoarding, plastered with placards for 'Deathless',
that bitter beer that tastes quite sweet to its drinkers
so long as they chew with it plenty of fresh distractions,—
just at the back of the hoardings, just behind them, it's real!
Children are playing, and lovers holding each other,—aside,
gravely, in pitiful grass, and dogs are following nature.
The youth is drawn further on; perhaps he's in love with a youthful
Lament . . . He emerges behind her into the meadows, she says:
'A long way. We live out there . . . . .'
                        'Where?' And the youth
follows. He's touched by her manner. Her shoulder, her neck,
        perhaps
she comes of a famous stock? But he leaves her, turns back,
looks round, nods . . . What's the use? She's just a Lament.

Only the youthfully-dead, in their first condition
of timeless serenity, that of being weaned,
follow her lovingly. Girls
she awaits and befriends. Gently, she shows them

was sie an sich hat. Perlen des Leids und die feinen
Schleier der Duldung.—Mit Jünglingen geht sie
schweigend.

Aber dort, wo sie wohnen, im Tal, der Älteren eine, der Klagen,
nimmt sich des Jünglinges an, wenn er fragt:—Wir waren,
sagt sie, ein großes Geschlecht, einmal, wir Klagen. Die Väter
trieben den Bergbau dort in dem großen Gebirg; bei Menschen
findest du manchmal ein Stück geschliffenes Ur-Leid
oder, aus altem Vulkan, schlackig versteinerten Zorn.
Ja, das stammte von dort. Einst waren wir reich.—

Und sie leitet ihn leicht durch die weite Landschaft der Klagen,
zeigt ihm die Säulen der Tempel oder die Trümmer
jener Burgen, von wo Klage-Fürsten das Land
einstens weise beherrscht. Zeigt ihm die hohen
Tränenbäume und Felder blühender Wehmut,
(Lebendige kennen sie nur als sanftes Blattwerk);
zeigt ihm die Tiere der Trauer, weidend,—und manchmal
schreckt ein Vogel und zieht, flach ihnen fliegend durchs Aufschaun,
weithin das schriftliche Bild seines vereinsamten Schreis.—
Abends führt sie ihn hin zu den Gräbern der Alten
aus dem Klage-Geschlecht, den Sibyllen und Warn-Herrn.
Naht aber Nacht, so wandeln sie leiser, und bald
mondets empor, das über Alles
wachende Grab-Mal. Brüderlich jenem am Nil,
der erhabene Sphinx—: der verschwiegenen Kammer
Antlitz.
Und sie staunen dem krönlichen Haupt, das für immer,
schweigend, der Menschen Gesicht
auf die Waage der Sterne gelegt.

Nicht erfaßt es sein Blick, im Frühtod
schwindelnd. Aber ihr Schaun,
hinter dem Pschent-Rand hervor, scheucht es die Eule. Und sie,
streifend im langsamen Abstrich die Wange entlang,
jene der reifesten Rundung,
zeichnet weich in das neue
Totengehör, über ein doppelt
aufgeschlagenes Blatt, den unbeschreiblichen Umriß.

what she is wearing. Pearls of Pain and the fine-spun
Veils of Endurance.—Youths
she walks with in silence.

But there, where they live, in the valley, one of the elder Laments
takes to the youth when he questions her:—'We were once,'
she says, 'a great family, we Lamentations. Our fathers
worked the mines in that mountain-range: among men
you'll find a lump, now and then, of polished original pain,
or of drossy petrified rage from some old volcano.
Yes, that came from there. We used to be rich.'

And lightly she leads him on through the spacious landscape
of Lamentation, shows him the temple columns, the ruins
of towers from which, long ago, Lords of the House of Lament
wisely governed the land. Shows him the tall
Tear trees, shows him the fields of flowering Sadness
(only as tender foliage known to the living);
shows him the pasturing herds of Grief.—and, at times,
a startled bird, flying straight through their field of vision,
scrawls the far-stretching screed of its lonely cry.—
At evening she leads him on to the graves of the longest
lived of the House of Lament, the sibyls and warners.
But, night approaching, they move more gently, and soon
moon-like emerges the all-
guarding sepulchral stone. Twin-brother to that on the Nile,
the lofty Sphinx, the taciturn chamber's gaze.
And they start at the regal head that has silently poised,
for ever, the human face
on the scale of the stars.

His sight, still dizzy with early death,
can't take it in. But her gaze
frightens an owl from behind the pschent. And the bird,
brushing, in slow down-skimming, along the cheek,
the one with the ripest curve,
faintly inscribes on the new
death-born hearing, as though on the double
page of an opened book, the indescribable outline.

Und höher, die Sterne. Neue. Die Sterne des Leidlands.
Langsam nennt sie die Klage:—Hier,
siehe: den *Reiter*, den *Stab*, und das vollere Sternbild
nennen sie: *Fruchtkranz.* Dann, weiter, dem Pol zu:
Wiege; Weg; Das Brennende Buch; Puppe: Fenster.
Aber im südlichen Himmel, rein wie im Innern
einer gesegneten Hand, das klar erglänzende »*M*«,
das die Mütter bedeutet . . . —

Doch der Tote muß fort, und schweigend bringt ihn die ältere
Klage bis an die Talschlucht,
wo es schimmert im Mondschein:
die Quelle der Freude. In Ehrfurcht
nennt sie sie, sagt:—Bei den Menschen
ist sie ein tragender Strom.—
Stehn am Fuß des Gebirgs.
Und da umarmt sie ihn, weinend.

Einsam steigt er dahin, in die Berge des Ur-Leids.
Und nicht einmal sein Schritt klingt aus dem tonlosen Los.

Aber erweckten sie uns, die unendlich Toten, ein Gleichnis,
siehe, sie zeigten vielleicht auf die Kätzchen der leeren
Hasel, die hängenden, oder
meinten den Regen, der fällt auf dunkles Erdreich im Frühjahr.—

Und wir, die an *steigendes* Glück
denken, empfänden die Rührung,
die uns beinah bestürzt,
wenn ein Glückliches *fällt.*

And, higher, the stars. New ones. Stars of the Land of Pain.
Slowly she names them: 'There,
look: the *Rider*, the *Staff*, and that fuller constellation
they call *Fruitgarland*. Then, further, towards the Pole:
Cradle, Way, The Burning Book, Doll, Window.
But up in the southern sky, pure as within the palm
of a consecrated hand, the clearly-resplendent *M*,
standing for Mothers. . . .'

But the dead must go on, and, in silence, the elder Lament
brings him as far as the gorge
where it gleams in the moonlight,—
there, the source of Joy. With awe
she names it, says 'Among men
it's a carrying stream'.

They stand at the foot of the range.
And there she embraces him, weeping.

Lone he ascends to the mountains of Primal Pain.
And never once does his step sound from the soundless fate.

And yet, were they waking a symbol within us, the endlessly dead,
look, they'd be pointing, perhaps, to the catkins, hanging
from empty hazels, or else
to the rain downfalling on dark soil-bed in early Spring.—

And we, who think of *ascending*
happiness, then would feel
the emotion that almost startles
when happiness *falls*.

Translated by J. B. Leishman and Stephen Spender

Die Sonnette an Orpheus

Erster Teil

3

Ein Gott vermags. Wie aber, sag mir, soll
ein Mann ihm folgen durch die schmale Leier?
Sein Sinn ist Zwiespalt. An der Kreuzung zweier
Herzwege steht kein Tempel für Apoll.

Gesang, wie du ihn lehrst, ist nicht Begehr,
nicht Werbung um ein endlich noch Erreichtes;
Gesang ist Dasein. Für den Gott ein Leichtes.
Wann aber *sind* wir? Und wann wendet *er*

an unser Sein die Erde und die Sterne?
Dies *ists* nicht, Jüngling, daß du liebst, wenn auch
die Stimme dann den Mund dir aufstößt,—lerne

vergessen daß du aufsangst. Das verrinnt.
In Wahrheit singen, ist ein andrer Hauch.
Ein Hauch um nichts. Ein Wehn im Gott. Ein Wind.

The Sonnets to Orpheus

First Part

3

A god can do it. But can a man expect
to penetrate the narrow lyre and follow?
His sense is discord. Temples for Apollo
are not found where two heart-ways intersect.

For song, as taught by you, is not desire,
not wooing of something finally attained;
song is existence. For the god unstrained.
But when shall we *exist?* And he require

the earth and heavens to exist for us?
It's more than being in love, boy, though your ringing
voice may have flung your dumb mouth open thus:

learn to forget those fleeting ecstasies.
Far other is the breath of real singing.
An aimless breath. A stirring in the god. A breeze.

5

Errichtet keinen Denkstein. Laßt die Rose
nur jedes Jahr zu seinen Gunsten blühn.
Denn Orpheus ists. Seine Metamorphose
in dem und dem. Wir sollen uns nicht mühn

um andre Namen. Ein für alle Male
ists Orpheus, wenn es singt. Er kommt und geht.
Ists nicht schon viel, wenn er die Rosenschale
um ein paar Tage manchmal übersteht?

O wie er schwinden muß, dass ihrs begrifft!
Und wenn ihm selbst auch bangte, dass er schwände.
Indem sein Wort das Hiersein übertrifft,

ist er schon dort, wohin ihrs nicht begleitet.
Der Leier Gitter zwängt ihm nicht die Hände.
Und er gehorcht, indem er überschreitet.

7

Rühmen, das ists! Ein zum Rühmen Bestellter,
ging er hervor wie das Erz aus des Steins
Schweigen. Sein Herz, o vergängliche Kelter
eines den Menschen unendlichen Weins.

Nie versagt ihm die Stimme am Staube,
wenn ihn das göttliche Beispiel ergreift.
Alles wird Weinberg, alles wird Traube,
in seinem fühlenden Süden gereift.

Nicht in den Grüften der Könige Moder
straft ihm die Rühmung Lügen, oder
daß von den Göttern ein Schatten fällt.

Er ist einer der bleibenden Boten,
der noch weit in die Türen der Toten
Schalen mit rühmlichen Früchten hält.

5

Raise no commemorating stone. The roses
shall blossom every summer for his sake.
For this is Orpheus. His metamorphosis
in this one and in that. We should not make

searches for other names. Once and for all,
it's Orpheus when there's song. He comes and goes.
Is it not much if sometimes, by some small
number of days, he shall outlive the rose?

Could you but feel his passing's needfulness!
Though he himself may dread the hour drawing nigher
Already, when his words pass earthliness,

he passes with them far beyond your gaze.
His hands unhindered by the trellised lyre,
in all his over-steppings he obeys.

7

Praising, that's it! As a praiser and blesser
he came like the ore from the taciturn mine.
Came with his heart, oh, transient presser,
for men, of a never-exhaustible wine.

Voice never fails him for things lacking lustre,
sacred example will open his mouth.
All becomes vineyard, all becomes cluster,
warmed by his sympathy's ripening south.

Crypts and the mouldering kings who lie there
do not belie his praising, neither
doubt, when a shadow obscures our days.

He is a messenger always attendant,
reaching far through their gates resplendent
dishes of fruit for the dead to praise.

9

Nur wer die Leier schon hob
auch unter Schatten,
darf das unendliche Lob
ahnend erstatten.

Nur wer mit Toten vom Mohn
aß, von dem ihren,
wird nicht den leisesten Ton
wieder verlieren.

Mag auch die Spieglung im Teich
oft uns verschwimmen:
Wisse das Bild.

Erst in dem Doppelbereich
werden die Stimmen
ewig und mild.

13

Voller Apfel, Birne und Banane,
Stachelbeere . . . Alles dieses spricht
Tod und Leben in den Mund . . . Ich ahne . . .
Lest es einem Kind vom Angesicht,

wenn es sie erschmeckt. Dies kommt von weit.
Wird euch langsam namenlos im Munde?
Wo sonst Worte waren, fließen Funde,
aus dem Fruchtfleisch überrascht befreit.

Wagt zu sagen, was ihr Apfel nennt.
Diese Süße, die sich erst verdichtet,
um, im Schmecken leise aufgerichtet,

klar zu werden, wach und transparent,
doppeldeutig, sonnig, erdig, hiesig—:
O Erfahrung, Fühlung, Freude—, riesig!

9

Only by him with whose lays
shades were enraptured
may the celestial praise
faintly be captured.

Only who tasted their own
flower with the sleeping
holds the most fugitive tone
ever in keeping.

Make but that image the pond
fleetingly tendered
knownly endure!

Not till both here and beyond
voices are rendered
lasting and pure.

13

Banana, rounded apple, russet pear,
gooseberry . . . Does not all this convey
life and death into your mouth? . . . It's there! . . .
Read it on a child's face any day,

when it tastes them. What infinity!
Can't you feel inside your mouth a growing
mysteriousness, and, where words were, a flowing
of suddenly released discovery?

Dare to say what 'apple' has implied!
Sweetness, concentrated, self-repressing,
slowly yielding to the tongue's caressing,

growing awake, transparent, clarified,
double-meaning'd, sunshine-full, terrestrial:—
O experience, feeling, joy,—celestial!

16

Du, mein Freund, bist einsam, weil . . .
Wir machen mit Worten und Fingerzeigen
uns allmählich die Welt zu eigen,
vielleicht ihren schwächsten, gefährlichsten Teil.

Wer zeigt mit Fingern auf einen Geruch?—
Doch von den Kräften, die uns bedrohten,
fühlst du viele . . . Du kennst die Toten,
und du erschrickst vor dem Zauberspruch.

Sieh, nun heißt es zusammen ertragen
Stückwerk und Teile, als sei es das Ganze.
Dir helfen, wird schwer sein. Vor allem: pflanze

mich nicht in dein Herz. Ich wüchse zu schnell.
Doch *meines* Herrn Hand will ich führen und sagen:
Hier. Das ist Esau in seinem Fell.

17

Zu unterst der Alte, verworrn,
all der Erbauten
Wurzel, verborgener Born,
den sie nie schauten.

Sturmhelm und Jägerhorn,
Spruch von Ergrauten,
Männer im Bruderzorn,
Frauen wie Lauten . . .

Drängender Zweig an Zweig,
nirgends ein freier . . .
Einer! o steig . . . o steig . . .

Aber sie brechen noch.
Dieser erst oben doch
biegt sich zur Leier.

16

The reason, friend, you feel so alone . . .
With our words and our pointings, little by little,
we're making—who knows?—perhaps the most brittle,
most perilous part of the world our own.

Who among us can point to a smell?—
Yet there's many a power we obscurely dread
which you can feel . . . You're aware of the dead,
and you shrink away from the conjurer's spell.

Look, our tasks are really the same:
dealt out a puzzle of parts, to endeavour
to make it a whole. Hard to help you. Never

plant me in your heart. I should grow too well.
But I will guide *my* master's hand and exclaim:
This is Esau here in his own rough fell.

17

Undermost he, the earth-bound
root of uprearing
multitudes, source underground,
never appearing.

Helmet and hunting horn,
words of the aging,
rage between brothers-born,
women assuaging . . .

Branch on branch, time on time,
vainly they spire . . .
One free! Oh, climb . . . oh, climb . . .

One, though the others drop,
curves, as it scales the top,
into a lyre.

18

Hörst du das Neue, Herr,
dröhnen und beben?
Kommen Verkündiger,
die es erheben.

Zwar ist kein Hören heil
in dem Durchtobtsein,
doch der Maschinenteil
will jetzt gelobt sein.

Sieh, die Maschine:
wie sie sich wälzt und rächt
und uns entstellt und schwächt.

Hat sie aus uns auch Kraft,
sie, ohne Leidenschaft,
treibe und diene.

19

Wandelt sich rasch auch die Welt
wie Wolkengestalten,
alles Vollendete fällt
heim zum Uralten.

Über dem Wandel und Gang,
weiter und freier,
währt noch dein Vor-Gesang,
Gott mit der Leier.

Nicht sind die Leiden erkannt,
nicht ist die Liebe gelernt,
und was im Tod uns entfernt,

ist nicht entschleiert.
Einzig das Lied überm Land
heiligt und feiert.

18

Master, there's something new
droning and drumming.
It has its heralds too,
praising its coming.

Ill though our ears understand
such perturbation,
now the machines demand
their celebration.

Source of our weakness
now, and in vengeful rage
ruining our heritage,

us shall these things at length,
us, who supply their strength,
serve in all meekness.

19

Change though the world may as fast
as cloud-collections,
home to the changeless at last
fall all perfections.

Over the thrust and the throng,
freer and higher,
echoes your preluding song,
god with the lyre.

Sorrow we misunderstand,
love we have still to begin,
death and what's hidden therein

await unveiling.
Song alone circles the land,
hallowing and hailing.

21

Frühling ist wiedergekommen. Die Erde
ist wie ein Kind, das Gedichte weiß;
viele, o viele . . . Für die Beschwerde
langen Lernens bekommt sie den Preis.

Streng war ihr Lehrer. Wir mochten das Weiße
an dem Barte des alten Manns.
Nun, wie das Grüne, das Blaue heiße,
dürfen wir fragen: sie kanns, sie kanns!

Erde, die frei hat, du glückliche, spiele
nun mit den Kindern. Wir wollen dich fangen,
fröhliche Erde. Dem Frohsten gelingts.

O, was der Lehrer sie lehrte, das Viele,
und was gedruckt steht in Wurzeln und langen
schwierigen Stämmen: sie singts, sie singts!

22

Wir sind die Treibenden.
Aber den Schritt der Zeit,
nehmt ihn als Kleinigkeit
im immer Bleibenden.

Alles das Eilende
wird schon vorüber sein;
denn das Verweilende
erst weiht uns ein.

Knaben, o werft den Mut
nicht in die Schnelligkeit,
nicht in den Flugversuch.

Alles ist ausgeruht:
Dunkel und Helligkeit,
Blume und Buch.

21

Spring has come again. Earth's a-bubble
with all those poems she knows by heart,—
oh, so many . . . With prize for the trouble
of such long learning, her holidays start.

Stern was her teacher, he'd over-task her
from time to time; but we liked the snows
in the old man's beard; and now we can ask her
what green, what blue are: she knows, she knows.

Eager to catch you, Earth, happy creature,
play with the children now outpouring!
Conqueringly foremost the happiest springs.

All she has ever been taught by her teacher,
all that's imprinted in roots and soaring
difficult stems,—she sings, she sings!

22

We wax for waning.
Count, though, Time's journeying
as but a little thing
in the Remaining.

End of unmeasured
hasting will soon begin;
only what's leisured
leads us within.

Boys, don't be drawn too far
into attempts at flight,
into mere swiftness.—Look

how rested all things are:
shadow and fall of light,
blossom and book.

26

Du aber, Göttlicher, du, bis zuletzt noch Ertöner,
da ihn der Schwarm der verschmähten Mänaden befiel,
hast ihr Geschrei übertönt mit Ordnung, du Schöner,
aus den Zerstörenden stieg dein erbauendes Spiel.

Keine war da, daß sie Haupt dir und Leier zerstör',
wie sie auch rangen und rasten; und alle die scharfen
Steine, die sie nach deinem Herzen warfen,
wurden zu Sanftem an dir und begabt mit Gehör.

Schließlich zerschlugen sie dich, von der Rache gehetzt,
während dein Klang noch in Löwen und Felsen verweilte
und in den Bäumen und Vögeln. Dort singst du noch jetzt.

O du verlorener Gott! Du unendliche Spur!
Nur weil dich reißend zuletzt die Feindschaft verteilte,
sind wir die Hörenden jetzt und ein Mund der Natur.

Zweiter Teil

5

Blumenmuskel, der der Anemone
Wiesenmorgen nach und nach erschließt,
bis in ihren Schooß das polyphone
Licht der lauten Himmel sich ergießt,

in den stillen Blütenstern gespannter
Muskel des unendlichen Empfangs,
manchmal *so* von Fülle übermannter,
daß der Ruhewink des Untergangs

kaum vermag die weitzurückgeschnellten
Blätterränder dir zurückzugeben:
du, Entschluß und Kraft von *wieviel* Welten!

26

You that could sound till the end, though, immortal accorder,
seized by the scorn-maddened Maenads' intemperate throng,
wholly outsounded their cries when in musical order
soared from the swarm of deformers your formative song.

Wrestle and rage as they might on that fated career,
none was able to shatter your head or your lyre:
hard stones hurled at your heart could only acquire
gentleness, soon as they struck you, and power to hear.

Though they destroyed you at last and revenge had its will,
sound of you lingered in lions and rocks you were first to
enthral, in the trees and the birds. You are singing there still.

O you god that has vanished! You infinite track!
Only because dismembering hatred dispersed you
are we hearers to-day and a mouth which else Nature would lack.

Second Part

5

Flower-muscle, gradually releasing
the anemone's pale meadow-day,
till at length into her lap unceasing
sky-light pours its polyphonic ray;

muscle stretching out that starry-flowered
quietude for endless welcoming;
so at times by fullness overpowered
that the restward call of evening

almost fails to bring your far-extended
petal-edges back to you once more:
world of will and power uncomprehended!

Wir Gewaltsamen, wir währen länger.
Aber *wann*, in welchem aller Leben,
sind wir endlich offen und Empfänger?

9

Rühmet euch, ihr Richtenden, nicht der entbehrlichen Folter
und daß das Eisen nicht länger an Hälsen sperrt.
Keins ist gesteigert, kein Herz—, weil ein gewollter
Krampf der Milde euch zarter verzerrt.

Was es durch Zeiten bekam, das schenkt das Schafott
wieder zurück, wie Kinder ihr Spielzeug vom vorig
alten Geburtstag. Ins reine, ins hohe, ins torig
offene Herz träte er anders, der Gott

wirklicher Milde. Er käme gewaltig und griffe
strahlender um sich, wie Göttliche sind.
Mehr als ein Wind für die großen gesicherten Schiffe.

Weniger nicht, als die heimliche leise Gewahrung,
die uns im Innern schweigend gewinnt
wie ein still spielendes Kind aus unendlicher Paarung.

10

Alles Erworbne bedroht die Maschine, solange
sie sich erdreistet, im Geist, statt im Gehorchen, zu sein.
Daß nicht der herrlichen Hand schöneres Zögern mehr prange,
zu dem entschlossenern Bau schneidet sie steifer den Stein.

Nirgends bleibt sie zurück, dass wir ihr *ein* Mal entrönnen
und sie in stiller Fabrik ölend sich selber gehört.
Sie ist das Leben,—sie meint es am besten zu können,
die mit dem gleichen Entschluß ordnet und schafft und zerstört.

We, the violent, are not so fleeting.
Through what lives though must we pass before
we reach that state of open-hearted greeting?

9

Boast not, judges, of racks no longer required,
of throats no longer locked in the iron's embrace.
Not one heart has it heightened, that newly-acquired
spasm of mercy's milder grimace.

Things it has slowly collected, the scaffold one day
offers us back, like children their long-ago gifted
birthday toys. He'd enter the pure, the uplifted,
gate-wide open heart in a different way,

the god of genuine mercy. Mightily, spreading
flamelier out from his origin.
More than a wind for the great ships steadily heading.

Potent no less than that gentle unconscious awaring,
silently winning us over within
like the quietly playing child of an infinite pairing.

10

Long will machinery menace the whole of our treasure,
while it, unmindful of us, dares to a mind of its own.
Checking the glorious hand's flaunting of lovelier leisure,
now for some stubborner work sternlier it fashions the stone.

Not for an hour will it stay, so that for once we may flee it,
oiling itself in a quiet factory, fitly employed.
Now it is life, no less, and feels best able to be it,
having, with equal resolve, ordered, constructed, destroyed.

Aber noch ist uns das Dasein verzaubert; an hundert
Stellen ist es noch Ursprung. Ein Spielen von reinen
Kräften, die keiner berührt, der nicht kniet und bewundert.

Worte gehen noch zart am Unsäglichen aus . . .
Und die Musik, immer neu, aus den bebendsten Steinen,
baut im unbrauchbaren Raum ihr vergöttlichtes Haus.

12

Wolle die Wandlung. O sei für die Flamme begeistert,
drin sich ein Ding dir entzieht, das mit Verwandlungen prunkt;
jener entwerfende Geist, welcher das Irdische meistert,
liebt in dem Schwung der Figur nichts wie den wendenden Punkt.

Was sich ins Bleiben verschließt, schon *ists* das Erstarrte;
wähnt es sich sicher im Schutz des unscheinbaren Grau's?
Warte, ein Härtestes warnt aus der Ferne das Harte.
Wehe—: abwesender Hammer holt aus!

Wer sich als Quelle ergießt, den erkennt die Erkennung;
und sie führt ihn entzückt durch das heiter Geschaffne,
das mit Anfang oft schließt und mit Ende beginnt.

Jeder glückliche Raum ist Kind oder Enkel von Trennung,
den sie staunend durchgehn. Und die verwandelte Daphne
will, seit sie lorbeern fühlt, daß du dich wandelst in Wind.

18

Tänzerin: o du Verlegung
alles Vergehens in Gang: wie brachtest du's dar.
Und der Wirbel am Schluß, dieser Baum aus Bewegung,
nahm er nicht ganz in Besitz das erschwungene Jahr?

Even to-day, though, existence is magical, pouring
freshly from hundreds of well-springs,—a playing of purest
forces, which none can surprise without humbly adoring.

Words still melt into something beyond their embrace . . .
Music, too, keeps building anew with the insecurest
stones her celestial house in unusable space.

12

Choose to be changed. With the flame, with the flame be enraptured,
where from within you a thing changefully-splendid escapes:
nothing whereby that earth-mastering artist is captured
more than the turning-point touched by his soaring shapes.

That which would stay what it is renounces existence:
does it feel safe in its shelter of lustreless grey?
Wait, a hardest is warning the hard from a distance,
heaved is a hammer from far away.

He who pours forth like a spring shall be known of his Knowing;
ravished, it leads him through cheerful creation, that closes
often as not with beginning and opens with end.

Parting's child or descendant is each glad space they are going
gazingly through. And now, feeling her metamorphosis,
laurelled Daphne wants you, changed to a wind, for her friend.

18

Dancer: you transmutation
of all going-by into going: what you have wrought!
And your finishing whirl, that tree of mere animation,
how it took over the year you had flyingly caught!

Blühte nicht, daß ihn dein Schwingen von vorhin umschwärme,
plötzlich sein Wipfel von Stille? Und über ihr,
war sie nicht Sonne, war sie nicht Sommer, die Wärme,
diese unzählige Wärme aus dir?

Aber er trug auch, er trug, dein Baum der Ekstase.
Sind sie nicht seine ruhigen Früchte: der Krug,
reifend gestreift, und die gereiftere Vase?

Und in den Bildern: ist nicht die Zeichnung geblieben,
die deiner Braue dunkler Zug
rasch an die Wandung der eigenen Wendung geschrieben?

19

Irgendwo wohnt das Gold in der verwöhnenden Bank,
und mit Tausenden tut es vertraulich. Doch jener
Blinde, der Bettler, ist selbst dem kupfernen Zehner
wie ein verlorener Ort, wie das staubige Eck unterm Schrank.

In den Geschäften entlang ist das Geld wie zu Hause
und verkleidet sich scheinbar in Seide, Nelken und Pelz.
Er, der Schweigende, steht in der Atempause
alles des wach oder schlafend atmenden Gelds.

O wie mag sie sich schließen bei Nacht, diese immer offene Hand.
Morgen holt sie das Schicksal wieder, und täglich
hält es sie hin: hell, elend, unendlich zerstörbar.

Daß doch einer, ein Schauender, endlich ihren langen Bestand
staunend begriffe und rühmte. Nur dem Aufsingenden säglich.
Nur dem Göttlichen hörbar.

27

Gibt es wirklich die Zeit, die zerstörende?
Wann, auf dem ruhenden Berg, zerbricht sie die Burg?
Dieses Herz, das unendlich den Göttern gehörende,
wann vergewaltigts der Demiurg?

Did not its crown, that your swaying might settle to swarming,
suddenly blossom with stillness? Above that, too,
was there not sunnily, was there not summerly warming
all the warmth that exhaled from you?

Nay, it was able, your tree of rapture, to bear.
Are they not, all its fruits that so peacefully shine,
jug streaked with ripeness, vase further ripened, still there?

And does not your mark in their paintings still meet the discerning—
that of your eyebrows' darker line
swiftly inscribed on the wall of your own swift turning?

19

Gold dwells somewhere at ease in the pampering bank,
mixing with thousands on intimate terms. But to any
coin that blind man begging, to even a penny,
seems but a desolate place, a chink in a dusty plank.

Money shines out from the shops in its own dimension,
plausibly masking in silk, carnation, and fur.
He, though, silently stands in the breath-suspension
of all the money breathing, asleep or astir.

Oh, how does it ever close at night, that perpetually open hand?
Fate to-morrow will fetch it back and display it,
bright, poor, endlessly fragile, year after year.

Could but at last some gazer, astoundedly coming to understand,
celebrate its persistence!—Only a singer could say it.
Only a god could hear.

27

Does it exist, though, Time the destroyer?
When will it scatter the tower on the resting hill?
This heart, the eternal gods' eternal enjoyer,
when shall the Demiurge ravish and spill?

Sind wir wirklich so ängstlich Zerbrechliche,
wie das Schicksal uns wahrmachen will?
Ist die Kindheit, die tiefe, versprechliche,
in den Wurzeln—später—still?

Ach, das Gespenst des Vergänglichen,
durch den arglos Empfänglichen
geht es, als wär es ein Rauch.

Als die, die wir sind, als die Treibenden,
gelten wir doch bei bleibenden
Kräften als göttlicher Brauch.

29

Stiller Freund der vielen Fernen, fühle,
wie dein Atem noch den Raum vermehrt.
Im Gebälk der finstern Glockenstühle
laß dich läuten. Das, was an dir zehrt,

wird ein Starkes über dieser Nahrung.
Geh in der Verwandlung aus und ein.
Was ist deine leidendste Erfahrung?
Ist dir Trinken bitter, werde Wein.

Sei in dieser Nacht aus Übermaß
Zauberkraft am Kreuzweg deiner Sinne,
ihrer seltsamen Begegnung Sinn.

Und wenn dich das Irdische vergaß,
zu der stillen Erde sag: Ich rinne.
Zu dem raschen Wasser sprich: Ich bin.

Are we really such tremblingly breakable
things as Destiny tries to pretend?
Does childhood's promise, deep, unmistakable,
down in the roots, then, later, end?

Ah, Mutability's spectre!
out through the simple accepter
you, like a vapour, recede.

We, though we wax but for waning,
fill none the less for remaining
powers a celestial need.

29

Silent friend of those far from us, feeling
how your breath is still enlarging space,
fill the sombre belfry with your pealing.
What consumes you now is growing apace

stronger than the feeding strength it borrows.
Be, as Change will have you, shade or shine.
Which has grieved you most of all your sorrows?
Turn, if drinking's bitter, into wine.

Be, in this immeasurable night,
at your senses' cross-ways magic cunning,
be the sense of their mysterious tryst.

And, should earthliness forget you quite,
murmur to the quiet earth: I'm running.
Tell the running water: I exist.

Translated by J. B. Leishman

ACKNOWLEDGMENTS

Every reasonable effort has been made to locate the parties who hold rights to previously published translations reprinted here. We gratefully acknowledge permission to reprint the following:

The Notebooks of Malte Laurids Brigge, translated by M. D. Herter Norton. Copyright 1949 by W. W. Norton & Company, Inc. Copyright renewed 1977 by M. D. Herter Norton. Reprinted by permission of W. W. Norton & Company, Inc.

Selections from *The Book of Hours* and *The Sonnets to Orpheus* are taken from Rainer Maria Rilke, *Selected Works, Volume II: Poetry*, translated by J. B. Leishman. Copyright © The Hogarth Press, Ltd. 1960. Reprinted by permission of New Directions Publishing Corporation.

Selections from *New Poems*, translated by J. B. Leishman. Copyright © The Hogarth Press, Ltd. 1964. Reprinted by permission of New Directions Publishing Corporation.

Selections from *Duino Elegies*, translated by J. B. Leishman and Stephen Spender. Copyright © 1939 by W. W. Norton & Company, Inc. Copyright renewed 1967 by Stephen Spender and J. B. Leishman. Reprinted by permission of W. W. Norton & Company, Inc.

Selections from *Das Stunden-Buch, Duineser Elegien*, and *Die Sonnette an Orpheus* are taken from Rainer Maria Rilke, *Sämtliche Werke*. Copyright © Insel Verlag, Frankfurt am Main 1955, 1956, 1959, 1961, 1963, and are reprinted by permission of Insel Verlag.